May 2014

Dear Robbie,

May this true love story about my grandparents be an inspiration to you and your family in faith, hope, and abiding love.

May your patriotism and love for your country always live deep within your heart.

Love,

Mrs. Inlee

Philippians 1:3-6

FOR THOSE WHO LOVE, TIME IS NOT

A WORLD WAR II
TRUE STORY
OF UNCONQUERABLE
LOVE AND FAITH

COMPILED AND EDITED BY KAY BRIGHAM

FOR THOSE WHO LOVE, TIME IS NOT

A WORLD WAR II TRUE STORY OF UNCONQUERABLE LOVE AND FAITH

editorial clie

Editorial CLIE
Galvani, 113
08224 TERRASSA (Barcelona)

FOR THOSE WHO LOVE, TIME IS NOT
A World War II true story of unconquerable love and faith

Cover design by Samuel Garrofé

Cover: USS *Buck* (DD-420), oil painting by Benjamin T. Stephenson

Photograph of Kay Brigham and granddaughter, Jacqueline, by Amy Brigham Boulris

Page Layout and design by Nicanor Gálvez

Depósito legal: B-9.747-2001

ISBN: 84-8267-189-8

Impreso en los Talleres Gráficos de la M.C.E. Horeb, E.R. n° 2.910 SE Polígono
Industrial Can Trias, c/Ramon Llull, 20 – 08232 VILADECAVALLS (Barcelona)

Printed in Spain

M.J. "MIKE" KLEIN

JACQUELINE C. KLEIN

COMPILED AND EDITED BY KAY BRIGHAM

FOR THOSE WHO LOVE, TIME IS NOT

THE WORLD WAR II LETTERS OF U.S. NAVY COMMANDER MILLARD J. KLEIN AND JACQUELINE C. KLEIN

MANY WATERS CANNOT QUENCH LOVE,

NEITHER CAN THE FLOODS DROWN IT

••• SONG OF SONGS 8:7 •••

To

Cissy and Mike

PREFACE

In 1995, the 50th anniversary of the victory in Europe and the end of World War II, Kay Brigham read for the first time her parents' letters, written in the years 1930-1943. The correspondence encompasses her father's First Class year at the United States Naval Academy, up to the time he went down with his ship, destroyer U.S.S. *Buck*, on October 9, 1943.

The letters are a time capsule of the human experience of a naval officer and his wife in the years of the Great Depression and World War II. In spite of censorship during the war, the letters bring history to life. The great message of the letters is that "many waters cannot quench love" (*Song of Songs* 8:7). The power of love and faith sustained a naval officer and his wife during lengthy separation and in the most threatening and perilous circumstances of the war. The letters speak eloquently for themselves and are a compelling story. Kay Brigham's introduction to the compilation of her parents' letters and addition of notes serve to give a focus and a historical context.

The perennial success of books and movies on the subject of World War II shows the enormous interest Americans have in the personal experiences of those who fought in that terrible conflict. These Americans include not only the "greatest generation" of veterans still alive today, but also their children and grandchildren. As the years pass, these letters gain even more historical value for future historians whose goal is to assess all the aspects of this crucial time of our nation's history.

The exploits of the U.S.S. *Buck* (DD-420) under M.J. Klein's command are chronicled in the following volumes: Samuel Eliot Morison, *History of United States Naval Operations in World War II,* vol. 9, *Sicily-Salerno-Anzio* (Boston: Little, Brown and Company, 1954); Theodore Roscoe, *United States Destroyer Operations in World War II* (Annapolis: United States Naval Institute, 1953); and *United States Naval Institute Proceedings* (March 1957).

Commander M.J. Klein was awarded the Navy Cross for the sinking of the Italian submarine, *Argento,* in August, 1943. His portrait hung in the Hall of Fame at the U.S. Naval Academy, Annapolis.

The letters of "Mike" and "Jackie" are essentially love letters. The most interesting are from Klein as a midshipman, Class of 1931, at the Naval Academy and as the Commanding Officer of the *Buck* in the thick of battle in the Mediterranean theater of World War II. The ones written from the Naval Academy reflect the life and education of a midshipman, as well as naval traditions and customs. Those written from sea in 1943 are the most poignant; even with the censorship, one senses that the fearsome conditions of warfare compelled the expression of the deepest emotions which sustain human beings, when they are passing through the valley of the shadow of death.

Most of Jackie's early letters were lost beneath the waters of the Mediterranean when the *Buck* went down. But we have her diaries which record her experience of falling in love with Mike. In addition, her letters of 1941-43 and two excellent original poems, "To One Missing in Action" and "My Balm of Gilead," testify to the strength of her Christian faith.

The context of the 1943 letters is enhanced by Klein's riveting action report of the destruction of the Italian submarine, *Argento*, by the *Buck*. Interspersed throughout the compilation of letters are action reports and explanatory historical notes. In addition, there are official Navy photographs taken aboard the *Buck* after the dramatic rescue of submarine *Argento's* crew, which included the commanding officer.

Kay Brigham's educational background includes the B.A. from Rollins College; Smith College Junior Year in Spain; M.A. in history from Claremont Graduate School (Woodrow Wilson Fellow); a year of graduate study at the University of California, Berkeley. She is the author of six books published by Editorial CLIE in Terrassa (Barcelona), Spain. Four deal with the writings of Christopher Columbus.

CONTENTS

Introduction 21

I Annapolis 1930-31 39

II Duty in Pacific Waters 1931-38 267

III Duty in Icelandic and North African Waters 1941-42 343

IV Warfare in the Mediterranean Theater 1943 461

    Action Report: Operation "HUSKY"--The Invasion of
    Sicily

    Action Report: Sinking of Italian Submarine,
    Argento, by U.S.S. *Buck*

Postscript 537

Appendices 543

    Commanding Officer's Instructions for Officers on U.S.S.
    Buck, 24 March 1943

    "Three Men on a Raft" in *The Stars and Stripes Weekly,*
    6 November 1943

    Letters from Survivors of the Sinking of the *Buck,* 1943-44

    Letter from Captain of German U-boat, 7 September 1999

ILLUSTRATIONS

Cover: *U.S.S. Buck* (DD-420), oil painting by Benjamin T. Stephenson

Back Cover: Kay Brigham and granddaughter, Jacqueline, photograph by Amy Brigham Boulris

Frontispiece: M.J. "Mike" Klein and Jacqueline C. Klein, mid-1930's

Page 41: Sailing at Annapolis, June Week, 1931

Page 269: M.J. "Mike" Klein and Jacqueline Coleman

Page 488: Group on bridge of *Buck* after sinking *Argento*, August, 1943

Page 506: Tract Chart of Attack and Destruction of *Argento* by U.S.S. *Buck*

Page 509: Last picture of Mike with family in Boston, September, 1943

Pages 513, 514: Last letters, dated September and October, 1943

Page 526: Navy Cross and Purple Heart

Page 532: "Missing in Action" Telegram

Page 534: Article in *Boston Herald*, October, 1943

Page 570: German submarine *U-616* that sank destroyer *Buck*, oil painting by Geoffrey Hunt

INTRODUCTION

MY DISCOVERY OF THE BOX OF OLD LETTERS

Our house lay in the path of Hurricane Andrew as it approached Miami. In the scurry to batten down before the storm, I wanted to be sure to save what meant the most: the family photograph albums, a few favorite books, and a box of old letters written by my parents during the years of World War II. Those letters were unread since then, but somehow I knew they must contain something precious. While stowing things back after the storm, I was strangely moved to sit down and read the letters, and I found a treasure.

JACKIE'S FOREWORD

On top of the pile of old letters was a Foreword my mother had written in June, 1950:

> My dear children:
>
> You were so young that day in October of 1943. You remember your father but vaguely. I can tell by your reminiscing that he is the shadowy figure that came home from the sea and gave our home a holiday air, laughed with us and entertained us, and, with a jaunty wave of his hand and a kiss all around, left us to wait long weeks in daily routine until he returned again. He is an attractive acquaintance to you, and I want you to know and love him as I did. I learned to know and love him through his letters, for,

should I count the days I had been with him before we were married, I should not need more than your fingers to count upon. I've kept all his letters, and he kept mine and took them with him and his ship beneath the blue waters of the Mediterranean. I shall tell you our story through his letters and, as well as I can remember, my answers to them.

Devotedly,

Your Mother

She also quoted a poem by Elizabeth Barrett Browning:

My letters! all dead paper, mute and white!
And yet they seem alive and quivering
Against my tremulous hands which loose the string
And let them drop down on my knee to-night.
This said,--he wished to have me in his sight
Once, as a friend: this fixed a day in spring
To come and touch my hand . . . a simple thing,
Yet I wept for it!--this, . . . the paper's light . . .
Said, <u>Dear, I love thee;</u> and I sank and quailed
As if God's future thundered on my past.
This said, <u>I am thine</u>--and so its ink has paled
With lying at my heart that beat too fast.
And this . . . O Love, thy words have ill availed
If, what this said, I dared repeat at last![1]

---

1. *Sonnets From The Portuguese*, XXVIII.

Although my mother told us much about our father, she never got around to compiling the letters as she had intended.

MEMORIES OF A LITTLE GIRL

The date was October 13, 1943. It was unusual for the doorbell of our home in Boston to ring at night. So I sprang out of bed and peered through the banisters of the staircase as my mother was opening the front door. There stood a Western Union boy. He handed the telegram to my mother, then quickly turned and ran into the night. My mother stared at the red stars stamped on the envelope for a few moments, then slowly opened it and read the telegram. She lowered her head and dropped her arms to her sides as the telegram fell from her hands to the floor. The Navy had notified my mother that her husband, Lieutenant Commander Millard Jefferson Klein, was missing in action.

THE EXPLOITS OF THE BUCK[2]

Although 94 survivors out of a crew of 260 were rescued after the U.S.S. *Buck* (DD-420) was torpedoed and sunk in the Tyrrhenian Sea off the coast of Salerno, the captain, Lieutenant Commander M.J. ("Mike") Klein, perished with his ship. At first my mother kept hope alive that he might have survived. But

2. The *Buck* (DD-420) had been built at the Philadelphia Navy Yard in 1938-39, a Sims-class destroyer of the 1936 building program. She had a standard displacement of 1,570 tons and measured 341 feet on the waterline, 35 feet beam, and ten feet draft. She had a top speed of 35 knots.

Admiral Royal E. Ingersoll, Commander In Chief, Atlantic Fleet, wrote forthrightly to my mother on October 18, 1943: "The circumstances of the loss of the *Buck* were such that I believe that there is absolutely no hope whatever that Mike could have been saved by another vessel or that he was made a prisoner. The ship was struck by a torpedo or hit a mine, the explosion of which apparently set off the *Buck's* magazines, and those of her crew who were not picked up at the time undoubtedly were killed by the explosions, or went down with the rapidly sinking ship before they could get clear."

Reports of survivors show that, just before the explosion, the *Buck* had been tracking an enemy submarine off the Italian coast. Morison described the loss of the *Buck* in *Sicily-Salerno-Anzio*:

Destroyer *Buck,* patrolling the Gulf [Salerno] on the night of 8-9 October, got a surface radar contact shortly before midnight. As she was tracking the submarine, one or two torpedoes struck forward of her single stack and exploded with great violence. Lieutenant Commander "Mike" Klein, the much beloved skipper, and most of the officers were killed in the explosion, and the destroyer began to go down. The men launched all life rafts that were intact, put such wounded as they could find aboard them, and abandoned ship. About four minutes after the hit, her stern stood straight up for 100 feet; she plunged down half way, shuddered, and then slipped under. As there had not been time to set all the depth charges on "safe", before they became inaccessible, some exploded, killing or wounding swimmers and blowing the bottoms out of all the balsa rafts. There were no other ships nearby. An Army transport plane spotted floating survivors at 1000 October 9 and dropped three rubber life rafts, a godsend to swimming survivors."[3]

Hours later an American destroyer and two other vessels arrived on the scene to pick up the survivors still alive. The October 9, 1943 entry in the War Diary of *U-616* would reveal that she was the German submarine that had torpedoed the *Buck*. *U-616*, commanded by Siegfried Koitschka, had surfaced off Salerno the night of 9 October to charge batteries. Suddenly a one funnel destroyer came into view, approaching at high speed and zeroing in on the submarine's position. The U-boat Captain observed black steam coming out the destroyer's funnel. Maneuvering *U-616* in a desperate crash dive, Koitschka fired out of the stern tube an experimental T-5 acoustic torpedo [*Gnat*] designed to leave no wake and react on the sounds of a ship's propellers. The new torpedo found its mark in the *Buck* and detonated.[4]

3. Samuel Eliot Morison, *History of United States Naval Operations in World War II,* 15 vols. (Boston: Little, Brown and Company, 1954) 9: 312.
4. The German perspective on the sinking of the *Buck* is described in two personal letters dated September 7, 1999 and March 20, 2000 and written by Siegfried Koitschka to Kay Brigham and Michael Klein. Later in the war an Allied destroyer group carried out a depth-charge attack on *U-616*, forcing the submarine to the surface. Koitschka scuttled and abandoned ship. He and the German crew were saved by American destroyers *Ellyson* and *Rodman*. The hunt for and end of *U-616* are chronicled by Clay Blair in *Hitler's U-Boat War* (New York: Random House, 1998) 524-25.

The "gallant" *Buck* had endured grueling North Atlantic convoy duty in the preceding two years, according to Morison's account.[5] Then on July 10-12, 1943, during the American amphibious assault on the Island of Sicily (Operation "HUSKY"), the *Buck* provided gunfire support for the landing of LCIs (Landing Craft, Infantry) against enemy shore positions. According to the report of a LCI captain, the *Buck* "went in at high speed with guns blazing and did a beautiful job of silencing these batteries." The report continues: "*Buck* closed the beach so near that the wash from her passing at 20 knots freed LCI-218 which had grounded on a false beach."[6] The Secretary of the Navy, James Forrestal, wrote the following citation about the Commanding Officer's performance of duty in that action:

> Skillfully directing the operations of his ship, Lieutenant Commander Klein provided accurate and effective gunfire support for the initial landing of the assault forces at Licata, Sicily, and later materially assisted the rapid advance of our troops by unerring and devastating bombardment of enemy shore positions. The excellent training of his command and careful preparations prior to the invasion were important factors in the successful accomplishment of this vital mission. Lieutenant Commander Klein's inspiring leadership and fearless devotion to duty were in keeping with the highest traditions of the United States Naval Service.

5. Morison 43.
6. See Sabin Report quoted in Morison 83.

Another daring exploit of the *Buck* was her destruction of the Italian submarine, *Argento*, on August 3, 1943, about two months before the *Buck* herself was sunk. The *Buck* began tracking *Argento* August 2 off the Island of Pantelleria. M.J. Klein as Commanding Officer wrote a detailed Action Report to the Admiralty on the subject of the sinking of *Argento*. The thoroughly professional tone of the official report was broken only once when the skipper, upon observing from *Buck's* bridge the forced surfacing of the enemy submarine, writes, "Suddenly dead astern at a range of about 1200 yards there appeared a contact. I wish to state that at this time I experienced one of the greatest thrills of my life." His informal verbal account was released by the Navy and published in the media all over the country several weeks later, after he was reported missing in action:

> While escorting a convoy late at night, the destroyer sighted a submarine, which submerged by crash-diving. Depth charges from the *Buck* ruptured the submarine's hull, and as it surfaced, round after round of hot lead and steel were poured into the conning tower. We turned for the submarine at a fast clip to ram, but we were too close at the time and the ship passed within fifty feet of the submarine as our machine guns kept up a withering fire on those exposed sections of the enemy vessel. Our big guns opened up and smashed the conning tower just about the time that two torpedoes were reported headed our way.

One was observed passing to starboard. The other must have been a wider miss. We could hear men shouting in the water, and as our gunfire lit up the scene, we could observe others jumping into the sea from the conning tower. One burst opened up a big hole below the tower and started a fire. We continued to pump shells into the submarine until I was certain that it was out of the war for keeps. When last seen, it had turned over. Our whaleboat was put over and in three trips picked up forty-five [including the submarine captain] out of a crew of fifty-one.[7]

The *Buck's* crew nicknamed their skipper "the slow Tennessean" because of his cool, calm manner while in action.

M. J. Klein was awarded the Navy Cross with the following citation from the Secretary of the Navy, Frank Knox, for the President:

> For extraordinary heroism as Commanding Officer of U.S.S. *BUCK* during an attack on an enemy submarine while on convoy escort off the Island of Pantelleria, August 3, 1943. Contacting the hostile vessel which was preparing to attack the convoy, Lieutenant Commander Klein skillfully maneuvered for vigorous and aggressive action, depth charging the submarine and forcing her to surface where the guns of the *BUCK* completed her destruction.

7. Associated Press, "The *Buck* Sank Submarine," Washington, 14 October 1943.

The forceful leadership and alert devotion to duty displayed by Lieutenant Commander Klein throughout the successful attack and in the subsequent capture of forty-six prisoners, including the commanding officer of the submarine, reflect great -credit upon his command and the United States Naval Service.

Posthumously M.J.Klein's portrait was placed in the Hall of Fame of the U.S. Naval Academy.[8]

MOUNTAIN BOY BECOMES A NAVAL OFFICER

Millard Jefferson Klein, Jr. was born July 25, 1908 on the campus of the Female College in Chappell Hill, Texas. His father was a professor of music on the college faculty. He changed the spelling of his surname from "Kline" to "Klein" as a way he wished to conform to the names of the great German composers. Professor Klein became ill with tuberculosis and returned to the family home in Knoxville, Tennessee where he soon died. His little son was only two months old.

Young Millard graduated from Knoxville High School. By the age of sixteen he had won a gold medal for marksmanship in camp and trophies for being the best rider in his company and

8. In addition to articles published in the media and Samuel Eliot Morison's accounts in *History of United States Naval Operations in World War II,* the exploits of the U.S.S. *Buck* are documented in Theodore Roscoe, *United States Destroyer Operations in World War II* (Annapolis: United States Naval Institute, 1953) and in *United States Naval Institute Proceedings* (Annapolis: United States Naval Institute, March 1957).

the best sharpshooter. From the age of ten, he dreamed of a life at sea. In 1927 he received an appointment to the United States Naval Academy.

Midshipman M.J. Klein, known as "Mike" to his classmates, rated about middle in academic standing in the U.S. Naval Academy Class of 1931. But his grades dramatically climbed upwards in the last year of his studies after he began correspondence with Jacqueline Reade Coleman from Richmond, Virginia. As a midshipman on a cruise he had first met "Jackie" at Virginia Beach the summer of 1930. Jackie made a few visits to Annapolis at Mike's invitation in the course of 1930-1931. They quickly fell in love with one another. He courted her aboard the subchaser moored on the Severn River that borders the Academy. Jackie later reminisced in a letter to Mike dated October 11, 1943, never received because the *Buck* had gone down two days before: "Little things came back to me so vividly of that wonderful November at Annapolis--when I couldn't listen to your explaining the mechanism of an airplane for wondering about you as you talked, and the strange, new feeling that came over me in the cosey bridge of the subchaser." (No wonder there were so many pictures of that subchaser in Jackie's photograph album!) Jackie inspired in Mike a sense of clear mission. He wrote from Annapolis:

> I discovered . . . just how much I need you if I am ever to properly fulfill my mission in life. We all do have a mission which God has planned for us, and it's up to us to find out his

plan, and then "carry on" to the best of our abilities. Until last Thanksgiving my plans were somewhat hazy. I knew that I was working, but I knew not what for. The future was merely an existence. I had some ambitions, but how much they have increased since you came along. All these plans are now formulated, and my only task is to finish preparing myself.... With you at the wheel and I'm in the engine room, a safe and happy voyage is assured.[9]

That year Mike went beyond the requirements of the regular academic program and wrote an essay entitled "The Future of Naval Aviation" which was awarded "honorable mention" in the Henry van Dyke Prize contest. The Naval Academy was successful in shaping the outlook of a future naval officer. As a midshipman Mike wrote to Jackie:

I am a man of the sea. I love the sea, my ships, and I am pledged to serve my country. War is my profession, and there are many joys which a military man does not have the privilege of enjoying.... How much I love the profession I have chosen. It is one in which the aim is not money. Military men are never rich. The only reason they are paid is for their livelihood.[10]

After graduation from Annapolis, Ensign M. J. Klein was assigned to duty on the U.S.S. *Roper* on the Pacific Coast.

9. 27 February 1931.
10. 9 January 1931.

Subsequently Mike was transferred to the U.S.S. *New York* in 1933 and was detached in December of that year with orders to the U.S.S. *San Francisco*. After four years on the *San Francisco*, he served a tour of duty in the Navy Department, Office of Chief of Naval Operations, Washington, D.C. Following that, he served as Gunnery Officer on the U.S.S. *Benson* until he was transferred to command the U.S.S. *Buck* in 1943.

TIA JUANA WEDDING

Mike's plan after his graduation from the Naval Academy was to establish a good reputation as a naval officer and save money to marry Jackie. In just a year, or after the first promotion, surely he would be able to afford that little house by the sea for his bride. But it was not to be just one year of separation before their marriage. Three long years passed before they saw one another again. The reason for the long delay was that Mike's widowed mother had unexpectedly appeared in San Diego and broke the news that she was no longer able to work and must be supported. The situation, which he accepted as a dutiful son, made it impossible for him to save anything from his salary for his anticipated marriage. On the long tours of duty at sea, he dedicated himself totally to his naval career and over the course of the next three years received commendations and a promotion.

But the separation of three years was a hard test for Jackie and Mike. She wrote in a letter July 20, 1933 that she was "just the sort of home brew that is very apt to have a spontaneous combustion when kept on tap too long." He responded on July 24, 1933: "If we are ever reunited and find that we love each other as we did during that glorious First Class year, it will be a grand test of real love and devotion and self sacrifice."

There were long months of utter silence during which Mike sent Jackie no letters or communication of any kind. She returned the engagement ring. He begged her to take it back. At last in September of 1934 Mike made arrangements to get leave and meet Jackie in Los Angeles. They would determine in that reunion if they still loved one another. She made the trip by train with her mother from Virginia to California. Mike and Jackie discovered immediately that the embers of their love still burned brightly. They sought the counsel of Mike's paternal uncle in San Diego. The uncle advised the young couple to go over the border to Tia Juana, Mexico and be married without a moment's delay and without his mother's consent.[11] So over the border they went in the company of Jackie's mother (consoled only by the promise of a subsequent church ceremony), and late in the evening of September 22, 1934 they were married in the Spanish language by a Mexican judge. In the course of their nine year marriage, two daughters, Kathleen (Kay) and Virginia (Cissy), were born in Long Beach, California and a son, Michael,[12] in Boston, Massachusetts.

11. In Jackie's scrapbook is an explanation of the problem in a quote from Buck's *East Wind, West Wind:* "There is no man able to stand unmoved between two proud women, one of them old and one of them young, and both loving him supremely."
12. After Michael's birth, the men aboard the ship fashioned a medal of scraps, connected by red string: one bar stamped "Girl," below it another bar stamped "Girl," and below the two bars a huge star stamped "BOY."

FOR THOSE WHO LOVE, TIME IS NOT

And so in 1995, the 50th anniversary of the end of World War II, I have taken up the project my mother only began with her Foreword. She had hoped to compile her husband's letters so that her three children might "know and love him as I did" through his letters. And what have I learned from these old letters written by my father to my mother over a half century ago? First, I have come to know and love even more that "shadowy figure that came home from the sea and gave our home a holiday air."

Most of Jackie's letters to Mike went down "beneath the blue waters of the Mediterranean" when the U.S.S. *Buck* was sunk. However, her letters of 1941-42 and a few of the last ones to her husband survive. The envelopes, postmarked October, 1943 before and shortly after the sinking of the *Buck,* bear the following stamps of the War & Navy Departments V-Mail Service: "Returned to writer," "Unable to deliver," "Unclaimed," "Deceased." These few letters and the testimonies of those who knew her confirm Jackie's strength of character and great faith as a Navy wife. What support her letters gave to a naval officer on active duty in wartime! She boldly and constantly prayed God to place His guardian angels in charge of the ship and to bring her husband safely home. She held on to the promise, "Ask, and it shall be given you" (Matt. 7:7), and the power of faith to move mountains. Yet she was always cognizant and accepting of God's perfect will. There was never bitterness or anger in her heart. A little nugget in her scrapbook illustrates the attitude she strove for:

Time is too long for those who grieve;
But for those who love, time is not.

Jackie shared those words with Mike when despair seized him at the thought of long separation from her. He wrote as a young ensign en route to San Diego for his first tour of duty in the Pacific:

> Somehow those words of yours, "For us time is not," [and] "Carry on," have been so comforting, the most comforting I have ever known. During the day when I'm missing you so, and at night when I'm dreaming too, I just think of those words and imagine seeing your dear sweet self telling them to me. Then my soul is quiet, and I am resolved to indeed carry on, as but I can, even though we are separated by such a distance.[13]

Wartime separation compelled a greater realization of love's meaning. Jackie wrote in 1941:

> I knew I loved you the first time I kissed you that cold November day back in 1930 in Mrs. Lietch's front parlor, and that knowledge has never left me. Yet it is only in separation that love knows its own depth.[14]

13. 27 June 1931.
14. Postmark, Nov. 9, 1941.

In Jackie's heart there was thankfulness for the joy and privilege of having known, though briefly, a true love in Mike. Her peace and comfort came in knowing that her beloved husband was "safe" in Christ, and that she would be reunited with him in heaven where there would be no more war, and all tears would be wiped away. The following poem, "To One Missing in Action," attests her faith:

I put you in God's loving care,
In His great Universe somewhere
You are still there.
You are o'ershadowed by His wing
In heav'nly climes; or in this ring
Of earth's circling.

He can restore you to my sight,
The battle's angry roar despite,
He has the might.
Though Laz'rus, death's dark valley trod,
It was within the power of God
To raise from sod.

Yet it may be this earthly span
Is but a test for mortal man;
A race you ran.
Who, in the fight, all sacrificed,
Have stood the test and gained the prize
Of Paradise.

If He returns you to my breast,
I shall rejoice in thankfulness,
And be e'er blessed.
But if He wills you wait me there,
Serene, the test of life I bear,
Expectant here.

Jacqueline C. Klein (1943)

UNCONQUERABLE LOVE

There is little historical data about the war years to be gleaned from the letters. Wartime censorship prohibited any such information. Yet the most impressive truth of the letters was expressed centuries ago by King Solomon in *Song of Songs* 8:7: "Many waters cannot quench love." For the Old Testament poets the phrase "many waters" was imagery suggesting not only the ocean depths but also perilous, threatening forces or circumstances in human experience. And so the letters are essentially a testimony to the power of love. It is unconquerable love. A love that imparts a sense of mission and significance to life; a love that inspires utmost devotion to a duty that requires sacrifice and resourcefulness; a love that grows ever stronger and sustains the human spirit in the midst of the most fearsome circumstances of this world, even in the face of death. Mike expressed it thus:

<u>Nothing exists</u> which could destroy this love and faith which I have in you, and it has become part of my life, accepted as God's gift, in answer to my dreams and prayers.[15]

Kay Klein Brigham
Miami, Florida

---

15. 11 May 1931.

I

ANNAPOLIS 1930-31

Jacqueline on deck of the Subchaser

Sailing at Annapolis, June Week, 1931
Jackie second from left, Mike second from right

ANNAPOLIS
OCT 27
6 AM
1930
MD.

U. S. Naval Academy.
23 October, 1930.

Dear Jacline,

No doubt you will be somewhat surprised to receive this letter, and perhaps you have long ago forgotten the writer. However, I sincerely hope not, and perhaps before I have continued much farther you will remember.

I have intended to write this letter for some time, but certain events have occurred which made it impossible. It was my intention to pay a visit to Richmond during the latter part of September with John Lunsford. However, soon after we arrived in Knoxville the first part of September, he "shoved off" for Florida, and I did not hear from him again until one morning he called and said that he was leaving for Richmond in fifteen minutes. As that was rather short notice, I could not have possibly accompanied him. After I returned to the Academy and shortly thereafter another disappointment came my way.

U.S. Naval Academy
23 October, 1930

Dear Jackie,

No doubt you will be somewhat surprised to receive this letter, and perhaps you have long ago forgotten the writer. However, I sincerely hope not, and perhaps before I have continued much farther, you will remember.

I have intended to write this letter for some time, but certain events have occurred which made it impossible. It was my intention to pay a visit to Richmond during the latter part of September with John Lundsford. However, soon after we arrived in Knoxville the first part of September, he "shoved off" for Florida, and I did not hear from him again, until one morning he called and said that he was leaving for Richmond in fifteen minutes. As that was rather short notice, I could not have possibly accompanied him. After I returned to the Academy and shortly thereafter, another disappointment came my way. I had fond hopes of making my last year a very pleasant one--that is to say, I hoped I would not have to study a great deal and could in general take life easy, with three hard years behind me. However, at the end of the first two weeks I found my name published all over the bulletin boards, to the effect that I was unsatisfactory in only four subjects. I rather suddenly reversed my above attitude, and since then I've really been "boning" as we say, in preparation for the examinations, the latter being completed some fifteen minutes ago. I have gone into the subject of why my intentions were good, as regards this letter, at some length. I don't know why, but now that my mind is free from academic work over the weekend, here it is at last.

I have rather pleasant memories of a nice afternoon at Ocean View, Va., some two months ago, which may be given as the reason for this letter, and I hope I may be forgiven for the seeming forwardness. I have thought frequently of that afternoon, with the desire that I might have the privilege of spending another. To use a Navy expression-- "Here's the dope."

Day after tomorrow our football team plays Princeton at the latter's home field in N.J. The regiment of midshipmen will accompany the team to Princeton and hence will not be at the Academy this week-end. However, the following week-end, the one of 1 November, Navy plays West Va. Wesleyan here at the Academy, followed by an informal dance in the afternoon and a "hop" that night. I would be awfully glad to see you, if it is possible for you to come, and I'm sure we can have an interesting time.

If you can possibly accept and will write to that effect, I'll answer with all the information as to your connections from Washington to Annapolis, where I will meet you, and any other details which may be useful.

Give Helena my best regards. I suppose she as well as you know that John has resigned from the Academy. He leaves tomorrow morning for Knoxville. I talked with him for over three hours one afternoon in an attempt to get him to reverse his decision, but to no avail.

Hoping to hear from you soon, I am

Yours Sincerely,

Millard Klein

Here's a new Navy song that is soon to be published and which will very soon be broadcast. Everyone thinks it's great.

We're all for one and one for all,

We stand together or fall,

All hands will always be on deck,

Should any comrade call.

We carry on, though we're right side up or sinking,

Sunlight or dawn, in our hearts a toast we're drinking.

Chorus

To the Navy, the Navy forever and a day,

Navy, the Navy at home or when far away.

And here's to our sweethearts wherever they may be,

Stand up! Stand up!

Lift your glasses high.

Drink up! Drink up!

Drain the bottoms dry.

We'll drink a toast wherever we may be

To the Navy and to victory.

U.S. Naval Academy

30 October, 1930

Dearest Jackie,

Until today I had been expecting your letter with considerable anticipation, and in only one respect was I disappointed. I had scarcely dared to hope that you would accept my invitation. In the last four years I have made the discovery that things worth while, as well as nice people, are not always so easy to obtain. However, way down in a corner of my heart, there was a faint glow of hope that perhaps I would see you very soon and enjoy a more pleasant afternoon than we did at Virginia Beach. Quite true, I was disappointed when I returned from class to find your letter awaiting me with the answer "No," but nevertheless I enjoyed your letter very much, and already today I have reread its contents several times.

I am quite sorry that I made the error in stating that we first met at Ocean View. You must excuse me, because Norfolk and surrounding country is strange to me, and Ocean View and Virginia Beach mean practically the same. Then, too, you must remember that in writing my first letter to you, I was somewhat excited and just not exactly responsible for the difference between the above two terms. Enough to say. I am absolutely sure that I am writing to the right girl.

Your term "swelegant" in reference to our new song is a new one to me, but I liked it very much. I imagine that you can say it, with even more pleasure to me. Your clipping from the paper was also new, and I'm happy to know that everyone is getting the "dope" about our new song.

Since writing the foregoing I've been for my daily "ride in the air." This is a privilege which First Classmen have that I enjoy very much. Since I have great ambitions to go to Pensacola next June and become an aviator, flying is my most interesting subject at the present time. I may not make it, but nevertheless I intend to try plenty hard. Our time in the air is devoted mostly to gunnery. A machine gun is rigged in the forward cockpit, and instead of live ammunition a film is placed in the cartridge drum, which records every point of aim which the gunner uses. A second pursuit plane usually flies alongside of the gunnery ship and then performs various stunts in order to confuse the gunner. When the practice is completed, the film is projected upon a screen, and a mark assigned to the midshipman concerned, according to his accuracy.

The Future! A challenge not to be taken lightly. It hardly seems possible that soon I will be out of school and facing the world which we know so little. One comes to realize a certain lack of vision, and how I try to fight against it! How much easier it would be to take life easy and not study, but drift along! I dread to think that in losing courage I might lose sight of all the big things I have planned.

I want to see you very much, and I hope that perhaps in the near future you will be able to come. After this weekend, we will be in Baltimore the two following Saturdays, but after that-- "start that red tape asking out."

In the meantime, I hope you will find time to write to someone who likes to hear very much.

Yours Sincerely,
Millard

P.S. Perhaps it would be best to belay[1] the singing until a later date. I will be willing to try in person!

---

1. "Stop" in midshipman lingo.

U.S. Naval Academy
5 November, 1930

Dearest Jackie,

Today has been the most satisfactory, as regards the academics, and I have been searching for the cause. Several days ago I had another successful day, and, as they are rather unusual, I have been considerably worried. However, I have arrived at a conclusion. On both the above mentioned days, I received a letter early in the morning, and the world suddenly assumed an entirely different aspect. In fact, I am quite unable to explain the extent of its new glory and cheerfulness, but it proves my old theory--that correct mental attitude is essential for success, and those two letters certainly appear to have changed mine.

I am quite happy to learn that you are an aviation enthusiast. I am quite interested in the subject, since I hope to enter its ranks, and I'm afraid that you encountered something which may become monotonous, since you gave me permission to speak more about aviation. The gunnery you spoke of is quite difficult, and long and constant practice is necessary to perfect an aerial gunner. There are so many different components which enter into the problem and which tend to spoil the gunner's aim. The course and speed of our own ship, the course and speed of the target, and that all important consideration, direction and velocity of the wind,

whose magnitude reaches huge proportions at high altitudes. A gunner must also consider, in firing at a diving target, that this target has a speed very much greater than his own, and must take the components of each velocity into account. This is done by wind vane sights, which automatically solves the velocity and direction of the wind, and by use of ring sights, the various components of the different velocities are solved. My first experience in the air with a machine gun produced 10 hits out of 115 shots. Not so good! However, my second attempt brought better results--85 hits from 115 shots. Gunnery in the air means destruction or success, so it behooves those concerned to properly prepare themselves. Of course, the actions of the pilot in maneuvering the ship may materially give the gunner an added advantage over an enemy and must be attempted always. For instance, if a gunner may attain the "blind angle" of an enemy, which is aft under the tail, he has a position which means certain destruction for the target.

Since you have never been in the air, why not wait about two years, and I'll fly up to Richmond some week-end, and we'll take a spin? Have you a place where a seaplane may safely land?

Saturday morning at the completion of the first period, we embark for Baltimore to engage the "Buckeyes" on the gridiron. After our creditable showing against Princeton, a good crowd is expected, and the regiment desires a victory. More correct mental attitude? Tschergi and "Bullet" Lou Kirn, our star backfield men, have been hitting the "ole line" plenty hard, and if they continue, our season will end in a "Navy Way."

The "hop" last Saturday night was a huge affair, and I thought of you so often. After dinner I came to my room and turned on the radio--Guy Lombardo from N.Y. was playing "I still get a thrill thinking of you." I was so contented and comfortable, just drifting and dreaming, that I went to sleep and almost did not arrive at Dahlgren Hall in time. However, I did my best to imagine that you were there, and we were having the best time of our lives.

What is happiness? Isn't it in loving the world or <u>parts of it?</u>

Your "slogan" was fine. Its words certainly mean a great deal, and with them always in your mind, you cannot follow that line of least resistance. I am reminded of something I learned long ago, and the last verse has been just a little revised.

This I say to you,
Be arrogant! Be true!
True to April lust that sings
Through your veins. These sharp
springs matter most. After years,
will be time enough for sleep,
Carefulness and tears.

Now!! while life is raw and new,

Drink it deep! drink it clear!

Let the moonlight's lunacy

Tear away your cautions. Be

Proud, and mad, and young and free!

Grasp a comet! Kick at stars,

Laughingly! Fight! Dare!

Arms are soft, breasts are white,

Magic in the April Night.

Purple, green and flame will end,

In a calm, gray blend.

Only--graven on my soul

After all the rest is gone,

There will be the ecstasies,

Of you alone.

Hope I'll have another day soon. What do you know of "Should I"?

Millard

U.S. Naval Academy

13 November, 1930

Dearest Jackie,

Last Monday morning my eyes were refracted, in order that I might take the required eye examination for aviation, and consequently the past three days have been rather easy. No classes, no studying--just listen to the radio, dream, and hope that I would receive a letter from you. However, this morning I began the "old grind" again and was expecting a fall at the hands of the academic department. Just before entering the first period class, your very nice letter arrived, and at four o'clock today another successful day was recorded. In fact, my steam professor nearly fainted when I presented the correct solutions for the day's problems. He remarked that it appeared that I only had one good day a week. I almost told him the "why" of it all.

Your "possum" hunt sounded most interesting, and although I have never participated in one, I imagine they are "lots o' fun." Won't you take me on one sometime?

'Tis on such nights as these that the mysteries of steam, navigation, and etc., hold no interest for me. A large pile of books before me have been neglected this night, and I too have been star gazing. A beautiful full moon is shining just outside my window, and the Chesapeake, a few hundred yards distant, presents a beautiful picture. Beautiful rays of Blue and Gold, our colors, go dancing across the white caps, and each one seems to have a message. A gentle fall breeze is whispering among those oak trees of "Lovers Lane," and the gravel walk appears as a silver thread in the moonlight. In the distance, slow moving white lights tell of the passage of a seagoing vessel, and perhaps many are the strange tales they could tell! Ships that pass in the night always hold a strange fascination for me.

Our aviation lesson today follows from your letter, expressing a desire to know something in general of planes. The accompanying sketch represents a simple diagrammatic view of a T4M-1 seaplane, the component parts being designated. No doubt you know many of the terms already, but perhaps you will gain something new.

Perhaps you would like to know how an airplane operates in the air. All the control surfaces are illustrated in the sketch with the exception of the ailerons. The ailerons are movable auxiliary wings, fitted to the after side of both the upper wings, and conform to the general shape of the wing. Their purpose is to produce a movement about the lateral axis. In "taking off," the motor is first "warmed up," and the plane "taxied" along the surface, to determine if the motor is functioning properly. When this is determined, and other parts of the plane are working properly, the engine is speeded up, whereupon the plane elevates its nose until it is taxing on the "steps" of the pontoons. When this condition is reached, it is only necessary to give a slight touch to the elevator, a slight amount of added gas, and she soars into the air.

All planes are now fitted with either of two set[s] of controls. The stick control, or the wheel control. Also, practically they are fitted "dual control," which means they can be operated from either of the two cockpits. We will consider the wheel control as it is very analogous to an automobile. Consider the plane in the air, and we desire to climb. The elevator, which is a horizontal surface, controls movement up or down. It is so connected to the wheel that by bringing the wheel to you, the elevator is depressed and the nose of the plane "points up." The opposite condition holds when it is desired to decrease your elevation. Now suppose we desire to turn right. We rotate the wheel to the right, which turns the rudder, a vertical surface, to the left. At the same time we push in on the right foot pedal. This elevates the aileron, which depresses the right wing, and the movement to the right begins. Opposite motions produce a turn to the left. A combination of the above tactics will produce a turn and a climb simultaneously.

Since you were unable to come to the last "hop," I have been constantly thinking since that time of another opportunity for you to pay us a visit. Your arrival and subsequent events I have reviewed in my mind so very many times. They are indeed very pleasant thoughts, and I never tire of them. I am reminded of:

Small spheres hold small fires;
But he loved largely, as a man can love
Who, baffled in his love, dares live his life,

Accept the ends which God loves for his own,
And lift a constant appeal.

On Wednesday night, 26 November, we have our Thanksgiving "hop," and I would indeed be honored if you will consent to be my "drag" on that occasion. The following day, Thanksgiving, will be devoted to athletic events and informals during the afternoon.

Won't you make my Thanksgiving a very happy one? If you will, I'll be very, very thankful.

Millard

P.S. In your P.S. you said: "Should I confess-etc." Why!--Why stop there?

WESTERN UNION TELEGRAM

ANNAPOLIS, MD. 1930 NOV. 19 P.M. 8:51

MISS JACKIE COLEMAN, RICHMOND, VIR.

WHO DID IT?

MILLARD

Excerpt from Jackie's Diary:

November 20, 1930

--I'm all excited! I'm going up to Annapolis for the Thanksgiving hop on Millard's bid... Millard writes the cutest letters--interesting yet full of life. I haven't ever seen him but once, but one can judge a lot by letters. I do hope I "get by" at Annapolis next Wednesday. It's not just the place. It's something I've derived from his letters that makes me want to know the writer. He's chock full of personality and character.

WESTERN UNION TELEGRAM

ANNAPOLIS, MD. 1930 NOV. 21 P.M. 3:10

MISS JACKIE COLEMAN, RICHMOND, VIR.

WON'T YOU PLEASE HURRY. I WANT TO

SEE YOU SO MUCH. LETTER FOLLOWS

MILLARD

Excerpt from Jackie's Diary:

November 21, 1930

--A telegram from Millard saying "Won't you please hurry. I want to see you so. Letter follows" --and how I want see him!

United States Naval Academy.
Annapolis, Maryland. 21 November, 1930.

Dearest Jackie,

Today has been such a happy one—
Everything has gone so smoothly of late, and all
my days now seem to be very successful.
Your letter of yesterday made me very
happy, and I am dreaming happy dreams of
your arrival, and stay at the Naval
Academy. I'm sure we will have a grand
time. Your telegrams were greatly enjoyed.
Your name to many of my friends is now
"Eureka", and my description of you has
been so glowing, that all my friends are
looking forward to meeting you next Wednesday

Perhaps a little information for you,
would now be appropriate. When you arrive
in Washington, you may journey to Annapolis

United States Naval Academy.
Annapolis, Maryland.   21 November, 1930

Dearest Jackie,

Today has been such a happy one. Everything has gone so smoothly of late, and all my days now seem to be very successful.

Your letter of yesterday made me very happy, and I am dreaming happy dreams of your arrival and stay at the Naval Academy. I'm sure we will have a grand time. Your telegrams were greatly enjoyed. Your name to many of my friends is now "Eureka," and my description of you has been so glowing that all my friends are looking forward to meeting you next Wednesday.

Perhaps a little information for you would now be appropriate. When you arrive in Washington, you may journey to Annapolis either by train or bus. The former departs from the Washington, Baltimore, and Annapolis Station every hour. The bus for Annapolis departs near midday. The exact time may be determined by inquiring at the W B & A Station. The buses are more pleasant, but they do not run as regularly as the trains.

The midshipmen are free at 3:30 on the afternoon of Wednesday, so if you arrange to arrive on the four o'clock train, I can meet you. This train will leave Washington at two o'clock. When you get on the train and arrive at Annapolis, tell the conductor to put you off at No. 2 gate at the Naval Academy. If you arrive at four o'clock, I'll be there. <u>Will I</u>???

As regards accommodations for the night: Most girls who come to the Academy either stay at Carvel Hall or at private homes. The former is rather high in their rates, so I would suggest that you stay at a private home. I know several nice families in Annapolis, and I have already spoken to one of them concerning you. She would be delighted to have you. A classmate is "dragging" a girl who will be staying at the same place, so you won't be lonesome, in case you wish to talk to someone. The above is only a suggestion, and if you desire to stay at the hotel, it will be quite all right.

In case you arrive at Annapolis before I am free from classes, I will here give the address of the lady mentioned above, and you can inquire the way:

Mrs. Lietch

157 Prince George St.

Annapolis, Md.

If you do arrive before four o'clock, you can either go to the above address, or to the hotel, as you prefer. The hotel, Carvel Hall, is only across the street from No. 2 gate, mentioned above. 157 Prince George is only one block over from No. 2 gate, and anyone can tell you where it is. You will be saved all inconvenience if you arrange to arrive at four o.clock. Gee, I want to meet you myself and welcome you to Annapolis.

Your last letter was wonderful, and it's been right over my heart since its arrival. As my telegram said: "Won't you please hurry?"

I hope I haven't omitted any details, which will make your arrival very pleasant and without any unnecessary delays.

A half dozen "plebes" have the time completed in hours, minutes, and seconds, until four o'clock next Wednesday.

The Naval Academy and a midshipman await your coming with happy hearts.

Millard

November 22, 1930

Four postcards depicting scenes at the Naval Academy sent and initialed by plebes with the following messages:

"The Plebe class awaits your arrival with keenest anticipation."

"Who knows maybe some day you'll be walking out that door.[2] We can hardly wait the time."

"Dear Jackie, I am enthusiastically awaiting your arrival. Lover's Lane is just in the foreground."

"Only 104 hours or 6240 minutes or 374,400 seconds till he shall greet you."

2. Chapel Doorway, U.S. Naval Academy.

U.S. Naval Academy

Annapolis, Maryland

27 November, 1930

Dearest Jackie,

Perhaps you will find this letter different from all preceding ones received from me, but I hope you will understand the emotions producing this. Tonight, there is a feeling in my heart which I have never experienced before. It is something undefinable, like the Navy Spirit we hear so much about, but it is a glorious feeling, and one which I hope will always remain there. I will attempt to explain it to you. This feeling in my heart appears to envelop my whole being, to make myself bigger and better. Nothing in this world seems unkind, and I am, oh, so happy!

If I had only the words of Browning to tell you my true feelings, how very much happier I would be.

Tonight you are speeding toward Richmond, away from the Naval Academy, but memories of your first visit will remain with me always. Memories, to a midshipman, are his most valuable possession--memories of home, memories of mother, memories of athletic contests are all so sacred. However, a corner of my heart has now been reserved for memories of your first visit. They include the time of our first meeting on the steps of Carvel Hall, a short time later, when I arrived at a certain conclusion, which has changed my whole life--in fact, this corner contains every detail incident to your arrival, stay, and departure. This corner is reserved for these memories--the remainder of my heart belongs to you--to do with as you desire. Yours, which you told me was left behind, is my most sacred possession, and its possession only means "dreams come true."

When ships come in, and dreams come true, how happy we are! Tonight I am saying, "What is happiness?" Is it not in loving the world or parts of it?

Fate has indeed been kind to me, and today has changed my entire plans for the future. I am a most exact person, when regarding the future, and I usually have plans formulated a long time in advance. I imagine that every young man has certain dreams, certain ideals, which he strives to attain. I have, and you have given me only more ambition to always seek that which is beyond. I want you to be proud of me, as I am proud of you. I want to be worthy of you, and to do that, I must certainly attain goals which have not yet been attained. To that end your image will always be before me, and just watch me!

Tomorrow at nine o'clock, when you arrive at your office, I will be in Luce Hall vainly attempting to locate myself in some foreign ocean, which the academic department has so kindly placed me. Your little ribboned anchor will be there on the desk before me, and perhaps I may pause a few moments, at intervals, and review the incidents of this afternoon. They are the happiest of my entire life, and my thoughts will be travelling over the distance between us, wishing you happiness in the future. I want you to be so happy, and when that is so, then too will I be happy.

Sorry, my heart just will not concentrate on aviation or engineering tonight. Next time, I will continue.

Jones was just here. I apologized for our not showing up this afternoon and explained that we [got] very interested in the soccer game and forgot all about our engagement. He sends his regards. He also said: "Well, perhaps I'll see her again soon, provided she will accept my invitation to visit the Academy soon." Whereupon I said, "Oh, yes. <u>That's fine</u>." To myself I said: "Not so fine." Jones is a nice boy, and he really feels hurt that he did not recognize you yesterday.

Living the hours and days just for you, dearest one.

Millard

Excerpts from Jackie's Diary:

November 27, 1930

--This is really the 28th, but I'm very talkative today, and my other diary is so irregular and has no key. What I'm going to say is what I should like to shout from the housetops, but I want to have it all to myself, so this seems to be the only outlet... Mother and Mrs. Caskie[3] read me as a book anyway, and besides I love them so much I must have no secrets from them. I hope he tells his mother. I do so much want her to love me.

Heretofore I've thought I knew what love was--love of a man and a maid. But now that in reality I know, it's plain to me that I hadn't the faintest idea. There's been some I preferred, but even during all my ecstasy I knew it to be only a passing fancy. In fact, I didn't want it to last. But Millard's love--and he said he loved me, and I do believe him, for I love him so much that there must be some answer--I want to last forever and a day. Of course, I've been kissed and have kissed others, but since his lips met mine, I've quite forgotten the others and never, never want another's to mar the kiss he

3. Jackie lived with Mrs. Caskie from 1928-1934. The Palmer-Caskie House, built in 1808 and now listed on the National Register of Historic Places, is located at 2 N. Fifth St., Richmond, Virginia.

left upon mine. Love--true love-- came upon me so unexpectedly. Going to Annapolis was, of course, a thrill. And his letters implied things at times which I took for the usual bull, but when he said, "I'm in love with you," something in me snapped, as a curtain swung seemingly back revealing my heart, touched for the first time. I answered right back, "I love you"--the first time I had told any man that, and I do, I do, I do!! Heretofore I always evaded saying it, for it's a tremendous confession, and I never could find the courage to say it until I really meant it. But confessing to him came so honestly, so sincerely, and I do love him so! He gave me the pictures which I shall love and keep always and told me he had saved them three years for me, and now I must keep them for "us." "Our Pictures." Oh, is it too much to even dream someday that we might have a little home with them hanging upon its walls? I must stop. I've outstepped bounds now. And I'm going to write to my love.

November 29, 1930

--When I arrived home this P.M., I spied a letter from Millard on my dressing table. Nothing unusual, perhaps, for he's written often before--but it sent the most delicious thrill over me that I could hardly wait to tear it open. And he says he's so happy! and wants me to be proud of him, as if I wasn't already so chock full of pride now that I'm nearly bursting. He's given me his heart, and I've given him mine. He says he wants to be worthy of me--when I've been praying that I may be worthy of him. Oh God, that's my prayer--let me be worthy of his love, let him always want mine, and let me never hurt him in any way, but prove my love for him by being all he thinks I am! It's strange that I have chosen "my man" forever and ever and know it in so short a time. I know this is real. I know it. I love him, I love him, I love him!!!!! I shall keep this letter always, and when it and these pages are yellowed with age, and we are old and grey, I can look back and see how happy I was--or rather, just when supreme happiness began for me, and I can say smilingly, "I knew true love when it came along." And maybe he may read them with me, and we can look back over years spent together.

United States Naval Academy.
Annapolis, Maryland.   29 November, 1930

Dearest Jackie,

Tonight I seek your companionship by the only method at my disposal, and although it is an indirect method, I find happiness, and my heart is contented. The adjacent windows of Bancroft Hall are dark. My radio is playing softly, and my thoughts are my companions. They are wonderful thoughts, and you seem almost near. I can even imagine that you remained for the week-end, and at the present moment we are together at the "hop" in Luce Hall.

This afternoon we defeated George Washington University upon the gridiron by 20-0. At the end of the third period, I departed from the game and came to my room. Mail is delivered in the Hall at three o'clock, and you see, I was expecting a letter. I entered my room almost afraid, for I wanted one so badly. Not since you left last Thursday, have I been so happy when I read your letter. It made me proud, happy, and sad. Proud that I am privileged to know you, happy that the future appears so bright, and sad that I cannot see you every day. I took your letter to the same subchaser, where we were last Thursday morning, and there I eagerly devoured every word. Each one seemed to convey a thousand thoughts, and every word is sacred to my heart. Should you write these things? If you only knew how my very being grows bigger, how I long to fight, and dare, all for you. If I may only gain the goals I have chosen for myself, all my dreams will be fulfilled, for I have found you!

Next Saturday we journey to Philadelphia to play University of Penn. If we continue our good work, we should gain a victory, and then on the following Saturday, be prepared to face the crucial test of the season--our game with the Army. The latter played a wonderful game against Rockne's wonder team at Chicago today, and they appear to have a marvelous defensive, as well as a strong offensive attack. A smashing run of 65 yds. by Schwartz of Notre Dame turned the tide in favor of the Irish late in the fourth quarter, when it seemed that a scoreless deadlock would result. The old "Nyvee" spirit *must* assert itself on 13 December at the Polo grounds, and the Navy crash thru! A victory will mean much to myself and classmates and will be a wonderful memory to take with us from Annapolis.

Dearest One, I seem to be unable to speak of things which do not pertain to you. I'm missing you so, and my thoughts are directed to that happy moment when I shall see you again. Will it not be at the Polo grounds in New York on 13 December, exactly two weeks from today? Two weeks from tonight we may again be together, at this very moment. Just the thought sends a little shiver of joy up my spine. Please be real good to that boss of yours and tell him that a certain midshipman's happiness depends on you. As soon as you tell me you can go, I'll send your ticket, and we can complete our plans concerning what we shall do following the game.

My work continually fascinates me this year, and so ceases to be work in the true sense of the word. The ways by which one comes to know the mind of each individual and then, through this avenue, mold and change his thought, character, and even the guiding principles of his life, is to me the one profession that comes into contact with the sure currents of life. Technical training has given me a far-reaching vision of the needs of the future men and women and the means by which their needs may be taken care of.

Your destiny lies in following the great and not the small.

Small spheres hold small fires;
But he loved largely, as a man can love
Who, baffled in his love, dares live his life,
Accept the ends which God loves for his own,
And lift a constant appeal.
Elizabeth Barrett Browning

Since last Wednesday, life has been getting fuller and fuller. Life has so much loveliness to sell, 'twere a shame to waste any of it. If one has no other purpose in life, it is enough to study character in all its manifestations.

I have drifted and dreamed this evening away in writing this letter to you. In two minutes the lights go out, so perhaps I had best close.

In my prayers, I will pray for you--in my dreams, I'll dream of you. So, in good night, perhaps my feelings may be carried to you in these words:

And in the wine you drink,

The lips you press,

End in what all begins and ends in;

Yes!--think then you are

What yesterday you were;

Tomorrow you shall not be less!

May I say--<u>I love you</u>?

Millard

Excerpts from Jackie's Diary:

December 1, 1930

--Another letter from Millard today making me love him more and more if it were possible to love him any more than I do. He said he read my letter on the subchaser--the one I wanted to break loose from its moorings and drift away with just us two. I really believe that's when I fell in love with him. I got my first thrill when he put my hand to his breast while we were dancing, and when the next day we came into the warm cabin on the bridge of the ship from the cold wind, and he taught me how to use the annunciators and wheel--that's when the queer feeling for the first time crept over me. I suddenly knew nothing in the world mattered but him. I was afraid to let myself believe this, until he told me he loved me back in the living room at Mrs. Lietch's house. At his confession of love, a wave of realization that this was true--he was the only thing that mattered--swept over me leaving me for a moment speechless--plainly dumb with the wonderment of it all. I could only lean forward and press my lips to his and whisper that I loved him too. And then the flood of joy!!! He ended by saying, "May I say, I love you?" Oh, that he may always and always say that and want to say it, for I love him so! I do, I do!!!

December 2, 1930

‑‑I got some books on aviation to read today, for I want to be of some help, if I may, to Millard. They're very interesting, but frighten me so when they talk of men killed in giving their lives for aviation and progress and country. If anything should ever happen to him, I suppose I would go on existing, but now that I'm really living, I'd surely die in a sense. I just couldn't stand it. But I am going to have courage and faith. With God all things are great, all things possible, and into His hands I commend my heart, my happiness, my very life, for Him to guide, keep, and love forever.

December 4, 1930

‑‑I was a wee bit disappointed today when I found no letter waiting for me. But I shouldn't be selfish. I don't want him to let me interfere in any way with his work. I'm enjoying reading books on aviation; so I want to help in some way. I wonder if he'll ask someone else for the games? I wish I could go just to see him. I want him to have a girl‑‑lots of them, but I hope he doesn't tell them things he told me‑‑kiss them‑‑fall in love with them.

Dearest Jackie,

The days are rapidly passing, and I can scarcely realize that the academic year is so far advanced, and Xmas is so near. Xmas leave will have come and gone before I am hardly aware of the fact, and then the five long, hard months which follow. I hope that I realize happy days are passing, and that I am taking advantage of golden moments.

The Naval Academy is becoming a very enthusiastic place, and the present days remind me of those when we were preparing for the Army in the fall of '27. My class is the only one now at the Naval Academy which has ever seen an Army game, and we are responsible to see that the underclasses realize the full significance of such an event. The old "Nyvee" spirit is going to assert itself, and I am positive we will be very proud of our team after the game on 13th December. I wish that I might define the "spirit of the service." It is something deeper and far reaching than one can suppose. No one attempts to define it; but as the first consciousness of it comes upon them, a new sense of power is readily apparent. Nothing can make you feel this spirit more than an Army game. Like many of the best things in life, its value to those concerned consists not in defining, but in feeling it. I believe the last sentence might be applicable to those "three little words."

This afternoon I received my greatest thrill in aviation since I have been flying. Heretofore we have always gone aloft in the huge bombing planes I showed you on our dock. These planes are very stable in the air, as one of their inherent characteristics, and a ride in one is not much more than an automobile spin. However, this week ushered in our training with the light fighting and scouting planes, which may properly be called "Hawks of the Sea." In time of war these planes constitute the eyes of the fleet; they seek out the enemy, determine his strength and other general information, vital to the commander-in-chief in forming his battle line. These "Hawks" then engage the enemy planes in a "battle of the sky," and my imagination can vividly picture such an encounter. Speedy little yellow flashes seeking to gain the altitude advantage and the "blind sector," continually spitting a rain of machine gun bullets, which mean death and destruction. Maneuverability and controllability are the vital factors here. This afternoon I went aloft in one of these speedy little fighters, and we quickly mounted to over six thousand feet. I now was introduced to my first stunts of the air. Dives, barrel rolls, and breathtaking spins left me a little dazed as to all that was actually happening. It's wonderful, and I'm all ready for another tomorrow.

Dearest little girl, you have made me a different man since that first moment on the steps of Carvel Hall. The dawn of each day seems to be the signal for me to arise and obtain those things which will make for those happy days I have planned. When next I see you, I am going to outline these plans. And how may you help me? You indeed were correct in your explanation of how you might, and by trusting and believing in me, you will aid me more than words can express. How much one is inspired when some loved one believes in him!!

Your letter was so very nice--kind, interesting, sincere, and I would not take anything for one paragraph of it. When something goes wrong and all the world seems dark and cruel, that single paragraph will be sufficient to dispel all such blackness and doubt.

May I allow Elizabeth Barrett Browning to bring my message to you this night?

How do I love thee? Let me count the ways.
I love thee to the depth and breadth and height
My soul can reach, when feeling out of sight
For the ends of Being and ideal Grace.
I love thee to the level of everyday's
Most quiet need, by sun and candle-light.
I love thee freely, as men strive for Right;
I love thee purely, as they turn from Praise.
. . . I love thee with the breath,
Smiles, tears, of all my life!--and, if God choose,
I shall but love thee better after death.
*   [Sonnets from the Portuguese, XLIII]*

In my last letter to mother, I sent your message and love, and at the same time added a few thoughts of my own. Evidently mother was very surprised at this letter, as she had never received such a one from me before. In fact, I wrote over six pages, and at this she was also very surprised. However, she expressed her appreciation for your message and sends her love to you, and she wants to meet you so much! My picture of you was so vivid that she stated she could very easily imagine you as you really are.

"Sixteen days, a sleep and a butt," as we say, until the great Army game and also another event which is even more important and vital to me. On that day I will see you again, and I'll wager that I see you first this time. Just as soon as I hear that you are really coming, I'll send my additional plans for your O.K.

Jackie, I want to see you again so very much. I try and receive your message every day at the scheduled time, and every night I seek that little dipper after dinner. It seems to bring me a message, and then to my room and study. Every once and awhile I glance at my locker door and imagine that promised picture just beside my mother's. Such happy thoughts make my happy days, and with my good night I pray for your happiness and say--Jackie, I love you.

Millard

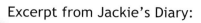

December 7, 1930

--Sunday afternoon. I've been home for two nights and consequently could not write my thoughts. Friday evening I found a letter from Millard for me. I shall keep it always as it's the most beautiful thing I ever read. Love's rather funny. Yesterday I thought no human could love more than I did, and yet today I feel I love him even more and couldn't love anything more; but perhaps tomorrow I'll feel it grown even stronger as I did today. He says next time he sees me he will outline the plans for happy days he's made. All days are happy for me now, and should any unhappy ones dawn for me, I shall find comfort in knowing his lips told me he loved me; pressed mine; his arms held me to his breast. I can never, never be sad with memories like that! He says I may help him in trusting and believing in him. I do that already. I trust and believe in him as I do in Truth and Love Divine. And he quoted Elizabeth Barrett Browning to bring his message to me--and it's also my message to him.

How do I love thee? Let me count the ways.
I love thee to the depth and breadth and height
My soul can reach, when feeling out of sight
For the ends of Being and ideal Grace.

I love thee to the level of everyday's
Most quiet need, by sun and candle-light.
I love thee freely, as men strive for Right;
I love thee purely, as they turn from Praise.
... I love thee with the breath,
Smiles, tears, of all my life!--and, if God choose,
I shall but love thee better after death.

And he's written his mother about me, and she wants to meet me. I hope I may meet her and that she will not be disappointed in me. I have nothing to offer him but love, but, oh, worlds of that. I want her to love me, too.

He hadn't gotten my letter saying I couldn't come to the game when he wrote his. I feel I must see him, hear his voice, touch his hand! I want him to come by Richmond either going or coming this Xmas. I simply must see him! I had my pictures taken Saturday for him. I tried not to pose, but imagined he was looking at me through the lens of the camera, so through my eyes I kept saying, "I love you, Millard. I believe in you!"

I really feel Millard nearer me when we exchange messages in the morning, and when I send him my good night kiss at my open window at night, proving more than ever that there's a wonderful Being who taught man to love and that all things are possible. Oh God, watch over him always and make him always happy!

United States Naval Academy.
Annapolis. Maryland. 5 December, 1930

Dearest Jackie,

"Three Little Words" was a surprise yesterday, but a very pleasant one. Since its arrival, no other record has been on the victrola, and the other side hasn't even been played yet. A quartet of "plebes" have the words memorized, and every night shortly before ten o'clock, you may know what they are doing, and of who I am thinking. Thanks so very much. Nothing could have been more acceptable.

Yesterday afternoon a classmate of mine passed away in the U.S. Naval Hospital where he had been ill for some time. Recitations have been suspended for the afternoon, and the funeral will be held in the little cemetery beside the Severn. Remember it? My entire class will pay respect to the body as the salute is fired over the grave. It's terrible to think that one so young and with such a happy future has gone forever. My heart goes out to his mother!

Yesterday was a wonderful, happy day. I was on watch, and your letter arrived at 0800, and "Three little words" at 1000. Between the two I spent a most enjoyable day during my off-hours. Even the long hours on duty seemed to have fleet wings, and when "duty days" are pleasant, it is time to stop and wonder why!!

I was real disappointed that you will be unable to attend the Army game. I was almost sure you would be there, and that we would enjoy several happy hours. However, I can easily understand that you are very busy with your position and with Xmas so near. I only pray for the days to quickly pass when I shall see you again, and I'll be with you in New York anyway. Right after the game I'll send you a telegram, and you'll know that I'm thinking of you, whether we gain a glorious victory or go down in defeat. It's going to be a wonderful battle, and I surely wish you were going to be there wearing the Blue and the Gold.

Your invitation to visit Richmond during the holidays was appreciated so very much. Since your letter arrived, I've been thinking of everything possible whereby I may see you, even for just a short time. If I cannot, Santa Claus will have made a certain midshipman very unhappy. A classmate of mine, Matty Hall, is planning to go home with me for the holidays, but I think I can persuade him to remain in Washington for a day or so. Mother, too, must be satisfied, and I think a letter telling her that Santa Claus is in Richmond will be satisfactory. Xmas leave begins on Saturday, 20 December, at noon. I could arrive in Richmond that night, provided I can make the proper connections from Washington. Then I can arrange to leave Richmond late Sunday or early Monday owing to the schedules. If this will be satisfactory, I think I can say that on the night of 20 December, I will be in Richmond, the home of the only little girl in all the world, who matters to me and who I want to see so badly. May I ask one thing? If the above plan is acceptable to you, and I come to Richmond, I do not want you or your mother or anyone else to consider me a visitor--just a southern boy coming home to the South, and all he asks of Richmond is <u>you</u>? Gee, I can hardly wait! Do you know how I feel? I want to put on my coat, dash out of Bancroft Hall, and run, and run, and run, until I find you, and then I want to stop and stay right there forever.

The next morning

I know that you are going to be of much value as regards my aviation paper. I'll greatly appreciate any information you can secure for me, and I know I can make use of it.

We "shove off" for Penn. in fifteen minutes. As soon as we return tonight, I'll write you about the game. All my love, dearest One.

Millard

Excerpt from Jackie's Diary:

December 8, 1930

~Oh, he's coming!!! He's coming!!!! He is to arrive Dec. 20th. I just can't wait, it seems! I hope his mother won't mind him being a day or so late. I think it's sweet of her to spare him to me for them. I want to see him so much! I hope mother doesn't go to Florida before he comes, but anyway I could have him here at Mrs. Caskie's, but I want mother to meet him and him to meet her. I wonder if he'd like a party Saturday night, but he's here so short a while I want him all to myself. I'm selfish and I don't care if I am! So there!

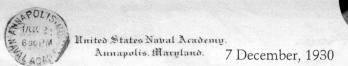

United States Naval Academy.
Annapolis. Maryland.   7 December, 1930

Dearest Jackie,

Have you ever had a thrill run up and down your spine, which is undefinable? I'll tell you under what circumstances I have had these little undefinable thrills run up and down my spine. After a glorious athletic contest, whether in victory or defeat, we stand with our caps over our hearts and sing our Alma Mater--"Navy Blue and Gold." A thrill of proudness always envelopes me at this time, and I have always experienced this on such occasions. Shall I call the next a thrill of happiness--a thrill of joy? This occurred one afternoon in front of a certain glowing kitchen stove with you. The next one occurred this morning when your letter arrived, and I read the story of the young naval officer. His heroic deed was wonderful and to me illustrates the spirit of the Service. Yesterday at Penn. we swamped the University of Penn. 27-0. The Navy team "clicked" in fine fashion, and we demonstrated what Navy "fight and spirit" can do. The Army coaches present, no doubt, learned that they will have lots to worry about next Saturday at the Yankee stadium. How I wish you were going to be there, for the battle of the year is going to be waged! A happy year will be in store for us, if at the end of the game we may sing "The End of a Navy Day" and whistle "taps" for the Army, all of which signifies a glorious Navy victory.

I can never express my proper appreciation for your efforts in collecting data for my paper. I hardly expected you to go in for it on such a large scale, and I can surely make use of everything you have sent me. Next year, during the last big dress parade during June week, you will be there. If I am privileged to win, you will gain all the credit. The information you are giving and the inspiration will warrant everything in your favor, and very little for me.

Apollo, wonder-man? I hardly come up to anything near that title, and please don't tell your mother such things. You see, she will be only disappointed, and I do so want to make a good impression. As for my mother being disappointed in you, she will love you just as I do, and just because you are Jackie, and just because I love you so.

Examinations begin this Thursday for the month of December and extend to the following Thursday. We have two on Friday, morning and afternoon--something to dampen football enthusiasm. However, we should, by this time, be fully accustomed to doing several things at once.

Jackie, dearest, every day I think such wonderful thoughts of you. No longer do studies become monotonous. I live to learn and strive for you. Every night I seek consolation in "our stars," because we are apart and dream of that happy moment when I shall see you again. In the meantime, every day at 9:15 A.M. I seek my message from Richmond, and at night I never forget the little dipper. The big dipper holds much more. Won't you use it in the future?

"We are ready now," to use the words of Capt. J.K. Taussig, commander of the first U.S. destroyer division reaching foreign waters during the Great War.[4] Last night as we marched thru the streets of Annapolis, returning from Penn., we awoke the "early to bed boys" by songs of the Army and our own songs. Everyone was feeling fine and happy, and such spirit cannot help [but] be transmitted to our team. The team represents the Regiment. "So goes the Regiment, so goes the team!" is an excellent phrase which will hold true. Next Saturday, when we march into the stadium, our heads will be high in the air, "tails over the dashboard," and a "heavy drag all along."

"Happy days are here again," the radio tells me, and how true that will be when the 20th of December finally arrives. Perhaps in a few hours I will again see the O.A.O [One-And-Only], and then Santa Claus's gift will be complete for a happy Xmas.

Always, always, dearest One, will I love you.

Millard

---

4. World War I from 1914 to 1918.

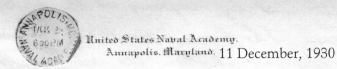

United States Naval Academy,
Annapolis, Maryland. 11 December, 1930

Dearest Jackie,

2000 T.S.B.'s [midshipmen] are straining on the reins and are hardly able to wait until Saturday. Everyone is talking, eating, and sleeping football, and it is said by officers that spirit at the Naval Academy has reached a climax never before attained. Our team has the spirit of the Regiment and the will to win.

Tonight in the shadow of the station ship and abreast of "our subchaser," a huge bonfire illuminated the Naval Academy, and 2000 howling midshipmen staged a wild snake dance. Members of the team, who will bear the brunt of the offensive Saturday, gave us a few words, and in none too dainty language.

We are facing three exams before we depart at 0500 Saturday morning, and the outcome for many will decide their Xmas leave. However, no one has their mind on Academics, and classes are merely routine.

Dearest Jackie, this is not a letter, and I know you can appreciate why I am unable to write one. After things have quieted down, when the game is over, I'll do better. I'll send you that telegram and then write you a nice long letter from some skyscraper.

The Army game is merely a stepping stone to Xmas leave and you.

A T.S.B. signs off and says good night--to dream of Navy victories and you.

Millard

Will I receive my picture Monday?

Excerpt from Jackie's Diary:

December 11, 1930

--If I don't hear from Millard every day I'm disappointed, and I mustn't be, because he can't let my letters interfere with his work, and I don't want him to try to write me when he's pressed for time. I just can't wait until the 20th. My eyes just ache to see him. He's so enthused over the game Saturday. His Navy spirit is so beautiful; he just loves anything connected with that life, and so do I. Rudy Valle played "Anchors Aweigh" tonight, and something inside me made me want to sing it out just as loud as I could. I was in White's eating supper, so I couldn't very well do that, but I turned the radio on louder and sang it softly anyway. Some people near me smiled at me. I suppose they knew I was rooting for Navy. Maybe they knew I was in love with a little sailor lad. I dunno, but I am so much so that maybe I just show it in everything I do. I've seen "War Nurse" three times this week. It reminds me so of the hospital. We used to take our training just as these girls took their war nursing. I could see in every type of nurse portrayed, some girl I knew while in training. The leading lady was my ideal of a nurse, so I imagined she was I. It was hard, though, because she had me so far beat. And the hero was an aviator!! But he didn't come near up to my aviator. I really am so in love with Millard that I'm simply overwhelmed. He sent me *The Log,* and I want to always keep the following poem from it. If he hasn't another copy, I want to send this to his mother.

The Mothers of the Navy

Only a girl.

And what is she

To crave the singing of the sea?

Only a girl.

Only a girl.

What tho' the salt spray is sweet to her?

The angry waves repeat to her,

"Only a girl!"

Only a girl.

But tho' she may not share the sea,

Her heart is true to the old Nyvee.

Only a girl.

Only a girl.

She said to me: "I'll raise a sturdy son to be

A Midshipman of this Navee--

As I am

Only a girl."

So through the years of his childhood

She taught him the things that stay;

She taught him the lore of the Navy,

The beauty of "Anchors Aweigh."

She told him the stories of history--

Of Farragut, Perry and all;

Of the men who have builded the Service,

Have built so it never shall fall!

She led him beside the white breakers

All lashed into foam with the storm;

She told him 'twas his for the taking,

'Twas to this life alone he'd been born.

Though her feet never felt the deck's movement,

Nor the fires in the hold warm her face,

Yet the velvet and lace on her bosom

Clothe a heart that can tremble and race

When the ships of the Navy come steaming

And the flags of the Navy unfurl,

For she's given her all to the Service

Tho' only a girl.

I'm going to write him a little note so he'll get it just before the game. No, I believe I'll send him a telegram Friday, saying, "Here's to a good old `Nyvee' victory."

And now I'll send a kiss to him out my window that will tell him again that I love him more than anything in the world.

WESTERN UNION TELEGRAM

ANNAPOLIS, MD. 1930 DEC. 13 A.M. 8:40
MISS JACKIE COLEMAN, RICHMOND, VIR.
WE ARE READY NOW.
MILLARD

WESTERN UNION TELEGRAM

NEW YORK, N.Y. 1930 DEC. 13 P.M. 8:38
MISS JACKIE COLEMAN, RICHMOND, VIR.
KINDA UNHAPPY. WISH YOU WERE HERE
MILLARD

United States Naval Academy,
Annapolis, Maryland. 14 December, 1930

Dearest Jackie,

A few minutes ago two thousand midshipmen returned to "Crabtown" with heavy hearts and lagging spirits. We trailed our scarlet band, and even "Anchors Aweigh" and "The Song of the Navy" failed to rouse our spirits, and we came thru the streets of Annapolis, heads erect, no one was speaking a word, still proud, even in defeat, that we are midshipmen, U.S. Navy.

A fighting Navy team, with the will to win, played a heroic defensive game and held the 210 lb. fast charging line of the Army at bay for over three quarters. Our light backs, time and time again, and with tears streaming down their faces, tried valiantly to pierce the All-American line of the highly touted Army. The will was there, and a frantic, imploring, cheering section urged them on, but perhaps fate saw fit to sweep our line off their feet, on one occasion, and allow an Army touchdown. Perhaps that will to win was not sufficiently strong to wear down the brawn of the Army. We have accomplished it before, and on this we based our hopes yesterday.

I was unable to restrain the tears yesterday when the final whistle blew. My last college game was over, and the game with the Army had been unsuccessful for the Navy. Dreams of three years were blasted, and I was not the only one who stood sorrowfully in the stands with tears in their eyes and watched those Kaydets [West Point cadets]. Away on the Asiatic station, the China station, the Philippines, men of the Navy also wept, for we wanted a victory, Oh, so much.

Last night I wanted you so very much. New York may appear a very hard place to be lonely in, but the great White Way and the towering skyscrapers held no charms for me on that night. After the game I caught the subway to Times Square and wandered along, trying to lose my thoughts, and then sought solace after dinner in sending you my telegram. That aided some, but I wanted you, just you, to tell me that you were still proud, still glad you are a true "Navy girl." We fought and are proud in glorious defeat, but it's hard. Gee, how I wanted you by my side, and then, I would have been happy in defeat, and only then!

It's a sorrowful Naval Academy, and outside the corridors are strangely quiet. We still have three exams coming up Monday, Tuesday, and Wednesday, and many of the boys are hardly in shape to match their wits against the Academic Dept. I'm ready, however, for anything, and now it's only one week.

Dear Jackie, just one week until I see you. How very long it has seemed since I saw you last, and my heart will be very, very happy when I start decreasing the miles that lay between us. Mattie and I will leave Washington at 2:55 P.M. on next Saturday, which will place us in your "Podunk" about six. I really can't believe that I'm coming, and perhaps I may wake up and find that I have only been dreaming of that dream girl once more and that I haven't found her. Perhaps, when I see you again, I'll know that it isn't a glorious dream and that I really know you.

Now I'll answer the call of this Ordnance book, and in between the lines I'll see your smile, and perhaps the lines, instead of telling me something of guns and shells, will say,

Jackie, I love you.
Millard

Excerpt from Jackie's Diary:

[Not dated]--Yesterday dear old Navy lost to the Army 6-0, but after she had put up a valiant fight. Before the game I got a telegram from Millard saying, "We are ready now."--so like him, full of courage and faith. And afterwards came another saying, "Kinda unhappy. Wish you were here." When I read that I wanted to rush out and not stop until I had him in my arms. I wished I had gone to the game, under any circumstances, just so I might be with him. I may flatter myself by thinking I would cheer him, but love is bold, and I love him so much I feel I have the power to do anything. There isn't an hour of the day that I don't think of him and grow to love him more.

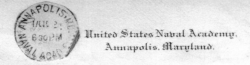

United States Naval Academy,
Annapolis, Maryland.   17 Dec., 1930

Dearest Jackie,

This afternoon we completed our examinations with our most difficult subject--Electrical Eng[ineering]-- and what a relief! Visions of Xmas leave and you have made the days pass so slowly, and it has been quite impossible to study properly. This afternoon during the three hour exam, I produced your two letters, received this week, and devoured each word once again. Each one was so typical of you, and I completely forgot I was even taking an exam, until some minutes early. I might add that I made a very good mark, too.

How can I thank you for your past two letters? The last one, written after receiving my last telegram, cheered me so much, and I faced the work almost happily. I returned to the Academy last Sunday in very low spirits. Your letters Monday morning made my world <u>all rosy once again.</u> A whole volume was contained in that second letter. Only the girl whom I love so dearly could write such a letter--one who is with me in victory or defeat, success or failure. With such a wonderful influence it will be quite impossible for me to ever do anything other than those which will make you proud of me. Jackie dearest, if you will only always love me, this world may present difficulties, but none which I cannot surmount. I, in loving you, can only think of you and how, by my efforts, to make you the happiest girl in all the world. The Navy and the

Service are proud of you, as well as I, and we are yours forever and a day. Saturday I'll sing to you "Sweethearts and Wives," and in it you will see our love for those who wait for us ashore--those who are true and noble and who share our joy and pain.

Am I dreaming, and will I soon awake to find that I've been so happy in a wonderful dream? Surely Saturday is not the day that I will see you again. Three days seem a terribly long time, but not near so long as the endless days which have crept slowly by since you departed from old "Crabtown." This will be the happiest of all my Xmas's, and I'm hoping you, too, will be happy, and I'm sure old Santa won't forget you.

We leave Washington Saturday afternoon at 2:45 P.M., and I hope the train's a flyer. Just think every turn of the wheels brings me closer to Richmond and you!

If I'm dreaming, please don't wake me too soon. Till Saturday I'm thinking of you every moment, and then, I'll still be doing the same thing.

Three little words, and then I'm off to bed.

Always, always yours,

Millard

POSTAL TELEGRAPH

ANNAPOLIS, MD. 9:28 P.M. DEC. 19, 1930
MISS JACKIE COLEMAN, RICHMOND, VIR.
THE BIG DIPPER SMILES DOWN AND SAYS
EIGHTEEN HOURS.
MILLARD

WESTERN UNION TELEGRAM

KNOXVILLE, TENN. 1930 DEC. 23 P.M. 12:27
MISS JACKIE COLEMAN, RICHMOND, VIR.
HOME AND MOTHER IS FINE, BUT HOME,
MOTHER, AND YOU IS PART OF MY DREAMS.
MILLARD

WESTERN UNION HOLIDAY GREETING

KNOXVILLE, TENN.

MISS JACKIE COLEMAN, RICHMOND, VIR.

OUR BRIGHT STAR IS OUT TONIGHT, AND I'M
SEEKING A WEE BIT OF HAPPINESS BY JUST
HOPING YOU ARE WATCHING TOO. XMAS EVE
AND I'M UNHAPPY, SO I NOW KNOW THAT I'LL
ALWAYS BE UNHAPPY TILL I'M WITH YOU. MY
THOUGHTS AND HEART UNITE IN WISHING YOU
A MERRY XMAS.

MILLARD

Excerpts from Jackie's Diary:

December 24, 1930

--Christmas Eve! And how much I have to write tonight! December 20th and 21st shall always be remembered as long as I live, for Millard came to me on his way home to Knoxville. He and Matty got here about six o'clock in the evening, and from then until he left me the next night at 10:20 P.M. I was truly in heaven. Saturday night (20th) so many people came in, but finally I was alone with the O.a.O. [One-and-Only] man in all the world for me. I still thrill at the memory of his arms about me, his lips to mine, and his eyes looking in mine. His picture is here now on the desk beside me--watching me. How I want him now! Sometimes I feel I simply must see him. And to think all my life will probably be spent bidding him good-bye. But I'm going to be a good sailor girl, and though I'm only make-believing--be gay, and though underneath my heart is crying, "Don't go, don't go!"--smile! He sang me the song called "Sweethearts and Wives" and how it did thrill me. I'm his sweetheart now, and someday I'll be his or no one's wife! He told me that someday he was going to make me so happy. He's already made me the happiest girl in all the world, and my hopes and prayers are that I may make him as happy--that he will love me for ever! He gave me the loveliest Navy pin which I shall always cherish. It shall always be over my heart feeling each throb as it beats for him. It seems when I'm in his arms that we're the only two people in the world. Nothing's untrue, unkind--only beauty reigns. His arms are so strong, his eyes so true. I'm sorry I cried a bit when he left, but I'm not used to having him leave me yet. I must learn to be brave. I will! His telegram announcing his safe arrival home and his dear mother's well-being is written upon my heart, for he said his home, his mother, and I were part of his dreams.

Christmas Eve! And my prayer is that the Child of Bethlehem will watch over him always, will guide us ever, and love us all!

December 28, 1930

--Christmas day is over, and what a day. I was sick with a cold and all alone here at Mrs. Caskie's during the morning--and to top it all received a telegram from Millard saying he was unhappy too without me. I am and should be the happiest girl in the world, but it seems all wrong that we have to be apart. I want him. I love him so!. . . God's been so good to me. Given me the life and love I want. Given me the most wonderful mother and dad, the most wonderful boy in all the world to love, and be loved by the dearest brothers and friends. And all that I want and I am grateful. I do so much want to show my thanks in some way. Tonight I went down to Mrs. Carson's for supper. Of course, they teased me about the Navy, and how proud I am there's reason too! Madeline insists that wearing a man's pin means engagement. My pin means I am in love with Millard— frightfully so, and that someday I do hope to become his wife, but it is in no way binding to him. I don't want to be a millstone around his neck, and it will be quite a long time before he's reached a goal and can take on responsibility of marriage, and that is if he should want me. I love him so much that I want him to go on to those ideals he has planned for himself. And for once in my selfish life I am willing to put myself last. It's much harder to have to wait for him, but I'm, oh, so happy that I have him to wait for. And I'll wait forever and a day and be faithful and true, for I love him more than anything in life.

POSTAL TELEGRAPH

ANNAPOLIS, MD. 1931 JAN. 2 A.M. 10:03
MISS JACKIE COLEMAN, RICHMOND, VIR.
SO LONELY AND WANTING YOU SO BADLY
MILLARD

2 Jan., 1931

Dearest Jackie,

The Naval Academy once again, and it was with a rather heavy heart that I entered the gray walls of Bancroft Hall at five-thirty this afternoon. Everyone appeared more or less unhappy, because they had departed from home and loved ones and were entering into five long months of hard work. It usually requires a few days to become accustomed to the daily routine again, and then the days come and go, just as though we had never been home and leave never came. This is indeed the dreary time for life at the Naval Academy, and how I have missed you!

My visit in Knoxville was very pleasant. Everyone was very nice to me, and I should have had a marvelous time. Every minute was occupied with something, and on the exterior I was a smiling, happy midshipman on leave. However, there was something lacking, and your picture, in part, provided that which I missed so much. All the time, after you arrived Xmas day, you occupied a chair that was drawn up close to my bed. The little ribboned anchor was draped over one corner, and the toy battleship, symbolic in her strength and power, lay alongside at the bottom. Every night you were the last of my thoughts, and on awakening you were always there, still smiling so patiently. I would smile back, bid you good morning with a tender kiss, and then I would spend a few moments of blissful happiness, congratulating myself upon having such a wonderful girl as you. Since my return, you now occupy a place beside my mother on my locker door. I stand off and look at them every few minutes and consider how very lucky I am.

The hardest thing I have ever attempted to do occurred when we said good-bye, and I started for Knoxville some ten days ago. It is impossible to describe the emotions which arose within me and revolted against the mere suggestion that we should be parted. I have come to love you even more than life itself, and since leaving Richmond, I have spent many hours just yearning for you. It seemed impossible--Mattie is so happy with Martha--to be cheerful and say that I was enjoying myself. I was, but how I wanted you--the only girl who will ever matter to me in this world. Dearest Jackie--your very name is so sacred--I love you with all my heart and soul and body. Since returning, I dread to start the grind again, because you are not near. If you were only close by where I could see you when things go wrong, how much easier all would be. However, our happiness depends to a large extent upon the next five months. You see, I just want you so badly, it's hard to do something which keeps up separated.

How can I thank you for the few golden, happy hours you granted me with you in Richmond. I've only known what real happiness really is since you came to Annapolis, and even this soon you have exerted a wonderful, powerful influence over me that will mold happiness for me the rest of my life. Your mother, father, and brothers are fine, and I like them all so very much. Your mother is so sweet, patient, and forgiving. I feel in love with her because of these things, and because she's <u>your</u> mother. And Stuart,[5] he is swell. I hope you will succeed in making a real Navy man out of him.

I am hoping you had a most merry Xmas, and that the new year will be the happiest of all for you, and us. I know that it has much in store for both of us, if my dreams are realized, and nothing can happen which will shatter them, as long as your faith and trust is in me. I could never, never betray such a faith, and my heart and being just swell with pride when I think of it. How much better we can work and accomplish so many things, when we are working for some one.

Right now, the one thing I am most interested in is when I am to see you again. I want to so badly, and I have something for you, and I just couldn't send it through the mail. Could you imagine what it is? Our next "hop," which is solely a first class "hop," occurs on Saturday 31 January. That afternoon we meet V.M.I. in basketball, and before the "hop," Bucknell in boxing. Shall we say that is the next time I am to meet you at #2 gate? Please say yes. 31 January seems awfully far away, but I'll try to work, and perhaps it will come quickly.

---

5. Jackie's youngest brother, age 8.

Your picture is my prized possession, and your cigarette holder and lighter I prize very highly. I will always keep the latter as your first gift to me, and the picture is you. That's all I need to say about the picture.

My love to your mother and the family. Please write me real soon.

Dearest One, I'll always be in love with you.

Millard

2 Jan., 1931

Dearest Jackie,

The radio began playing "Three Little Words" a few minutes ago, and I could do nothing else but write you, since that is the only means I have of talking to you. I have removed your picture from the locker door, and now you are right in front of me on my desk.

Tonight a huge new moon is shining just outside my window, and the twinkling stars appear so friendly too. Since you came, the moon and stars have become my best pals, because I know they are smiling down at you too, and that they are telling my message to you every night.

What shall we talk of tonight? The Navy, of course! Suppose I tell you of our battleships, and how they are classified according to their class. Battleships of a certain class are termed "sister ships," and all battleships are named after states. We have eighteen battleships, two of which will be scraped during the present year.

Sister Ships: *New York, Texas; California, Tennessee; Maryland, Colorado, W. Va.; Florida, Utah; Nevada, Oklahoma; Arkansas, Wyoming; Miss., Idaho, N. Mex.; Penn., Arizona.*

The guns of a battleship are divided into three main groups: the main battery, secondary battery, and the anti-

111

aircraft battery. The main battery furnishes the main offensive strength and consists of guns ranging from 12" to 16" of 45 caliber to 55 caliber. The secondary battery is to protect the ship from torpedo and destroyer attack, while the anti-aircraft battery is self explanatory. The latter consists usually of 3"50 caliber guns, but a special 5"55 caliber gun has been developed which has proven superior to the 3" in defense against air forces. Its burst in the air produces a great concussion in the air, and a direct hit is not necessary in order to destroy a plane. Since the air is to be so important during our next war, a means to successfully combat this danger must be devised. This new 5" gun is the latest to be devised.

My heart goes out to you tonight. How much I think of that wonderful evening with you in Richmond. The radio softly playing--just you and I. How very happy I was, and how I pray that the days will pass swiftly, and I can again whisper in your ear--Jackie, I love you so.

Millard

UNITED STATES NAVAL ACADEMY
ANNAPOLIS, MARYLAND
4 January, 1931

Dearest Jackie,

Sunday night and the morrow brings the first day of the academic month of January--the last of the present term. When it is completed, there will remain for me one term, four months, in which I will conclude my long argument with the various academic departments. It has been a long hectic fight, and it continues up until the last day. So far I have been just a jump ahead, and I hope, during the last term, that I will be able to progress to two jumps, just to be sure of myself.

The end of the first term concludes a naval career for many midshipmen. At this time, all those who are not passing in all subjects are called to the commandant's office and sign their resignation papers, which have already been prepared for them. In a very few days, they start their return journey for home and the farm. I have often thought that February would be a most inopportune time to "bilge out," because it is usually exceedingly cold, and a new outlook upon life would be hard to obtain.

Your telegram was surely appreciated. I was hoping it was from you, when I was told to report to the main office for a telegram. I've opened it innumerable times, and it is now tucked into one corner of your picture, and in the other corner is your last letter. Your picture has helped me so much already.

You see, you are always smiling, and hence I smile too. Jones says that I'm never grouchy any more, even when things go wrong.

The past few days have not been exactly happy ones for me. Since I returned to the Academy, there has been that inexpressible longing in my heart, that makes me long for you so. I first experienced it when you departed from the Academy last Thanksgiving. When I left Richmond and arrived in Knoxville, mother's presence more or less comforted me, but now that I have neither her nor you, it's awfully hard to return to the daily routine of attending classes, drills, and etc. However, I still have my memories and those sacred spots where you and I were together. Last night, after taps had sounded and all of Bancroft Hall was in darkness, I found it impossible to sleep. I slipped on a sweater and stole out of the Hall into the cool darkness, with our stars and moon appearing so happy to see me. Our subchaser was my destination, and I remained in the tiny cabin nearly an hour, living over and over our moments there. I repeated my commands, and I could easily imagine your hands on the annunciators. When I returned, I was soon asleep, for I had been with you, and I had sent my message--I love you so.

Millard

Excerpt from Jackie's Diary:

January 7, 1931--I'm ready for bed every night now, as work at the office and other things keep me going until I flop exhausted. If there's strength to write, I write to Millard or just jump in bed and dream. The New Year holds much for us. I'm looking forward to supreme happiness, for I've found him. I've heard from him every day since Saturday (this is Wednesday) and Oh! the thrill of it. I want to see him so badly I'm going--I've just got to someway--to the Academy the 31st of the month. He wants me to come. He says he's got something for me, which he just couldn't send thru the mails. Mrs. Caskie says she bets it's a ring. I wonder--I'd be engaged to him this minute if he asked me to, but somehow I'd rather he wouldn't go to the expense of a ring, for I like the little band alone on my finger some day. I should love it though, for he would have given it to me. My, how I do count my chickens before they hatch! Oh, I hope he does want me to someday become his wife. People tease me about June naval weddings, but I know it wouldn't be then. I couldn't make his start in life weighted down. Besides he owes something to his mother. And yet--I want him so. It's all such a hodge podge. How I do cross bridges before I come to them. He hasn't even asked me yet. I let my dreaming run away with me sometime.... I'd rather wait a year or so, even though I love him more than anything in this world. Sometimes I wonder why I get all the best things in life anyway. I've done nothing to deserve it. I lived a rather selfish life, only thinking of myself, and yet life has always been one sweet song. Oh, there have been times when things upset me, such as having to give up [nurse's] training,[6] but I'm glad I did, for if I had been in training, I wouldn't have been able to go to Virginia Beach and meet the only one in the world for me. I don't know why I write these things. I don't want anyone to read them. But someday when I'm old, I'll get a lot of joy living these happy moments over again. I hope I get a letter tomorrow. I shall write then. And now to send my message to him by the stars and good night.

---

6. Jackie reluctantly gave up a nursing career, for her mother's sake, after her older sister, Virginia, contracted tuberculosis as a graduate nurse and died at the age of 22.

UNITED STATES NAVAL ACADEMY
ANNAPOLIS, MARYLAND   7 January, 1931

Dearest One,

I've simply devoured your past three letters, and think them all wonderful. You cannot possibly realize how very much happier my days are when I am in receipt of a letter from you. Mattie and myself are all smiles these days, even after Xmas leave, because he too hears quite frequently from Martha.

I think it quite remarkable that you should be thinking of our subchaser at approx[imately] the same time that I paid my visit to the tiny cabin. When two hearts beat as one, it is, however, only logical that they should think of those things which are most sacred. Our subchaser, our stars, and other spots here at the Academy will always be near and dear to me, because they represent the place where I first came to really know you, and that's why I love them so.

Stuart's little note was grand. Thank him for me and say that I hope he writes another real soon. He is one that will make excellent material for a midshipman and a future naval officer. I hope he will early begin his preparation, and, by his interest in naval subjects, his love for the Navy and the Service will grow with the years. My sketch, this time, is a complete submarine for you and Stuart.

Yesterday your Xmas card, which I mailed before I came to Richmond, was returned to me, looking as if it had travelled to China. I cannot understand why it was not delivered, but I immediately placed it in another envelope and sent it back. Better late than never!

I would give much to see our ships that you have had framed. Perhaps someday we'll have them in a - - - Well, I would like to see them anyway. I prized them for over three years, and I'm happy you like them too.

I want you to listen for the latest song, if you have not already heard it over the radio. It's title is "Yours and Mine." Here are the words: I think they are nice--

Just a home with morning glories,
Like the one you read about in stories,
And we'll call it
Yours and mine.

Where the flowers extend their greeting,
Where the blue birds hold their meetings,
We'll call it
Yours and mine.

When the sun gets up, then
We'll get up, and I'll help you cook,
When you sit down, then I'll sit down
In our breakfast nook.

There between your chair and my chair,

Maybe there will be a <u>high chair</u>,

And we'll call it

<u>Yours and mine.</u>

Submarines being our subject tonight, we will begin our recitation. Draw slips and man the boards.

Submarine characteristics

Submarines are classified as (1) coast submarines, (2) fleet submarines, (3) cruiser submarines and to their construction as (1) single hull, (2) double hull.

The superiority of a submarine over the usual surface vessel lies in its ability to maneuver, attack, and retreat while invisible to an enemy vessel. On the other hand, a submarine is a very vulnerable vessel not possessing the armament, protection, and speed of surface vessels.

The principal dimensions of a modern general purpose submarine are as follows:

Length over all---------240'

Breadth----------------22'

Mean draft-------------13'

Surface displacement----1000 tons

Submerged displacement--1250 tons

The armament of such a submarine consists of five torpedo tubes and one gun. Four of the tubes are in the bow pointed forward, and the other one is in the stern pointed aft. The gun is usually 4"-50 caliber and is located forward of the conning tower. Provision must be made for protection of this gun from salt water when submerged. This is accomplished by the "housing gun" or "wet gun." The housing gun is fitted on a special platform which can be lowered into a water tight compartment before the vessel submerges.

Remember a submarine or dirigible always displace their own weight. In other words, if a submarine weighs 1000 tons, the weight of water displaced by that submarine is 1000 tons. Next time we will consider the submarine's deadly weapon, the torpedo, and just what makes it operate.

Don't you love to observe people in general, and unconsciously you will find yourself enumerating the various qualities which they possess and which are readily apparent. Also I notice the qualities which they lack and which I love so well in those whom I have a high regard for. Life holds so much in secret, however; one can never say "I know." One can never know. Truth is evasive, and life is a lure. That's why we enjoy living so much. Even tho our present days are not so very happy, we look forward to happy days where we can love and be very, very happy all our days. There must and is always our quest onward and our destiny. All do not fulfill their capabilities, and therein lies a great sorrow--all do not see life, and there[in] lies a catastrophe. They stop short, and in so doing their destiny, their future happiness is as an undeciphered language of the past, written but unsolved--the key is lost forever.

My mind seems to be travelling fast tonight, but now it stops on you. I'm glad you mentioned Mrs. Caskie in your recent letter. Last Sunday night I went to the telephone booth, with the intention to call you. It seemed that I must talk to you. And then I remembered that you probably would not be home, and I could not remember Mrs. Caskie's name, although I had heard you mention her while I was in Richmond. Tell me what night you are home, and I'm going to call real soon.

Your guess as to my surprise for you was a good one, but far from being the correct one. I have it here in my room, and I look at it several times each day, and I imagine--Well, guess again!

Dearest, the days are slowly passing, and each night brings to a close a day during which I have done my utmost for you, and what a joy it is. I am happy in a job well done, and I know that there is one day less until---until I can see you more than I do now. That constitutes my hard job at present, and I can think of little else, because

I love you so.
　Millard

UNITED STATES NAVAL ACADEMY
ANNAPOLIS, MARYLAND 9 January, 1931.

Dearest Navy Girl,

Saturday, night and another week completed - Jones is in town, and the windows of Bancroft Hall are all strangely dark - I am alone with our moon and stars and my thoughts. In such a surrounding my loneliness can do nought but turn to you for my happiness on this Saturday night. My heart too, has recently learned the true meaning of loneliness, and I'm praying for the day when I can say I am lonely no more. Tis' on such a night as this that I realize that I am a man of the sea - I love the sea, my ships, and I am pledged to serve my country. War is my profession, and there are many joys which a military man do not have the privilege of enjoying. How very much we have to talk over when you arrive in Annapolis on Jan. 31! How much I love the profession I have chosen - It is one in which the aim is not money - Military men

UNITED STATES NAVAL ACADEMY
ANNAPOLIS, MARYLAND   9 January, 1931

Dearest Navy Girl,

Saturday night and another week completed. Jones is in town, and the windows of Bancroft Hall are all strangely dark. I am alone with our moon and stars and my thoughts. In such a surrounding my loneliness can do naught but turn to you for my happiness on this Saturday night. My heart, too, has recently learned the true meaning of loneliness, and I'm praying for the day when I can say I am lonely no more. 'Tis on such a night as this that I realize that I am a man of the sea. I love the sea, my ships, and I am pledged to serve my country. War is my profession, and there are many joys which a military man does not have the privilege of enjoying. How very much we have to talk over when you arrive in Annapolis on Jan. 31! How much I love the profession I have chosen. It is one in which the aim is not money. Military men are never rich. The only reason they are paid is for their livelihood. I truly love all this, but, Dearest One, there is something in my soul, far reaching and deeper than any love that I have for my ships and sea. It is my love for you. It seems to enfold me, to lift me above everything, and it is something I have chosen to give my all. My entire being is yours always just as long as you desire it. Your happiness is my happiness, and my life is directed toward that end. I would even be content to place my love in my heart and go far away, where I could always have your memory, if that meant for your happiness. No, I cannot say that! Without you--without you, I would be terribly unhappy, and just memories would not be sufficient. Jackie, I want you, just you for always and always. You know, I imagine that every man dreams of that dream girl who he hopes will someday come along. He dreams of her and hopes and hopes that some day she will come along. You've made me, Oh, so happy!

The "Song of the Navy" just came over from Cincinnati. I hope you were listening in too. A little thrill goes up my back whenever I hear it, as well as the "Navy Blue and Gold." They both express so much and mean so much to me.

Your telegram came this afternoon, and tomorrow night your telephone at #2 [2 N. Fifth St., Richmond] will ring, and the Navy will be on the other end of the line. Until then, good night my Navy girl. I'll dream of you tonight, and I bet if you could step in the room during the wee hours, I'll have a smile on my face, and I would be saying, I love you.

Millard

Dearest Jackie,

Life for me, at present, is just drifting along. I am attempting, to the best of my ability, to do those things I am required to do in the best manner possible, but I am just waiting, trying to make the days and hours pass swiftly until 31 January--19 days, 452 hours until four o'clock, 31 Jan. at #2 gate. I have a very vivid imagination, so I can easily imagine myself at #2 gate ages before the famous trolley arrives, and with joy in my heart--which joy I have not experienced since I arrived in Richmond that Saturday night. I'll be very restless, and I'll be wanting to meet the trolley somewhere between Washington and Crabtown. To use your own words--Just waiting, please hurry!

How wonderful it was to talk with you last night! I was so happy and wanted to say so much, I fear that I didn't say anything worth-while, perhaps with the exception of those "three little words." After all, that's all I called for--to know that I could talk to you and tell you what is written on my heart forever. I could hear you fine. You appeared to be in Annapolis, and I--the reason you had difficulty in hearing me is because, when I am talking to you, everything which I say is of such a sacred nature by reason of talking to you, and it seems that I must whisper everything.

--Section, rise!

--Sir, I report Section 301 (star section of the class) ready and prepared for recitation.

--Very well, Seat your Section! I trust the section is prepared on the intricate interior mechanism of our modern torpedoes. Draw questions and man the boards!

The torpedo, the deadly and effective weapon of the submarine, constitutes its offensive power, and its destructive effects strike terror to those who are so unfortunate as to encounter one upon the high seas. The torpedo is divided into three main sections, namely, the warhead, the body, and the tail. As the name implies, the warhead holds the deadly charge of T.N.T., which demolishes the vitals of a ship. The body of the torpedo, separated from the warhead by a bulkhead, contains the operating mechanism and the power plant of the torpedo. The tail consists of the rudder and the stabilizing fins, very similar to the tail of an airplane; and directly forward of the rudder, is the propeller which drives the torpedo thru the water. The body of the torpedo is very important, for there the power which drives the torpedo is generated. In this body there is the combustion pot, to which there is led a mixture of 55% alcohol and 45% water. This mixture is led to the "pot" by means of a small pump, and led thru several valves. The water and alcohol are stored in tanks just aft of the warhead. Before entering the pot, the alcohol and water passes thru a small area nozzle and is thus finely sprayed into the nozzle. The mixture when ignited provides a gas, or more properly a high velocity vapor which is led to and allowed to impinge on turbine blades. These turbine blades are connected to the shaft, and thence to the propeller. We now have learned how the propeller is turned, and thus how the torpedo moves. However, there are still many other problems to consider. For example, we must have a mechanism which will keep the torpedo on an even keel. We must have a mechanism which will keep it at any desired depth. We must have a mechanism to permit of curved firing, and one which will ignite our mixture in the combustion pot when the torpedo is fired from the tube. Exhaust gases must be allowed to escape, and a steering mechanism must be provided for.

There goes the bell.

--Section, march out. To be continued.

This morning I awoke very early, and our beautiful heavenly bodies were in their glory. In the early hours of the morning, when the world appears as a giant fallen asleep, one can do his clearest and best thinking. The sensations which arise do not cloud one's mind, but present unusual stimulus. One gets away from the veneer of life, back to the basic principles. The most terrible punishment in the world to me is my Conscience. We might call it mental worry, better. The future holds so much in store for me, and I seem so unprepared to face life. Here everything is provided. We have our worries as regards academics, but I know that life outside will be very much different. That's what constitutes my mental worry of above. You see, my dreams of the future contain you, and I must first attain my place in the great outside. Dearest Navy Girl, you must be so very happy, and I want to be the means to that end. All these things I thought of and deliberated on in the early hours of the dawn. My bay and ships provided the stimulus, and my mind extended to very happy days of days, I hope and pray will come.

How can I wait to see you? Just by working daily with all my heart, no matter how hard it seems, and realizing that I'm preparing myself for you--just you, my Dear Navy Girl.

With a kiss on each star for you, I say good night. In my prayers, I'll say: Dear God, always keep Jackie and be with her. She deserves the utmost happiness of any woman on earth, and please be always with me too, in those things I desire to do.

Millard

14 January, 1931

Dearest Jackie,

One week from tomorrow examinations for the month of January start, and their completion will complete the first academic term. After a few of the boys have left for home, and we are certain that we are not included in the kind invitation, the new term will be well underway and then four months later--a great day for me.

The work next term is considered the most difficult of the entire course, and I see that I am going to have to apply myself very strenuously. Radio Engineering, Steam Turbines, as well as Differential Equations, together with four other subjects does not present such an inviting appearance. With my paper yet to prepare, I see busy days ahead. During the time I have been here I have seen many [in] first class come within one and two months of graduation, and then be dismissed. To me that appears to be the worst calamity imaginable and would be a blow from which I would never recover.

Stuart's letter was fine. I have enjoyed both of his so very much. I show them to many classmates, and how we all laugh at his unique method of expressing himself. The misspelled words are quite all right, and I'm glad you did not make him correct them. Stuart is a fine example of American boyhood, and someday he'll do great things. Tell him that I will answer his letters real soon.

Do you play golf? If so, we will have a game someday, and I'll wager that you defeat me. I'm very poor, not having played extensively, but I find it a great game, and something I attempt to lose my loneliness in. On some days, when I don't do so well in classes--those are the times when I need you so and want you more than anything in the world. It is impossible for me to sit at my desk and attempt to accomplish anything. I have a nameless longing that completely envelopes me, and I <u>have</u> to do something. Take a long walk, where I can just be alone with you by my sea and ships--this is the best of all, I find--other times I attempt to lose myself in golf--just waiting--just trying to make the hours and days pass by--just waiting for you.

Huge chalk marks over my door proclaim 16 days and 385 hours until you arrive. Can I wait?

Your poem was much appreciated. I overlooked it when I read *The Log,* so I'm happy you thought to send it to me. If I can only know that you will always be waiting for me, my days will be happy, and I'll always attempt to come back. Gee, I can let my imagination hold sway and dream of the most happy days--days with you, when I can tell you every day, every minute, that I love you more than my life. To imagine that you kiss me good night appears as a glorious dream too, but every night I'll take one from our stars and send one in return.

May I say, dear one, that my life is yours, and I'll love you but better after death.

Millard

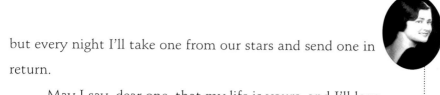

UNITED STATES NAVAL ACADEMY
ANNAPOLIS, MARYLAND

18 January, 1931

Dearest Jackie,

Sunday afternoon, and again I have Bancroft Hall mostly to myself, where I can watch the sailboats on the bay and be alone with my thoughts. How I love these sacred moments! Then I am alone with you, you're smiling at me, and I can say those things which my heart desires to say. I may say that these are my happiest moments of my present life. I am happy, yes, in my everyday life, for I am striving for a purpose, but when I can be alone with you and my beautiful thoughts--that's what I call true happiness!

Yesterday afternoon our record of six consecutive victories in basketball was broken by the highly touted "Duke" five, which journeyed to Annapolis to administer a sound beating. The final score was 40-27, and if we had not have had two of our stars out of the game, there might have been a different story. The day you arrive in Annapolis, we play V.M.I. at two-thirty. I forgot that the 31st is a Saturday, so you must plan to arrive shortly after noon if possible. We are free after 12:30 P.M., and I would like for you to see the basketball game. After the basketball game, there will also be wrestling that perhaps you will want to see. You see, I'm really giving many excuses for your early arrival, I want to see you so badly.

During the past month I have been slightly worried over a certain matter. Until now, I have not mentioned the matter to you--but the future must be faced, so here goes. Congress in a bill several years ago designated the maximum number of officers in the U.S. Navy. Last year that number of officers, 5,079, was reached. This means that if my class is commissioned as Ensigns, there will be 450 more excess officers in the Service. Although it is admitted there is a shortage of officers in the service, the number allowed for by Congress cannot be exceeded. So, in the New York paper some time ago, there appeared the announcement that over 200 of my classmates will not be commissioned next June. These men will be allowed to graduate, receive a year's pay, and then returned to civilian life. Thus the ambition will be blasted of serving our country in the Navy--the life and career we have chosen. Now, we shall see just where I stand in my class. Of course, the ones commissioned next June will be the highest in the class. My class consists of 465 members, and my standing is 230. In other words, there are 235 members below me in class standing. This would signify that I am more or less on the border line, if the report is true that over 200 will not be commissioned. It is by no means official, as the authorities here have not denied or substantiated this rumor. It is, if true, a situation which must be faced squarely. If I were not commissioned, it would constitute the greatest blow I have ever received. I have attempted to give my all since I have been here, and I have steadily improved every year, coming up over a hundred numbers each year. I was at more or less of a disadvantage when I entered, since I was only seventeen and had had no preparatory work before entering, but came directly from High School. Since so many had college work before entering the Academy, it is a disadvantage, as far as class standing is concerned.

I hope my troubles haven't been boresome, but I just had to tell you now, so that if anything happens, you will know. I pray that everything will come out all right.

Dearest One, my faith in life is embodied in you alone. When times are black, it is then I realize just how much that faith is, and that I love you, love you.

With my prayer at night, and yours in the morning, perhaps God will see that we are always happy.

Millard

WESTERN UNION TELEGRAM

ANNAPOLIS, MD. 1931 JAN. 21 P.M. 10:48

MISS JACKIE COLEMAN, RICHMOND, VIR.

HOW CAN I THANK YOU FOR YOUR LETTER. IT

HAS MADE ME SO HAPPY, AND I KNOW THAT

EVERYTHING MUST COME OUT ALL RIGHT. EXAMS

UNTIL YOU COME, SO MY MESSAGE WILL COME

TO YOU EVERY NIGHT BY WAY OF THE STARS.

TEN DAYS JUST WAITING. PLEASE HURRY

MILLARD

UNITED STATES NAVAL ACADEMY
ANNAPOLIS, MARYLAND

22 January, 1931

Dearest Jackie,

I returned from a two hour exam yesterday afternoon, weary and groggy, after such a strenuous battle with the Steam Dept., to find your letter awaiting me. How happy I was to receive it, and I quickly forgot how tired I was. I proceeded, before opening it, to take a shower and dress. Then with your picture and letter I dashed out of Bancroft Hall for dear old S.C. [subchaser] 234. The tiny cabin held out her arms to me, and within her sheltered space, I read your beautiful letter. You know troubles have ceased to be a worry to me, because I now have someone to go to, whom I know will aid me. I can't express to you how much I love you for that letter. It seemed to open a new world for me, and I know that things will happen in just the way which will make you the happiest. You are always so patient, so cheerful, so kind, and you help me so. If I had only known you two or three years ago, I would probably be standing near 30 instead of 230.

Dear Jackie, can I wait to see you? These numbers on my door change so slowly it seems unbearable. Can I wait to take you in my arms once more and whisper over and over and over that I love you with all my heart and life? If I can just always be working for you, and you believing and trusting in me, the days will be filled with glorious happiness, and God can but know that I love you as no one ever did before.

My heart seems to be filled with so much that I want to say, and it seems impossible to say it as I want to. If you will only hurry, I know that your presence will give me courage, and we can speak of days which are to come. Days in which I want to be worthy of you, and you to be proud of me.

Did you know that you have been gone for one whole night? A "plebe" who draws very well acquired the task of sketching you, so I permitted him to take the picture to his room. However, I went down and told you good night at five minutes of ten. I think he did a very good job, and I am sending his drawing to you. Evidently he has lots of talent.

This is necessarily short, for with six yet to go, I had best get busy, for when you come I want to have some good marks for you.

Dearest Girl of my dreams, I love you, I do, I do.

Millard

HIRAM PERCY MAXIM, President
CHAS. H. STEWART, Vice-President

F. E. HANDY
COMMUNICATIONS MANAGER

A. A. HEBERT, Treasurer
K. B. WARNER, Secretary

THE AMERICAN RADIO RELAY LEAGUE

HEADQUARTERS: HARTFORD, CONN., U. S. A.

RADIOGRAM

ANNAPOLIS, MD. JAN. 23, 1931 6 P.M.

MISS JACKIE COLEMAN

JUST ANOTHER WAY IN WHICH I MAY SEND
GREETINGS TO YOU. EVERY CLASS EVERY
DRILL MY SEA AND SHIP SEEM TO SAY ONE
HUNDRED AND NINETY TWO HOURS. YOU CAN
SEND A RETURN MESSAGE BY THE ONE WHO
DELIVERS THIS TO YOU. 88S
SIGNED MILLARD

UNITED STATES NAVAL ACADEMY
ANNAPOLIS, MARYLAND   24 Jan., 1931

Dearest Jackie,

9:45 Saturday night and at this very moment next Saturday I will have you in my arms, and I will be dancing with tears of joy in my eyes. It will be the first real happiness I have had since those wonderful moments in Richmond during Xmas. I can't believe yet that you are really coming-- that I am going to hear you laugh and talk, and to have the privilege of telling you of the love in my life which is the greatest thing I own. As the hours draw nearer for you to arrive, my heart beats faster and faster-- by the time you arrive it will be going at a furious rate, but how happy I will be. Gee, Jackie, every word I say attempts to tell you in some way that I love you--love you. It seems to be something which I am not capable of reaching--so far above me, and yet my whole being expands and throbs when I attempt to tell you that you've been my dream girl for a long, long time, and your faith in me is the greatest thing that can ever, ever happen to me.

I am surrounded by a huge stack of books, log tables, ballistic tables, navigation tables, and I have entered them, interpolated, until my poor brain is all awhirl. I just had to stop and give a few moments to you. Your face and smile has been in between each number and figure, and since I've studied now for four hours, just these few moments are so sacred.

I'll "spoon on" Mr. Williams if I should ever happen to meet him. If he should not be nice to you and allow you to come, he certainly would have an enemy in the form of the Navy. I knew however that he could not refuse. There is some way, I know, in which he can feel how sacred and vital you are to me, and how much I need you, even for the few short hours you are going to be with me.

To bed and wonderful dreams of happy days. The bay is beautiful tonight, so I will lay for awhile and watch her twinkling lights, each one of which blinks a message. Please, Dearest Jackie, Hurry. Then to sleep and may God give you pleasant dreams too.

Millard

28 Jan., 1931

Dearest One,

It seemed a new world dawned some ten minutes ago when our last exam was completed. What a relief that the first term is practically completed, and only one more to go! The exams this month were very difficult, and I pity the poor one who had to pass them. Everyone seems to believe that they were longer and more difficult than any heretofore. However, outside of a couple I did fairly well, so now lets forget and think of Saturday. Your two letters this week have been of wonderful aid, and I wish that I might have answered them immediately. I've been studying every available minute, however, and every night I have "knocked off" for the last ten minutes before taps to read your last two letters and bid you good night.

Such popularity must be deserved! Two days ago we drew our programs for the dance Saturday. You see it is to be a program dance--that is, the first ten will be; and the remainder will be "break." I did not intend to be very selfish, but I had intended to give away five and keep the other five for myself. Would that have been too selfish? However, I have been besieged by all my friends for a dance with "Jackie," and consequently I now have the first one only. I'll try to spare you to the other boys, until after the tenth dance, but the remainder--Can't I be just with you!

Is it really true that you will arrive in Annapolis Saturday afternoon? Please tell me that it is true--that it is now only two and 1/2 days until I see you again. It has indeed seemed centuries since that sad night when I told you good-bye at Richmond, and it seems impossible for me to believe that you are really coming. Jackie, darling, you are going to make me so happy this Saturday. Now that exams are completed I am walking on air and thinking of every moment that you are to be here. This Saturday and Sunday are to be the happiest days for me yet, because I am going to--It will wait, but won't you hurry!

Your reservations have been made, and I will meet every train Saturday after one o'clock until you arrive #2 gate.

Girl of my dreams, I love you. I love you.

Millard

UNITED STATES NAVAL ACADEMY
ANNAPOLIS, MARYLAND   1 February, 1931

Dearest Girl of my dreams,

It seems that each succeeding time I see you, the letters following have to be altered in some way to suit the emotions of my heart. Each group has been growing dearer and dearer, and this must be the maximum happiness for me. I can conceive of no greater happiness, and my heart is so very full of joy and happiness that I have you.

The tears could not be restrained as I slowly strolled back to Bancroft Hall tonight after your departure. It seems that we spend more time in saying good-bye than in anything else, and it just doesn't seem fair that we should be separated. Your letters make for my happy days, and I could not live without them--but--you are so much better--and when I say good-bye, I cannot keep that lump from my throat and the hollow empty feeling which I now experience. Jackie, my own, I love you so. If I could only tell you how much, perhaps I would in a measure be consoled. However, I want to tell you over and over, and yet again that I will love you forever and a day, and then but even better.

The happiest day of my life came this afternoon in the subchaser. We now have two to take care of. However, they are sister ships, and I'm sure the one of today knows all. You see, I was afraid that perhaps you wouldn't accept my ring. Since that day when I first told you that I loved you so, I have known that you are the only girl in the world for me--that I want you for my very own, and I want to make you the happiest woman in all the world. When you said that I might have that privilege, my heart and soul have expanded until tonight I hardly know just what it is all about.

Dearest One in all the world, the future lies before us. It is a future in which my life is yours, and all my efforts are to be directed toward your ultimate happiness.

May I say that the dreams of that little home, with you to say "Good Evening"--Oh, will such glorious happiness ever come. Just you is all that I am living for, and please let me love you always, always. I will anyway, but I would much rather you want me to.

I'm happy and sad as I go to bed. You are in Washington also preparing to retire, and my prayers go with you wherever you go.

Dearest, I love you. In my dreams I'll see you standing on that little porch, and perhaps there will be someone else.

Millard

THE AMERICAN RADIO RELAY LEAGUE
HEADQUARTERS: HARTFORD, CONN., U. S. A.

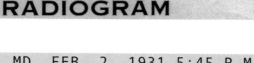
RADIOGRAM

ANNAPOLIS, MD. FEB. 2, 1931 5:45 P.M.

MISS JACKIE COLEMAN, RICHMOND, VIR.

HOPE YOU HAVE ARRIVED SAFELY AND ARE

NOT TOO TIRED FROM YOUR LONG JOURNEY.

HOPE YOU HAVE GOOD OPINION OF

ANNAPOLIS AND OUR NAVY. AM VERY LONELY

BUT HAVE MOST SACRED MEMORIES.

EVERYTHING REMINDS ME OF YOU: THE

CAMPUS, YARD, AND THE DEAR OLE

SUBCHASER. AM TAKING PICTURE OF IT

TOMORROW. STILL COUNTING 20 DAYS.

JONES SENDS HIS REGARDS. 88S

SIGNED MILLARD

2 February, 1931

Dearest Jackie,

I need you so. Since your departure last night, it seems impossible to keep myself within these walls away from you. All day I have paced this lonely deck of the third battalion, and you have been in my thoughts and dreams every moment. Dear one, why must we be parted? When I consider the bigness of my love for you, I wonder why fate is so cruel, in that we see each other so seldom. And yet, when I attempt to calm myself and assume the correct mental attitude, I know that everything is going to come out right for those who work and wait. It all depends on me. Already you have aided and helped me so much. I cannot state just how much. It's awfully hard to say good-bye and see you go, but I soon am able to apply myself, for I know that in doing so I am arriving much quicker at that wonderful moment when I can say: Jackie my own, my own wonderful Navy girl, I love you now even more than that first day when I told you those wonderful words and realized that I had indeed found the girl of all my dreams.

The second term of the present academic year began today at the usual hour. It is the last one for me, and I so much want to make it the most successful. I truly have much to do. Until April I want to work on my paper. In that time I should be able to collect my remaining material, as well as write it more than once, in order to eliminate mistakes. Then too, if I can succeed in obtaining that 2.5, I want to continue in fencing and rifle. The former attracts me most, but with only two years' experience, I do not have the chance I would have if I had entered during my "plebe" year. That year was such a struggle I hardly had time to go out of Bancroft Hall. Rifle starts in March, over beyond the experimental station. With eight years experience with the service rifle, I am able to hit the Bull's Eye occasionally, and it's lots of fun too.

Together with these things I am going to continue working on my dreams of the future with you. Won't you submit a few ideas? I know they will be wonderful ones, and I'm happiest when I'm busy planning--planning that Blue Heaven with its sea, flowers, and green shutters, or shall they be blue?

With a happy heart I now turn toward this pile of books, because I know it is for you, and you alone.

Good night, sweetheart.

Millard

Dearest One,

How I love your two letters of today! From their pages I see my dreams of days gone by and of the future. All during the day I wonder at it all and try to believe it all true. You have made me so very happy, giving me inspiration and the desire to do so much. Before you came, I had the ambitions for mother's sake, but the monotony of the days sometimes appeared unbearable, and I was a rather carefree young man, who managed to get along without advancing so very far. If one can examine my marks since last November, they will understand that a remarkable change has occurred in my life--a change which has produced the happiest of days, and I no longer dread the work of the Academic Departments, but rather welcome all that I can get. In this way I know that I am striving for an end. To this end was I born, for this cause came I into the world, that someday, when I can call you all my own, when I can give you all the glorious happiness which you deserve, then will I be happy and content in knowing that I have completed my dreams--well done. In your letters I have visions of that tiny home--the green shutters--of course, they will be green--the flagstone walk--the white picket gate--the flowers, the sundial--the ship's model--our pictures--all seem too wonderful to be true. Please, oh please, tell me that you love me again, and that you want all these things as I do.

Love, happiness, and sincerity--a most glorious combination which makes for eternal happiness for me. It means that I will always confide in you my joys and my sorrows, and in so doing I will receive in return that which I have already received from you--tender patience and love which is the glorious thing in the world, and thereby arriving at a proper solution for my troubles, or you giving me the desire to go on. For you I would go to the ends of the earth. My Navy Girl, if I could only tell you my heart's innermost thoughts and desires. It seems impossible to properly express them, so won't you read them for yourself--that I will love you always and always, as no one could ever have possibly loved anyone. It is apparent in every thing I do--my every action, my every thought, my desires--all proclaim that I'm yours forever and ever.

You know I am considered a very serious person by my classmates and friends. I suppose, as I told you, that is the reason so many come to me with various problems. In a measure, I imagine, that is a failing, but it is my characteristic, and all because all my life I have dreamed of you and had the desire and ambition to make something of myself in order that you might be proud of me, when I finally found you. I only hope that I have progressed along this route, and in doing so I have acquired the necessary background in order to compete with others in life. And now your principal characteristic which may be said to be exactly opposite from that of mine. This as well as all your others I love and cherish, and they help me so. They make me gay and happy with a cheerful outlook on that which I have done and that which is to come. This characteristic of yours is joy of living, happiness in making others happy, always cheerful, patient and forgiving, loving life and all mankind. All these I love so and admire you for them. Perhaps because some of them are so very different from mine is the reason they aid me so much in every way.

This afternoon I attempted for over an hour to raise Richmond on the radio. I called W3FJ over and over in hopes that perhaps you would be there waiting to send that__..__...
However I heard no answering W3ADO (our station call) and finally gave up in despair. Perhaps at some later date we can arrange for you to be at the other end of our signals. If you should, and 88 (___..,___..) should come over the air, it will mean love and kisses.

Your poem on "our" tiny home is indeed heaven to me. You know, Jackie, I can so easily imagine every little detail concerning that "tiny house." I turn to the right, a little white light, and there you are by our little gate to kiss me Good Evening. Does such happiness really exist? I hope so, for my life is for you, this tiny home, and perhaps the "someone else."

Will you send me the little song you sang to me while you were here? At the time I know it was beautiful, but I don't remember all the words. I want to learn them too.

This week has been a busy one, and I have attempted to start my last term in the right manner. It promises to be a difficult one, but I'll be right in there "fighting 'em" for you.

My love, good night. I'll see you in my dreams beside that lovely gate.

Millard

25 July is my birthday. Let me know the outcome.

7 February, 1931

Light Ho! Sailor,

Greenbury Point lighthouse is sending its friendly rays of light to seafaring men on this, another cold snowy Saturday night. It seems to welcome sailor men to a friendly port and at the same time warn: "Rocks and shoals ahead!" I have been watching her bright rays for the past few moments and thought of the many times her light has proved a welcome sight. On returning from two midshipman cruises, we have sighted ole Greenbury at 4 A.M. and known that we were at last home.

I seem to have dedicated every Saturday evening to you. I, too, seem to miss you so much on certain days and nights. I suppose after the week has been completed, I only want to be with you, to tell you of every incident and have you join in joys and sorrows. Then, too, Bancroft Hall is dark and silent. I am alone with my lights on the bay and my thoughts of you. At such a time, thoughts come easily, and I am most happy when thinking, planning, and dreaming of coming days with you. Oh, Jackie, it seems untrue that God has been so good to give me you. By chance we met--fate brought us together, and how quickly I realized that you were meant for me. The latter statement is so true, and I'll never, never give you up. I'll love you, live for you, strive for you all my days and at the same time be very thankful that I have that privilege. You have already aided me so much, and we have barely begun the great path of life. Can I say that we have started? Perhaps when I can say to you, "<u>my wife,</u>" then we will indeed have started. When we are living in our tiny home, with all the things you have planned, then life will have really begun for me. All my life until then is merely a preparation for you, working and striving to be worthy of a woman such as you, and I'm afraid I'll never quite reach the point when I can say I am. But, oh, the joy of trying and knowing it's all for you. I long for that day when I can call you my own, but I realize that I have yet much to accomplish. Until it is done, I need you so--all your wonderful faith, courage, cheerfulness, and patience.

I hope that I have not been premature in telling you that legislation for my commission has been passed. For two days "dope" to that effect has been circulated around, but as yet we have received no official notification of that effect. You see, this legislation is necessary because the officer quota for the Navy is already at the number designated by Congress a number of years ago. Unless this special legislation is passed, called the Britten Measure, introduced by our champion Senator Britten, my class will not be commissioned due to all vacancies being filled. The latter is not true, because there is a demand for officers in all branches of our Navy, but the limit allowed by law cannot be exceeded until new legislation is passed. Even though the Britten Measure is passed, and my class is commissioned, it does not permanently satisfy

conditions, because future classes must be provided for. This means that still additional legislation must be passed if the graduates of future classes of the Naval Academy are to remain in the Navy. I hope so much that the rumors are well founded, and when we are officially advised, I will let you know.

I enjoyed "twiddling the key" with our "radio man" so much yesterday. It makes it appear that I am so much closer to you, when I know I am talking with someone who is able to reach you easily by telephone. I appreciate his transmission of my messages to you, and more so of those I receive in return. I'm hoping I'll soon be able to talk to you myself, and I sure want to hear your signals. Shall I give you the letters? Here they are:

A ._

B _...

C _._.

D _..

E .

F .._.

G __.

H ....

I ..

J .___

K _._

L ._..

M __

N _.
O ___
P .__.
Q __._
R ._.
S ...
T _
U .._
V ..._
W .__
X _.._
Y _.__
Z __..

If you learn all these, you can send me a message yourself.

Two weeks from tonight I will be with you. Last week at this time found me with you, and tonight finds me writing you my hopes and dreams. It seems impossible to be away from you so much, and you so far away. My only consolation is your dear letters, which tell me that you love me and that I must carry on. How much easier it would be if you were near, but then I'm working and waiting.

Sure I recognized your clock. It's swell, and such clocks strike the hour just as we do aboard ship. Two strokes for each hour, and one stroke for the half hour. Of course we will have to have one, and it will be your choice.

The addresses you desire are: M. Hall, Jr., 3040 Bancroft Hall, and J.C. Bentley, 3217 Bancroft Hall. They have pleasant surprises in store for them.

I feel like rambling on and on. Outside huge flakes of snow are falling, and their effect is so soothing. Perhaps I can wax eloquent on my paper, so I'll bid you good night and see what I can do. In about a month I'll submit a rough copy for your corrections and approval.

Dearest Navy girl--so tried and true--I love you--I love you with all my heart. With dreams of you, our home, and clock, and pictures, I say good night.

Millard

11 February, 1931

Darling,

Now that I've become used to you and your letters, I can't imagine just what I would do without them. As long as we are parted, or I am away, you <u>will</u> always write me, won't you? Yours of this morning, which came just before the first class, was wonderful, and I consider it among the best. Day after day, I try and imagine that our happy days will quickly arrive, and when your letters come, those days appear so much nearer and so very much wonderful. I've also been thinking just what would happen to me without you. Without you, I would fear the worst. You've come to aid me in a manner which you can't realize. It's something in my soul, and it continues to penetrate deeper and deeper, day by day, my faith in life and the joy of living. You may have lost your heart to a sailor man, but he will keep it and cherish it as the most sacred thing in life, always and always. My heart, too, is yours forever, and it's beating for you every minute. So I have yours, and you have mine. In this wonderful condition, we'll lock our hands and begin that climb up the ladder. We are on the bottom rung at present, and perhaps we may have to strain ever so often to barely reach the next, but we always will, and if on reaching we fail to grasp, our mistakes will be corrected, and we'll get 'er next time.

Last night I was introduced to something new. The new term has ushered in an entirely new course--After dinner speaking as part of our English course. Every week twenty midshipmen are designated from a battalion, and in full dress we partake of an excellent dinner in a special room of the Hall which has been designated for that purpose. Two English professors are present to observe the speeches and mark same, while two invited guests are always present. Last night Comdr. Barleon and Lt. Comdr. Scott were the honored guests. The stage is thus all set. After the very excellent dinner referred to above, everyone but the midshipmen concerned are ready for the ordeal. Jones, Mattie, and Raysbrook were present last night, so all your pals were well represented. The subjects of the evening are left entirely to the midshipmen concerned, but it was suggested that our topics would relate to our own section of the country, so that conditions of the many states thus represented would be brought out in the course of the evening. This suited me, so I chose to talk upon the Great Smoky Mts. and their advent as a National Park, and various other details concerning life and methods in the mountains. When the marks for the evening were published this morning, I find that the professors considered my speech the best of all, and I received a 4.0. As it was my first attempt, I felt rather good. I must admit that several classmates have already decided to spend their next vacation in the Great Smokies, so I must have "greased" them up fairly well.

The final term marks were published today, and the standing in the class of the members. Here they are:

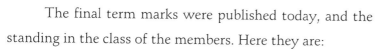

	Mark	Standing
Electrical Engineering	3.26	52
Engineering and Aeronautics	3.03	127
Ordnance and Gunnery	3.40	61
Modern Languages	3.10	153
Seamanship and Flight Tactics	3.20	219
Navigation	3.02	214
Hygiene	3.60	88

Aggregate Class Standing 1st Term: 143

If you remember I told you that I was unsatisfactory in Electrical Engineering for one month. From the above you will see that it is also my best subject, the class standing being 52. Last month I made a 3.90 which brought my average for the term up in the running. It's too bad, I guess, that I didn't do better my first two years, but it's now a trifle late to speak about that.

Yours till the end, dear,

Down by the sea.

I love that song, because you sang it to me, and it expresses so well so many things of which I have dreamed so long. In a few well chosen words, we can find expressed the hopes of a lifetime, and the above two lines express mine to you.

I'm yours till farther than the end, dearest One.

Millard

10 February, 1931

Dearest Jackie,

I'm afraid the good news I sent you over the radio was a bit premature. Today, the Academy was notified that the midshipmen's bill, the fate of which we have been anxiously awaiting, has been rejected by the committee, and hence will not even come up for a vote. Also, only those midshipmen will be commissioned as provided by law, approximately 150. The remainder will be returned to civilian life and given a reimbursement of $2,000. I'm afraid that lets me out, for good, and I'm sorry you know someone who is so dumb. However, I can only tell you that I've tried, and 230 just didn't happen to be good enough. It's a disappointment, not only because I choose the Navy as my career, but you have now come into my life. In the Navy we could have had that tiny [home] in a relatively short time, but now, who knows just what I can obtain in the way of a position.

I need you so, dear one. I feel so unworthy of you that I failed, but can you forgive me? I'm not going to worry, for I know you would not have me do so, and perhaps all will turn out best in the end.

Whatever happens to me, I'll love you until I die, even tho I am at the end of the earth. I do love you so much. For myself, I care not. It's you and <u>your</u> future I'm thinking of, and that's why today has been a big disappointment in my life.

If I could only see you now. I do need you so much.

Millard

ꙮ ♡ ꙮ

Valentine Card
Annapolis, Md.
February 13, 1931

I'm up in the air
As high as can be,
In hopes that my signal:
This LOVE flag, you'll see;
And now that you've found
This affection of mine
Won't you please promise
To be my Valentine?

[Written on back of card:] My Valentine day really comes next Saturday, but on the real day I'll send my greeting and love over the miles to you. This love flag will always be in my heart for you, and it's hoisted, Oh, so far.

Millard

Postcard and newspaper clipping

"Bill for Navy Gets Approval in House Vote"

Washington, D.C.

February 13, 1931

Dear Millard:

According to the following quotation from yesterday's issue of the *Evening Star,* you and the other members of your class will be given your commissions in June following your graduation. The House today (Feb. 12, 1931) amended the Navy supply bill so as to permit all midshipmen in this year's class at Annapolis to accept commissions. The vote was 91 to 50. This was an amendment to the Britten Bill.

Please accept my hearty congratulations and best wishes. Remember me kindly to your roommates and other friends there including the Hodges family.

Sincerely,

Uncle Jud

14 February, 1931

Darling,

Another Saturday evening, and did you know that at this very moment next Saturday I'll be with you? When we are parted I dream of the moment when we shall see each other once again. I count the hours and days and minutes, and I can hardly believe it true that at this very moment next Saturday, I'll be near you. I can talk to you. I can tell you I love you more and more. Oh, glorious happiness, please tell me it's all true.

Your telegram and letters have aided so much this week. I have felt rather blue and worried about the future in general, but when I receive such glorious words from you, all doubts and fears vanish, and I know that we cannot go wrong.

Perhaps that is why tonight I can write pleasant news. I'm sorry my past few letters have been so utterly void of cheer and joy. Having you, I should always be happy and proud that I am alive, to live for you and continually strive for your happiness. The latter is why I have been worried. For myself I care not--for you I care all--and loving you as I do, Oh Jackie, if I could tell you how much. It's something that grips my entire soul, body, and heart. It grips so very hard, that sometimes I wonder at my ability to remain away from you, at all.

I have now informed you twice that I would not be commissioned in June, and that month would find me a civilian. I refuse to again be the bearer of information which is or is not true. The Navy is the best place in the world for all types of contradictory statements to float around. For this reason I am enclosing a clipping from this morning's Washington paper, and also a card I received from my uncle in Washington. It seems authentic enough, but I refuse to accept it until the authorities at the Academy say we are to be commissioned.

The Britten bill which provided for our commissions was indeed thrown out, but this Navy supply bill appears to increase the officer ratio, which takes care of us and all succeeding classes. Let's hope it's true. I do so much hope it's true, because of you. You have been so wonderfully patient and cheerful when I have written you such sad news, and, dearest, if it is true, in a few months I'll be saving for the "tiny home," and perhaps in a year it will be ours. Can I say all this? Is it indeed true? Please tell me again that it is, and that you are mine--All mine, to make so very happy. We will be happy, the happiest man and wife that ever trod the great path of life together. You will always be so patient and cheerful--so beautiful and wonderful--and I--I will always love you with a love that increases with the days.

This has been a wonderful Valentine day. I first received the enclosed card from my uncle, and then read the clipping. At ten o'clock, I reported to the medical department for my aviation physical exam. I didn't tell you that I was going to take it, because I wanted to wait until I passed. For three hours they attempted to find something wrong with me. They tested my eyes by reading, by lining up lights, and examined them with instruments. I was a little afraid of my eyes, but I passed O.K. They spun me around in chairs in a vain attempt in getting me so dizzy that I couldn't walk a straight line or focus on a white square on the wall. I walked in front of ten doctors, and they listened to my heart with everything they could hear with. At one-thirty they said I could go get something to eat and that I was qualified physically to fly. Now all we need is a commission, and I'll be landing in that birdbath within a year.

I appreciated the Valentine so very much. It made my Valentine day so very happy. Mr. Bentley came dashing over to my room with his, and Jones had to wave his in my face and say that I didn't have a chance. Mattie, too, had to bring his up also, so we had a regular party, with everyone arguing which was the best Valentine. Jones insisted that his life buoy was the best of any, and Mr. Bentley was in there fighting too. I let them argue and then quietly asserted--which is the biggest? That's the best test of all. That sorta stopped all opposition.

I slept this afternoon until the mate brought your letter in, whereupon, I took same for a long walk--just you and me. I lived over my train ride next Saturday--my arrival in Richmond and the glorious moments with you. How much we can talk about, and how much we can plan for the future! It will be so glorious to plan every little thing and then watch each one materialize into a realistic something.

We have two exams next Friday and Saturday morning, respectively. I'm going to study real hard for them, so that at twelve o'clock I can dash for Washington, happy that my work is well done and much more happier that I am coming to you.

The future is bright because I have you. Without you, I would be nothing. With you--a sunny day, and not a cloud in the sky--I am everything.

Sweetheart, I just gave Venus a tender kiss for you. Please send one in return.

Millard

16 February, 1931

Jackie, dearest,

The day ends perfect when your letter arrives on the last mail at four-thirty. Jones arrived at that time before I did, and I entered later with high hopes of seeing your letter on my desk. To my disappointment there lay only an advertisement. I sought consolation in "Three Little Words," and did not offer to read my advertisement. Jones then asked if I didn't think I should open my mail. I picked up the advertisement, and this roommate of mine had placed your letter under the latter, where it could not be seen. I was too happy to receive it, even to scold him.

Tonight I have the "guard," as we say, and I'm attempting to write you this from my little desk that commands a view of the entire corridor of the third wing. All the boys are in their rooms studying for the classes of tomorrow. Being on guard I don't attend classes, so therefore do no studying. How very much nicer it is to write you than to study the mysteries of calculus, etc.!

The latest "Stuart act" is a "wow," as he would say. I can easily imagine him entering with shining eyes and a bright face to say that he constituted the "skunk" in the new powerful organization of "Animal Crackers." You know

sometimes I wish I were that age again. They do have a grand time, don't you think? I'm attempting to think of something to bring Stuart when I come next Saturday. You know the things he is interested in, so give me a suggestion and keep mum.

I'll attempt to arrive on the same train that I did during Xmas. However, it all depends on the connections I make to Washington over our wonderful trolley. They don't always operate on time. If I have to catch any other train, I'll let you know from Washington. I can hardly wait, and this week is going to pass so terribly slow. How beautiful our "ole barn" is going to look, when the rattler rolls in. I can still picture every post, and gate, and the long flight of steps. And then too, a certain spot down the long platform, where I held you so close on saying good-bye to you and Richmond, is dear to me, not because I was saying good-bye, but because you were there. We do have lots of places which have become sacred since your first visit to Annapolis, and certain ones will always be near and dear. For instance, the front room of Mrs. Leitch's will forever be stamped upon my heart, because there I first told you the words which gave me to you forever and ever. I can recall our exact position. I was sitting on the davenport and so very afraid. I wanted to tell you so badly and yet was afraid. You were so wonderful, I was awed at it all, but I had made up my mind. You were sitting in the chair on my left, and I've often wondered if you suspected what I was going to say. I'm sure you did, for it seemed that my love for you radiated itself in everything I did. I'll always remember the struggle I had with myself the Saturday night after leaving you--that first Saturday night. I didn't want to leave. Something drew me back to tell that I loved you, loved you with a love which has daily grown since that first day.

Dear One, I must tuck all the little middies in bed, so I'd better get started. When you are tucked in bed also, imagine that with a good night kiss, I said--

Good night, my love, sweet dreams.

Millard

WESTERN UNION TELEGRAM

ANNAPOLIS, MD. 1931 FEB. 20 P.M. 8:02
MISS JACKIE COLEMAN, RICHMOND, VIR.
SINCE I CAN'T WAIT ANY LONGER,
I'M COMING TOMORROW
MILLARD

WESTERN UNION TELEGRAM

ANNAPOLIS, MD. 1931 FEB. 23 P.M. 6:08

MISS JACKIE COLEMAN, RICHMOND, VIR.

TO WORK AGAIN AND WAITING FOR YOU

MILLARD

WESTERN UNION TELEGRAM

ANNAPOLIS, MD. 1931 FEB. 23 P.M. 7:31

MISS JACKIE COLEMAN, RICHMOND, VIR.

I JUST CAN'T GO ON. PLEASE TELL ME

ONCE MORE YOU LOVE ME

MILLARD

UNITED STATES NAVAL ACADEMY
ANNAPOLIS, MARYLAND 23 February, 1931

Monday Night and

Missing you so

My Darling,

I arrived tonight at 5:30, and when I entered these four walls, I fought a battle which is unexplainable. A nameless dread and a longing enveloped me, and it seemed impossible for me to return. I came to my room and prepared for dinner. In the meantime I had sent you my first telegram. It was impossible to go to the mess hall, so I slipped away and wandered around the yard. Oh Jackie, a thousand emotions were tearing at my soul, and I soon broke into a run. I don't know why--I utterly revolted at the idea of leaving you and again settling down to this monotonous routine. I ran over to the hospital and there called the Western Union to send their boy so I could send my second telegram. Please forgive me, but I was not responsible. I miss you so. If you were only nearer. In your home, when I retired, my soul was content, for I knew you were only across the hall from me. Now I know I cannot see you--you are many miles away--and Jackie, I love you so. I want you so. My every action and thought cries out to you that I need you. I want you near so that I may call, and you can tell me that you are near me, that you will always be. Only when this is true will I be content and enjoy real happiness. I realize more and more as I see you more that you are a part of me. To live and be happy, I must have you--you alone for always and always. Without [you] I cannot live--with you near I can be everything and be the happiest man in the world.

Jackie, please understand all these strange actions of mine. I cannot. If you were here, I would be normal. But all I can say is I love you with my body and soul. If I cannot realize that all I do for the rest of these school days is for you, I am lost. But I will realize that in order for us to be happy, I must carry on and continue the good work. Tonight it seems impossible. I have tried to study, but I cannot. Your wonderful, beautiful self looms before me, and my arms are stretched out to you with all the longing and pity that I possess. Can I wait? Can I continue these last three months? Oh, Jackie, please pray that I will. I will, I must.

I've found out tonight that I cannot go away for three years. Three years without seeing you would be an awful torture of attempted living. I cannot. I will not do it. I need you with me always.

My own darling little girl, I'm not in my right mind tonight, but this is what I've been doing. The Navy regulations state that a married ensign receives $182 per month. Oh, why do I even think of these things? When we are married I want to have everything to give you, to make you so very happy. It seems impossible to wait three long years--

three lonely years without you. I haven't really said the words to you yet, but I want you to be mine. Will you marry me? Oh, the joy to think that you will. Please, think of everything, and if we could possibly do on the above amount. If it cannot be done, let's find out before we try, but I need you so. Surely we don't have to wait so long.

Dearest, my heart is full. I'm struggling so hard. I'm going to pray that God is with us in all that we ever do, and for my success these last months. I can and I will, if you will only love me.

Until death do us part, I'm yours.

Millard

P.S. How's Oscar?

Postcard

Annapolis, Md.

Feb. 26, 1931

Dearest Jackie,

Your telegram was so dear. Thanks so very much. Just as soon as I complete these ole exams Friday, I'll write a real nice letter. My last wasn't so nice, but Monday night I missed you so.

Mr. Bentley is writing you why I am unable to sit down. Last night was hundredth night. (Plebes took charge.) Mr. Bentley took charge, and you are to be the judge in his case.

Millard

UNITED STATES NAVAL ACADEMY
ANNAPOLIS, MARYLAND

27 February, 1931

Friday Night

Dearest,

I've missed writing you these last few days, but I've tried to do well in all the exams and obtain the old "velvet" before May rolls around. After such a wonderful week-end, it's awfully hard to return to five examinations in as many days. I've studied every possible spare moment, and I hope results will be apparent.

Every succeeding letter from you seems to be dearer than all the others. Our last exam was at 7:55 A.M. this morning. Just as the bell rang for the formation your letter arrived, so I carried it along to the exam. Fortunately seamanship is my easiest subject, so I could spare a few moments to read this last- -I think the most wonderful of all your letters. When I completed reading it, I couldn't refrain from allowing a couple of tears come out. I clasped it tight to my heart and didn't care if an officer did come up to see what I was reading. Anyway I read it a second time and then sailed thru the various questions on aerology in less than an hour.

"So let's be happy and carry on!" Those words I think are the most characteristic of you and show so many of the qualities I love so well. Already, my darling, you have made me the happiest man in all this wide world. Just to know that you think of me every day is enough. I dare not think of the glorious day when I can say you belong to me. It will be happiness beyond my wildest dreams, and the hours we have spent together have just given me a bare glimpse into the wonderful future.

Your telegram of last Tuesday was all I needed in order to "carry on." These words in your telegram caused all doubts to fade and the old determination to reappear. Last Monday night is the first time in all my life that I have wavered. My soul was in an upheaval which I have never experienced before. It seemed that I just could not force myself to be away from you, although I realized its impossibility. "Can't" is indeed a very poor word, and please forgive me for using it. I didn't really mean that I was "quitting," but, oh, the difficulty of leaving you. After your telegram the old fight and determination quickly came, and I was all right. I can't yet exactly understand just what was going on within me that night I returned. It's a feeling I hope will never, never again return. The world seemed utterly void of hope and cheer, and it should have just had the opposite appearance, for I was returning to work for you--to prepare the way for our happiness. Now that the trail has been blazed this far, our happiness cannot be far off.

I'm happy you thought over my last letter and prayed too. That's why I can always give you my innermost thoughts and feel so safe that you will offer the correct solution. Jackie, I love you. It seems more and more as I see you and receive your letters, I cannot help but place you so very high, because that's where you will really belong as far as I am concerned the rest of my life. It seems that nothing is too good for you, and I will never, never tire of working for you. I only ask that you be near me and love me. Under those conditions I am great-- without [you] I am nothing, and I discovered last Monday night just how much I need you if I am ever to properly fulfill my mission in life. We all do have a mission which God has planned for us, and it's up to us to find out His plan, and then "carry on" to the best of our abilities. Until last Thanksgiving my plans were somewhat hazy. I knew I was working, but I knew not what for. The future was merely an existence. I had some ambitions, but how much they have increased since you came along. All these plans are now formulated, and my only task is to finish preparing myself. All this has to be done away from you, and therein lies the difficult part of it all. I tell myself constantly that it's all for you, and then I am comforted and happy and ready for everything.

I'm sure we could get along on an Ensign's salary. You see, you are to be the manager of "Us and Company," and with you at the wheel and I in the engine room, a safe and happy voyage is assured. So as you say, we will not say three years. Just as soon as I become settled wherever I go and become accustomed to my job and be assured that I am going to fit in, I will come to you, or if that is impossible, you will come to me. Oh, darling, when I even speak of the day when I can hold you close to me and whisper, "My wife, my own darling little Navy girl," I know that God is good, and all my efforts and dreams have not been in vain. I want you now, just as soon as I graduate, but I know it is best that we wait a few months-- but--three years. No, I won't wait that long.

Saturday Night

I didn't get to finish this last night, as the first class were addressed by the Dean of Yale, and I had to attend.

Once again it's Saturday night, and all is well and quiet in Bancroft Hall. Our boxing team meets its strongest rival in Penn. tonight, and most everyone has gone over to the gym. As for myself I couldn't pass up my Saturday nite with you by letter--so here I am.

It's now eight-thirty. At this very moment last Saturday night I was with you in that wonderful home of yours, and I was, Oh, so happy to be near you. Tonight, we are far apart, but in spirit I am just as close as I was this time last week.

This afternoon I played "pal" to a classmate and "dragged" for the first time since you came. Of course you remember Marian Wells and "Mike" Gaasterland. "Mike" had, of course, invited Marian down for the athletic events this afternoon and for the "hop" tonight. However, he went on watch last night, and his tour of duty lasted until six o'clock tonight. However, he asked me to take Marian to the swimming and wrestling. I did, and it seemed so terribly unnatural not to find you by my side. At the wrestling we had almost the same identical seats you and I had, and all the time I was thinking of those happy moments when I could take delicious little peeps (your words) at you as you watched the wrestling. Marian asked of you, and I readily agreed with her that you are a wonderful girl. You know so many people have asked me of you. At church that day, everyone liked you, and since I always sit with my boys, they asked who the charming young lady was. I'm quite happy that they do ask. It gives me an opportunity to tell them all about you, and when I do that, it is one time I rate a 4.0 for my speech.

I found out something today which takes a whole week away from the time I am to see you. The March hop is on 21 March instead of 28 March, as I told you in Richmond. So 21 days, 504 hours until I'm happy again.

I now have only a month to finish my paper, so I have to do a whole lot yet before it's completed. Even though I don't win, I'm enjoying writing it and giving a few of my ideas on how our next war is to be fought via the air.

I almost forgot to tell you of hundredth night. 100th night is the 100th night before the first class graduate. On that night the "plebes" take charge and run things as far as first classmen are concerned. Since I have been very lenient with the "plebes," I expected to get off rather light. Anyway 100th night was last Tuesday, and the "plebes" took charge at supper

formation. At the supper table I assumed the status of a "plebe," and the "plebes" the status of a first classman. First of all I started the dinner by shaving myself with a table knife and apple sauce, since they insisted that I needed a shave. Next I sat on infinity for some minutes, while tomato sauce was poured all over my nice hair. Ice cream had arrived by this time, so I sat on the deck while a generous helping was poured down my trousers leg and topped off with a glass of water. After the meal, Mr. Bentley quickly found me. I at least expected mercy from him, but none was forthcoming. I amused him by pushing a golf ball all over the deck with my nose, and I then assumed the angle /--that's why I'm unable to sit down except on a pillow. Mr. Bentley did all this, so I told him you were the judge as to his fate. I let on like I was terribly mad at him, but I wasn't. I expected it.

I love you, I do, I do. Dearest Jackie, happy days are ours in the future--Oh, so happy. Until they come, I'm dreaming of you, and when they come, we'll always just be sweethearts.

Millard

U.S. Naval Academy

Sunday Night

1 March, 1931

My Dearest,

How good it was to hear and talk with you tonight! Sunday night is always our "blue night," and it seemed that I must at least talk to you before retiring to my room for study. I hadn't planned to call you, but as I came out of the mess hall, I suddenly had the idea and the desire. I think it all due to the fact that you were hoping that I would call, and that I was thinking of you at the same moment. I'm quite happy the operator allowed us to talk over three minutes. If she knew how very happy I was, perhaps she would have given me the honor for the rest of the evening.

Mr. Bentley was over and I told him about the coming "chow." A very greedy look came into his eyes, and very ungentlemanly he licked his lips in anticipation. I'm looking forward to it myself very much, and I'm going to appreciate it so very much because it's from you. I'll love each part of the box, because I know that your hands put it there.

Today I have lived over our weekend together. It has been rainy and gloomy, so I have remained in my room and dreamed that I have been with you. They are wonderful dreams and next best to being with you.

Sorry because of my letter to you in which I asked you to be mine[?] Of course not, and I will never, never be sorry. You are the one woman in this world who was intended for me, and without you I can never be happy. I love you, Jackie, so much that my every minute of living is yours. My every action is for you with the purpose of our ultimate happiness. That's why I want you so, desire to make you happy and have you for my very own, to love and protect as long as I live. Because of all this, I want you as soon as possible, for then I will have you near me to share my joys and sorrows. Only then will happiness be complete for me, when I have you by my side forever and a day. If I cannot have you, then no one else will do, because I could never, never forget you; your dear face, kind ways--so patient and enduring--would be before me the rest of my days, and I'm afraid that I would have that awful feeling I experienced last week when I left you behind me. When I try and grasp just how much you mean to me, it is too much, too huge a task for me to attempt. I can only make an effort at the bigness of it all and wonder how I force myself to stay away at all. The latter sentence expresses it all too well, because I will always have to force myself to go away from you with the knowledge that I am doing it for you.

My own dear Jackie, I love you.

Millard

Dearest,

"Dreams, my ship; love, my compass; life, my ocean; and heaven my haven — I have faith in the fair sailing." In every letter you write there is always a sentence or a word which characterizes only you, and I always love them so much. I have a little note book in which I keep a record of all these sentences and phrases of yours, and when I want to be with just you, I go to these words because they express your thoughts and soul and life.

I have the utmost confidence and faith in my helmsman. She is to "Conn" my life for me, and with her steady eye, and patient nerve I know that no rocks will ever be encountered, and "fair sailing" will always be ahead. In case heavy weather is encountered, I'll be there with a word perhaps of advice, and the bow will always

U.S. Naval Academy

5 March, 1931

Dearest,

"Dreams, my ship; love, my compass; life, my ocean; and heaven, my haven--I have faith in the fair sailing." In every letter you write there is always a sentence or a word which characterizes only you, and I always love them so much. I have a little notebook in which I have a record of all these sentences and phrases of yours, and when I want to be with just you, I go to these words because they express your thoughts and soul and life.

I have the utmost confidence and faith in my helmsman. She is to "conn"[7] my life for me, and with her steady eye and patient nerve, I know that no rocks will ever be encountered, and "fair sailing" will always be ahead. In case heavy weather is encountered, I'll be there with a word perhaps of advice, and the bow will always be kept heading into the wind. And when the "blow" has passed, my confidence and faith will have only increased; and if another hard one is encountered, I'll have the word passed, "Jackie, conner of life, lay forward to the bridge."

---

7. Nautical, to direct the steering of a ship.

Sailor, how about a little "chow?" You never have to add more, and you have endeared yourself to numerous midshipmen who live adjacent to 3220. The entire box is excellent, and you were wonderful to think of us. The Chinese "chew" brought back sacred memories to me, of when I was with you that wonderful week-end. It seems ages ago. I'll bet you made the fudge which I discovered all nicely covered up in the bottom, and it's excellent. Every time Mr. Bentley comes into the room, he licks his lips, and that greedy look, mentioned before, comes into his eyes. I'm afraid that when this is all gone, we will starve to death, and there won't be a crumb after tonight, I'm sure. All the boys say you are a wonderful cook and join with me in thanking you with all our hearts. "Chow" in Bancroft Hall is heralded far and wide, and although it never lasts long, no matter the quantity, it's appreciated more than any other possible gift.

A new method of sending kisses! I like the evidence part very much, but it's not exactly like you, however. I've never seen the "red" on your lips, and they don't need a bit. Oscar's kiss was quite characteristic, and thank him for me. Has he forgotten me, after being with you for two weeks? If I were him I'd forget all about the Navy, when I had you for my "pal" all the time.

Your radio test receives indeed a 4.0. Not a mistake, and every letter was exactly correct. I didn't understand just who was giving the lessons and tests. Do you receive the signals over your radio at home? A high frequency receiver is usually necessary to receive radio code signals, although some times code is heard over the ordinary receiving sets. I'm proud of your knowledge, and when you come on the 21st, I'll bring out a little "buzzer" set and give you a test myself.

By the time you arrive my paper will be in fairly presentable shape. I've been busy on it all my spare moments this week, even forsaking my usual nine holes yesterday to write some. I also called on Lt. Comdr. Ramsey, commander of our flight squadron here, last Tuesday, and we held a long interesting talk. He has been in aviation since the war and, of course, is much interested in the subject as well as well-versed in all its branches. He has a service reputation of being one of the best of "flyers." I told him that I desired him to give me his ideas on how the next naval battle would be fought, considering aircraft, and gave him a few of my ideas for consideration. Altogether I learned very much about methods in the fleet and gained an excellent background on which to base all my allegations. The Asst. to the Commandant before coming to the Academy was First Lt. on the *Saratoga,* so he gave me some valuable information concerning the character and conduct of these mighty ships, so all important in naval aviation. I expect you to be all critical when you read the results of my efforts next 21st.

Mental attitude! How important I find it every day. After my battle that Monday night, when I returned to the Academy, leaving you behind forced me to assume the correct mental attitude before the following morning, or it would

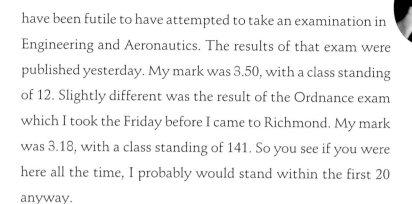

have been futile to have attempted to take an examination in Engineering and Aeronautics. The results of that exam were published yesterday. My mark was 3.50, with a class standing of 12. Slightly different was the result of the Ordnance exam which I took the Friday before I came to Richmond. My mark was 3.18, with a class standing of 141. So you see if you were here all the time, I probably would stand within the first 20 anyway.

I forgot to say that my paper must be headed with an appropriate motto. I've racked my brain, and the only one I can think of is: "Careful preparation is the best safeguard against failure." Won't you think of a better one to send me? And then I'll sign the paper Mr. and Mrs.---I mean M.J. Klein and Jackie Coleman.

You haven't told me where you would rather have me be--East or West Coast. In just a few more months I'll be preparing to buy that "tiny home" with the picket gate, so perhaps we had better decide on its approximate location-- East or West. Isn't that approximate? As far as I am concerned, its only requisite is you. Everything else is for you to decide. Darling, I'm living the hours and minutes and days until I'll have you forever. It's all I can think of. I love you so, Jackie. I wonder how I stay away from you at all, but I do know it's because I do love you so, and I have that single purpose in life--to make you so very happy.

Millard

U.S. Naval Academy

Annapolis, Maryland

Saturday Night

7 March, 1931

Jackie, Dearest,

My Saturday night letter is always such a comfort. When I am a midshipman no longer, and school days are gone, and I am away from you, I'll continue to always make my Saturday nights yours. To be a little more exact, all my nights and all the days are yours too, but I seem so much nearer when I am writing you on Saturday night. The week's work is completed, and our minds are more free from worry than at any other time in the week. Everything is so nice and quiet and dark, and I'm alone. Perhaps it's because we've been together more on Saturdays that I like especially to write you at this time.

Tonight our boxing team invades the lair of Syracuse for a dual meet. Our twelve year record of no defeats is still intact, but tonight is considered the stiffest meet of the season. We are hoping to keep the record clean and to produce two or three intercollegiate champions when the intercollegiates are held next month. I'm so sorry that you won't see one of our meets. They are very popular, and the gym is always filled to overflowing. Our last meet is next Saturday with Western Maryland, and the intercollegiates are to be held at Philadelphia.

You had best look to your laurels in this "golf" game. I played nine holes this afternoon and turned in my low score to date. However, you should not be particularly worried, for my low score is not so low when real golfers discuss their score. I'm certainly looking forward to our game so much, and we'll be setting the date not so very far distant. I imagine it will be early in June if O.K. with you.

I'm quite thrilled over "twiddling the key" with you tomorrow afternoon. I worked W3FJ this afternoon (our radio man), and he said that he had everything arranged for you to be at his station at five o'clock. Gee, it will be exciting to know that you are at the other end of my signals, and each Da and Dit will mean that I love you. So if you don't catch everything, it can all be condensed into those three little words. I hope you will do a little transmitting yourself and at least send me "Mike." It will surely be the best transmission that I have ever listened to.

Eighteen more "rivers" to go. Each river constitutes an exam, and the fewer rivers left to cross the better everyone feels. Three months and eighteen rivers can't be so terribly long, and perhaps it will come and go as quickly as I hope. I really can't imagine myself graduating. I've been going to school so very long, it will indeed be a novel sensation to receive the diploma which ends my school days. However, work will have only begun in perhaps a little different form from that which I have been used to, and in reality you are trying to be a naval officer for several years after graduation.

It's going to be fun though, and I'm going to work real hard from the start. There is a certain "something" which is known as "service reputation," and this reputation begins the day you graduate. It really means your ability as an officer and a gentleman, and your reputation precedes you to every new station to which you report for duty. This reputation as it is gradually established determines to a great extent the particular duty to which an officer may be assigned. If his service reputation is bad, he will certainly not be assigned to an important post where reliability and efficiency are necessary in the man who runs the machine. Hence it behooves one to start early and build up a fine "service reputation," if everything is to run smoothly in later years, when high ranks are finally obtained.

I've missed you so much this week! Perhaps no more than other weeks, but when the week-end is completed, I long for the happy hours which only you can give me. I can't yet really believe that you will someday be near me forever, and that every day, every hour will be a joy and heaven on earth just because I know that I have you, and you are near me always. I think it is always difficult for us to realize that sacred dreams have really come true, when they really do. Afterwards we can look back and wonder at the strangeness of fate [that] is causing things to work just right so that these dreams are finally achieved. Our meeting at Virginia Beach, my first letter, your first letter, and succeeding correspondence, your first arrival at Annapolis, Xmas leave in Richmond, your

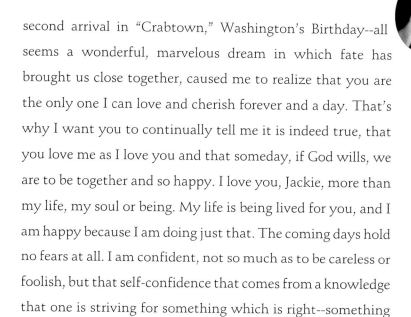

second arrival in "Crabtown," Washington's Birthday--all seems a wonderful, marvelous dream in which fate has brought us close together, caused me to realize that you are the only one I can love and cherish forever and a day. That's why I want you to continually tell me it is indeed true, that you love me as I love you and that someday, if God wills, we are to be together and so happy. I love you, Jackie, more than my life, my soul or being. My life is being lived for you, and I am happy because I am doing just that. The coming days hold no fears at all. I am confident, not so much as to be careless or foolish, but that self-confidence that comes from a knowledge that one is striving for something which is right--something that depends on future happiness. Oh, I miss you so, dear one. I want to hear you say over and over that you love me. I want to hold you so close always and tell you that I love you--love you with all my heart.

Sunday Night

I wanted to wait until I talked with you this afternoon before I mailed this. I was so excited almost as much as if I was going to see you at five o'clock. It was lots of fun, and I enjoyed every da and dit, for I knew that you were at the other end of space listening too. I am enclosing your transmission as I copied it down. You will observe that I had no difficulty in receiving "chow," "coming soon," and "88," as well as your name. It was fun, and I'm real proud of you as an amateur radio operator. I'll give you another test on the 21st, and you will soon be an expert.

I wrote our "radio man" a note thanking him for arranging the afternoon. What is he like? Did he tell you that I said to him this afternoon: "From one operator to another, watch your step!" He gave me a big Ha! Ha! and told me how nice you were, also something about beautiful brown eyes that I missed, and which he wouldn't repeat.

My week-ends are happy when I am able to communicate with you in some way. It makes me welcome the coming week with enthusiasm and causes me to cease being so lonely. May these next thirteen days pass so very swiftly. I am living already when I meet you at your arrival. I'll bet you that I'm not surprised anymore, unless you arrive sometime at night.

Please hurry, my darling. I want you so. I'm sending a multitude of kisses by our stars, and I'm cherishing those dear 88's you sent me this afternoon.

Yours forever and a day,

Millard

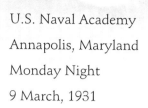

U.S. Naval Academy

Annapolis, Maryland

Monday Night

9 March, 1931

Dearest,

I returned from class today at 4:30 in the hopes that there would be a letter. I entered the door, and, yes, there was a letter, but not the one I was hoping for. This one was much smaller than your usual envelopes, so I turned away and wandered dejectedly down to the rifle gallery to try and bore in a few bullseyes. When I returned to my room about 6:15, I discovered this same letter had a very beloved handwriting upon it, and that you had changed stationery on me. I was so happy to receive it, and next time I will examine everything real carefully.

Your letter has made me wonder also just where we will be and what [we will be] doing this time next year. So much can happen in a year, and your dreams sound wonderful to me. I would rather have you tell them to me than anything I know, and every one of your plans is coming true about our "tiny home," and every little detail which you have mentioned. Gee, darling, I do so much want to make a fine start when I report to my first ship. All my debts will be paid when I start, because, since becoming a midshipman, part of our monthly money has been laid away, and this is ample to buy our complete outfit as an officer and pay any additional debts. So immediately I can start preparing for that wonderful day when I can tell you: Dearest Jackie, I'm now ready for you, ready to make you all my own and spend the rest of my life in making you so happy. Oh, darling, I want that day to come so quickly. I want you so everyday it seems that I cannot wait the time which seems necessary. It is necessary though, because as an Ensign in June I'll just be starting the long road of life, and I want to make sure I'll be a success before I ask you to join me. You see, I will not take any chance that perhaps you will not be happy, and this depends so much on me. But when I am sure that all is well, that I am safely embarked, way on and headed for the open sea, I'll call for you to man the wheel, and we will sail and sail always in deep water, away from rocks, and, oh, the happy days.

As long as I love you--do you realize just how long that is? I'm sorry there are no units in which I can express that interval, but you remember that little poem of Elizabeth Barrett [Browning] which ends: "I shall but love thee better after death." In my mind her love must have been something like mine, and she expresses most powerfully in that one sentence all the regard, esteem, and love which I will always have for you. And you--you will make me the happiest man on earth, because you love me, because you will be waiting when I return from long, lonely days at sea--waiting for me to come home to you beside that little gate, and I can tell you again, and yet again, that I love you.

My own Navy girl, very often something rises up within me which tears my soul almost apart. I long for you so. Your beautiful, kind, patient self continually is before my eyes, and it seems so cruel and unfair that I can't always be with you. But I'm hoping, praying, and working for that day of days in all my life when you are mine alone.

My old rival on the scene again! And he stopped by to say hello! It does seem that he likes to say "hello" very much, and especially to you. Yes, I do remember him rather vividly, but he never calls on me to say "hello." Strange isn't it that he should be so negligent? The very next time I see him, I think I will remind him that he has been so terribly inattentive. Mr. Bentley still gives my hair a massage twice a week, so I'm going to send him out to Carvel Hall for additional business. Don't you think that he would appreciate such kindness? Now there I go throwing off on my rival, when I should have the attitude, "May the best man win," but I just don't like him!

20 million stars throw you a kiss from a Navy boy tonight, and the whole sky pours out my love to you.

Millard

U.S. Naval Academy
Annapolis, Maryland
12 March, 1931

Jackie, Dearest,

Your letter, a nice long one of yesterday afternoon, was so welcome. Somehow it seemed so long since the last one, and I couldn't concentrate very hard on my golf game for thinking of the pleasure awaiting me in the Hall, if I found a letter from you. I did when I returned early at five o'clock, and I can't tell you [how] happy I was.

Isn't it fun being home for a nice vacation? I know you miss dear Mrs. Caskie, but a change of environment is often so welcome, and "home" has sounded sweet in my ears during the past four years. And especially when we are with loved ones, every moment is so happy and seems to pass so quickly. You see I'm just thinking of those happy moments I've spent in your home, and I know how quickly they passed.

I'm so glad you realized that I didn't fail you last Saturday night. I'll never do that, for there is nothing I could possibly do to derive more pleasure than being alone with you for an hour or so on Saturday night. Everything is so peaceful, and I seem so close. I look forward during the week to my Saturday night letter. One more Saturday night letter, and then you'll be here. Oh, that's so much better!

I've often said that graduation from the Naval Academy is so very improbable. There are so very many things which can happen to rob one of a lifetime ambition. All thru these four years, each year one or two men have been robbed of their commission, some within a month of graduation, and one, I recall, within a week. Yesterday morning a classmate of mine slipped and no doubt will be dismissed. It's always the fault of the midshipman concerned, and he can only blame himself. But it seems so hard after so long a grind. Do you remember the boy I pointed out to you as the biggest midshipman in our class? John -- yesterday morning he didn't get up at reveille and slept thru breakfast. The midshipman on watch in the office called him down to find out why he was absent from formation. John answered that he had been called to the main office for visitors. This reason was duly entered as the reason for his absence. An officer happened to check the list, however, and as a result John was reported for falsehood. 99 times out of a 100, this list would have never been checked, and a first classman would have got by. I'm hardly afraid to breathe anymore, and I'm watching every step.

I'm scarcely able to realize that in a short time my school days will be over forever. Most everyone is ordering their uniforms and outfit by now, and I haven't ordered a thing, as yet. Everything has been so unsettled that I've just been waiting, so I'll have to get busy real soon. With so much to buy, I hardly know where to begin, or just where to go. There appears to be a thousand companies bidding against each other as regards the price of an outfit, and it's rather difficult to choose the best, if such is possible.

I'm glad you like our "radio man," and that he gave you a pleasant afternoon. I hope to meet him soon myself, and I know he is very interesting. I feel that I owe him much for giving me the opportunity to "twiddle the key" with you. It was great fun, and I enjoyed it so much. With a little practice, you will be able to send so that I can receive your entire message next time. I didn't do so well on your first, except the 88's, and I didn't miss one of those. Sure, I received Ted's message to take it easy, or else I'd burn up his set. I was sending them rather fast and furious, so perhaps I needed the warning.

I betcha! That's a swell saying, and it sounds so good from you. I'm betting on you too to beat me, but I'm going to do my "darndest," so you had better get in all the practice you can. Gee, it will be fun to play with you, and that's one reason I want to hurry and graduate so we can have our tournament, and I'm going to get the "dope" on you before assigning any handicaps.

If my superior officers in the fleet have the confidence you have in me, I'll not fail to have a good "service reputation." Jackie, my own, you'll never, never have reason to regret any confidence and trust which you have placed in me. Every day I'm trying to live up to your standards, and as you would have me live, and I wouldn't betray your trust for anything in the world. Your love and trust I value above all worldly things, and it's the greatest thing in my life. It serves to make me happy that I am alive to have you; it keeps my head up, and I feel proud of everything I do, which is well done, because it was done with you behind it all. My darling, I do love you with all my heart, and soul, and mind. I wonder that the days before you came were so dark that they must have been impossible. How you changed everything for me, and how happy you've made me.

Of course, we'll go to a little romantic place for dinner--just you and I, and I'll enjoy it too so much better. Please tell me always the things you want, and what you want to do.

A moment's look at the bay by starlight, and we won't forget our subchaser--and then the glorious dances with you.

O[h], please, my own, hurry. I want to see you so badly. I love you, I do.

Millard

U.S. Naval Academy
Annapolis, Maryland
Saturday Night
14 March, 1931

Jackie, Dearest,

Our Navy boxing team started the present season as of old, but last Saturday we met our first defeat at the hands of Syracuse, as you know. Tonight we were again slightly disappointed, but still mighty proud of our "fighting" boys. At 7:30 we engaged Western Maryland in the last dual meet of the season, and knockouts and downs were in order for the evening. When the last bout began, the score stood three bouts for Navy and the same for Western Maryland. Our heavyweight champion, Mid.[shipman] Crinkley, was expected to crash thru in the last bout and give us the meet. However, he ran into some stiff opposition, and the bout was pronounced a draw, at which both sides registered much disapproval. Due to intercollegiate rules, an extra round is prohibited so the evening was considered a tie for all hands. Next week the intercollegiates will be held in Philadelphia, and we hope to produce a few intercollegiates.

This time next week-end I'll be telling you in person the many things my heart desires. It's now nine o'clock, and perhaps we'll be aboard that dear old subchaser of yours which has been such a good friend. It has seemed so terribly long since I saw you last; it seems impossible to realize that I will really see you again next week. It's always thus--the time drags by so slowly until you come, and then the moments suddenly become very swift and fly by without my realizing that they have gone. Dearest Jackie, I want to see you so much. Can't we some way move the 21st up a day or so? It always seems that I just can't wait. I love you, Jackie, Oh, so very much, and all the days without you seem so very hard. You've taught me what real happiness really is, just by allowing me to be near for awhile. I often think of every moment over and over again, and how happy I was when I knew you were sleeping just across the hall. The whole world seemed to be at peace. My heart and soul were content. Oh, may the days quickly arrive when you will always be near.

I'm quite proud of your bowling achievements, and I'm betting on you to win those two more sets. You'll have to teach me the bowling game. I've never played except with the large pins. Is it much different? The competition for the cup must be a very keen one, if so many ties have to be played in order to determine the winner. If you win this year, will that allow you to keep the cup for keeps? Next time I'm in Richmond, I'll expect to see it with your name as the high scorer.

And a 3.4 in tap dancing. I have so many things to congratulate you for. If I remember, you didn't dance for me last time, so that's something for the future, besides our golf game. I imagine it's lots of fun, and maybe you'll teach me some day. I'll try to be an apt pupil and learn quickly. At last we can go on the stage, if necessary, and in this day one cannot have too many accomplishments. You see, a 3.4 is a star mark, so I know you are plenty good.

I believe we have another "radio date" tomorrow afternoon. Don't forget, for I'll be there at three o'clock furiously calling W3FJ. I'll wager your sending is quite O.K. by this time, and there will be no difficulty in receiving your message. I'll again send you the results, and please put lots o' 88's, because I love 'em, and they are so easy to send.

This is going to be short tonight, because I've lots yet to do in getting my paper ready for you to read. With only a month to go, I've got to put on the finishing touches. I'm expecting you to be my hardest critic, so I want to make an excellent impression. Next Saturday night, I'll leave it with you, and you can read it after I've shoved. You can then perhaps form your criticisms much better.

Gee, I want you so, my darling. Every moment today I've thought of you and of every moment next Saturday. I'll be waiting till you arrive, because I'm in love with you.

Millard

HIRAM PERCY MAXIM, PRESIDENT
CHAS. H. STEWART, VICE-PRESIDENT

F. E. HANDY
COMMUNICATIONS MANAGER

A. A. HEBERT, TREASURER
K. B. WARNER, SECRETARY

THE AMERICAN RADIO RELAY LEAGUE
HEADQUARTERS: HARTFORD, CONN., U. S. A.

RADIOGRAM

ANNAPOLIS, MD. 16 MARCH 1931.

MISS JACKIE COLEMAN, RICHMOND. VIR.

WHAT A PLEASANT SURPRISE TODAY AND

THANK YOU VERY MUCH STOP I CAN HARDLY

WAIT TO SEE YOU AND THE HOURS SEEM SO

LONG 88S 88S 88S 88S AD INFINITUM

SIG MIKE

(ES JONES) I WONDER WHAT THIS MEANS..

MORE COMPETITION? CURSES!

U.S. Naval Academy

Annapolis, Maryland

Tuesday

17 March, 1931

Only 4 days till <u>you</u>

Dearest,

My, what a pleasant surprise awaiting me yesterday afternoon when I returned from class! I wasn't really expecting another wonderful box so soon, but it didn't take me very long to get real hungry all over again. I'll bet you made these yourself, and every time I offer someone else a bite, I brag just heaps about your many accomplishments. Thanks so very much. I've enjoyed every bite so much. Each one made me believe that I was in Richmond again living over those wonderful moments. Mr. Bentley and Jones and Mattie and Gaasterland and Mike say "Thanks." Imagine the condition of your box after that mob finished up!

Old man winter is paying us a nice white visit at present. It's our first real snow this winter, and everything is so beautiful in this white covering. It's awfully cold too, and I'm hoping the weather will be much warmer for your arrival this Saturday. This Saturday--you know that sounds almost "close," especially when not long ago I was saying a month. I'll be waiting, my own, waiting and counting every moment until you arrive.

I understand you are to be invited to the weekly meetings of the Richmond Radio Club. I'll wager in two months you'll be the best "ham" of us all and will probably have a station all your own. After you listen to the vernacular of a few radio fans for a few weeks, it will be in your blood, and after that it's too late. Your sending is really improved a lot, and with a little more practice we'll have no difficulty in receiving all of your messages. Don't forget we are to have a test of your ability real soon? I want to show you our radio station too, and it becomes a lot dearer since your messages have been coming through.

I spent about four hours last night in sacrifice of my studies to complete the first writing of "The Future of Naval Aviation." I probably will make many changes, and I know lots of errors exist in punctuation, etc., but I wanted to have it in rough form for your criticisms. One day this week I'm going over and call on Lt. Comdr. Ramsey, our squadron commander, and get his views on my paper. If they aren't favorable, we won't worry about it anymore. The length of the paper is about 3,500 words, and Jones says he's never seen such unadulterated "breeze shooting." However, I've tried to make everything logical as well as practical, and <u>maybe</u> it will go over.

<u>Now wait just a minute!</u> Seven strokes per hole! Up to the present time I haven't won any tournaments or matches, and most everyone beats me in this game of golf. In fact, I'm quite proud when I break a 45 on this course, and 32 is par.

Now that I've spilled the "dope" just how "rotten" I am, please, please come down on that handicap <u>just</u> a little. For example, if we played a hole and halved same, I would be exactly seven strokes behind, and wouldn't I look nice? I see right now I'm going to have to talk to you about this golf subject.

Is Mrs. Coleman coming with you this week-end? Tell her not to forget she has been invited, and that I'm more or less expecting her. Tell her we'll dance 'n everything and have a real jolly week-end.

Jackie, dearest, before I wake up and find that you have been only a marvelous dream, won't you hurry and come just so I'll sleep on and on forever?

Millard

U.S. Naval Academy
Annapolis, Maryland
Thursday Night
19 March, 1931

Dearest,

I'm getting quite excited with the time of your arrival drawing so near, and every minute seems so long. The ole numbers over the door proclaim two days, and as the hours pass, everything seems to be just a little brighter, because you're coming. Oh Jackie, please, please hurry. I just can't wait to see you.

I want so much to write lots, but I'm going after these exams tomorrow and Saturday morning--and after that ordeal--you. I'm even studying real hard, because it's you the mark is for, and you have always got to be high.

So, with your name appearing between the lines of all these Engineering problems, I'll say good night. Jackie, I love you so, and as the days pass, I count one less until you are always mine.

Millard

U.S. Naval Academy

Annapolis, Maryland

23 March, 1931

Dearest,

I'm missing you so! The time arrives for you to come-- a few brief wonderful moments, and again the world goes on as before, so utterly dark and cheerless in comparison to the glorious moments with you. The first few hours after your departure seem unbearable, and I'm wondering if I'll always have to bear the pain of parting and of saying goodbye. It's so hard, but I try to carry on, as I know you would have me do.

I attempted to bury myself in study last night in preparation for the seamanship examination this morning. I finally gave up in disgust and joined "Abie" in retirement. There in the darkness and stillness (I forget Abie's snores), I could think of you and wonder just what you were doing. I'm hoping you have arrived safely once again, and that no difficulties were encountered. I hate to think of you alone in Washington with two bags. I'm just waiting for the day when I can accompany you in all our travels, and I'll sure take good care of you.

Mrs. Hodges was quite angry with me, as she told me this morning in a letter, for not bringing you out Sunday afternoon. It seems that she had invited in a few people, and

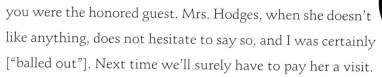

you were the honored guest. Mrs. Hodges, when she doesn't like anything, does not hesitate to say so, and I was certainly ["balled out"]. Next time we'll surely have to pay her a visit.

I want to write loads and loads, but perhaps I had better pass these coming exams first. I'm going to be real happy when there's no more. Navigation tomorrow and it's study, and pray for me.

I looked at the hop schedule last night, and the next one is on 4 April, and then no more until 2 May. I dare not think that I will have to wait until 2 May, so I just won't think anything. Loving you every minute. My own, I'm yours.

Millard

U.S. Naval Academy
Annapolis, Maryland
Thursday afternoom
26 March, 1931

My Dearest,

It's so nice to be able to write you once again without a flock of exams awaiting around the corner. They really cause a lot of uneasiness since they mean so much, and it's quite a relief to have them completed once more. Twelve more rivers--twenty-four more hours of exams, and the last danger will be crossed. But then the <u>real</u> work only begins, but it will be a decided change, and I'll be so happy preparing for <u>you</u>.

Your letter came this morning before the "juice" exam, and I attended my first exam in that subject in very high spirits. I managed to "crawl out" at four o'clock this morning for a little needed extra study, and when the first mail arrived, I was in need of a little ray of sunshine. Your letters always provide a great big ray, so I tucked it in over my heart and went cheerfully forth into battle. It was a victory too, not an overwhelming one, but decisive.

You are beginning to have the language of a real radio "ham," and I'm expecting you to be a leader in Richmond circles before so very long. All real radio "hams" talk a great deal in "Q" signals, and there's lots more for you to learn. I know you enjoyed the radio meeting so much, and I'd like to congratulate all the members upon their good fortune in having such a visitor as you, and I'll bet they are looking forward to future meetings too. I can't help but be just a little envious of them.

The midshipmen's spring golf tourney starts Sunday with the qualifying round. I think I'll have a try just for a little more practice and see how far I get. It's lots of fun, and you see I'm out to beat you. After all, that's why I've been practicing so much of late, so, young lady, look to your laurels!

Our choice of coast and of ships is to be turned in next Monday morning. We spoke of the West Coast when you were here and decided upon a ship in that vicinity. However, it's going to be difficult to request something which takes me so many, many miles away from you, and I'm wondering if I should. I've attempted to look forward to the bright future and choose our home where we will be the happiest. From all accounts the West Coast is a wonderful place to live with conditions so very much better than in this section. But, a whole year three thousand miles away from you on first thought seems unbearable, and I'm kinda hesitating. Let's have some more "dope," little girl, before I go and put the foot forward.

I discontinued writing a few minutes ago just to dream of you and your visit last week-end. During these past four days I haven't had a minute in which to just light the old pipe and sit and think of you. I get quite a lot of pleasure from just doing that--living over each glorious moment spent with you, and each one is so sacred to me. The difficult days of exams would be a joy if they would give me just a few minutes with you whether by letter or thought. The joy of trying and of work well done is so gratifying, because during each effort I can see you before me, and because you are there is why it's so pleasant. You'll always and always be there, and every act I ever do will be because I love you with all my heart. I do, I do love you so, dearest little girl. Oh, those glorious days to come with you. I try and imagine them every day, and then wonder why God has been so good to me. I thank Him too every night and ask Him to always make you the happiest woman in the world. He's promised to.

Has any word come from John[8] yet? I still wonder at him leaving such a home as your mother's, and I can easily imagine her feelings when he left. However, he is resourceful enough to prosper when he arrives in his beloved California, and I don't think Mrs. Coleman has to worry concerning his safety. Perhaps I can lend a helping hand out that way in a few months.

The sailing boats have at last arrived, and their clean, white sails dotting the bay give ample evidence that spring has really come. The next time you come you will be a helmsman in reality, and we'll go sailing, sailing away together. It's lots of fun especially in a stiff breeze--the lee rail awash, and the

8. Jackie's brother, age 17.

sharp clean bow of the half-raters[9] cut the running sea like a knife. We'll take a "vic" along, and maybe some "chow," and away to that old "devil sea."

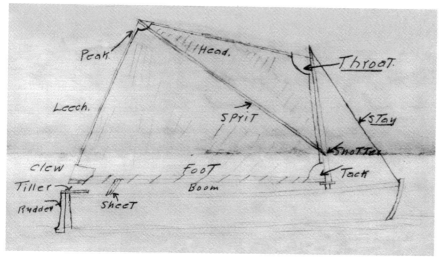

Here's a simple line sketch to show you the principal parts of a sail. There's lots of technique in sailing a sailboat properly, and you must learn to "tack," "wear," etc.

I'll be with you again Saturday night, my darling. Here's where I get a little needed sleep. Jackie, my own, I love you, I love you, I do. Every thought of mine is yours.

Here's a kiss for you by the biggest star in the sky.

Millard

---

9. A small sailboat carrying jib and mainsail and with no bowsprit.

U.S. Naval Academy
Annapolis, Maryland
Saturday Night
29 March, 1931

Dearest,

A most wonderful night in which to be alone with you!--a night in which I come to you for happiness and consolation after a trying and difficult week. A nice soft spring rain is pattering against my window, and happiness is complete, for you always seem so near during our Saturday nights together. I've often wondered why I chose this night just to be closer to you than any other time in the week, and I've decided it's because I need you so. When the week's work is completed, it's terribly difficult to be alone without you, especially with dreams of the past week-end fresh in my memory. I want and need you always at all times, but when work is completed I want just you to say well done, sailor mine! Then, nothing else matters, and I'm quite refreshed for any succeeding trials.

Last Saturday before you came, I had an English exam in the morning. If you remember I told you about writing your name instead of someone else and detecting my error shortly after. Our marks for that exam were published today, and I made a 3.79 with a class standing of 4. Just another example of your influence upon me, and why I am able to surmount any obstacles when your faith and belief is in me. If you will always have that faith in me, I'll never have any serious difficulties. Without it, I would be nothing.

I was so disappointed to learn that you lost the bowling championship, but next year is coming, and we'll get the cup back then. I'll wager that it wasn't your bowling that lost the match, and I would have given much to have seen the deciding game of the meet. Can we have a game sometime?

Monday outdoor rifle starts, and so begins my last season as a gunman. I hope the ole eye is still steady after such a long layoff, and that I'll be able to "plug in" a few bulls from the start. There are lots of mountaineers here besides myself, and the competition becomes quite keen for an opportunity to shoot in the actual matches. However, we'll try to hit the black.

I'm so happy to learn that John has returned home, and that your mother is happy again. Since his heart is set upon going, it will be very much better for him to depart in a proper manner. Perhaps he can be persuaded to finish the term at school before departing for the golden West. It's only two months, and he should be able to wait that long. If he would only realize the value of his school days and the aid which they will give him later, I'm sure he would finish his high school course at any rate.

"Mattie" and Raysbrook came in for the evening and spoiled it all, and now it's time to go to bed. I'll finish tomorrow.

Sunday Night

A great special delivery this morning, which was appreciated so much. You've been so good about writing during the past week, and I couldn't tell you how they have aided me. Every letter, and every word from you, is a bit of sunshine in my life which makes the days so happy. I often think that a better letter from you cannot arrive, yet there always does. Yours of this morning was wonderful, and I've read it over and over, each word being so very sacred. Our happy days are coming, my darling. I love you too much that I can be denied your presence so very much longer. I want you, I need you so, Jackie. I'm going to be the happiest man in all this world when I can call you all my very own. Oh, that happy day. I'm happy now because I know I have found the girl of all my dreams, but when we embark on the long road of life, I'm going to enjoy happiness supreme because of you.

It's going to be hard waiting for you until 2 May, but I was afraid that would be the verdict. In fact, I had already placed the days until that date upon my door and more or less reconciled myself to my fate. Every hour in the day your beautiful face looms up before me and inspires me on to do and dare. Since you came along, self-confidence has been so prominent in me that I am not the only one who wonders. Classmates ask what has happened which has pulled me from that lazy "rut" in which I was travelling before the days of

Virginia Beach. In those days I was content to ease along, just getting by and seeking that path of the least resistance. I found it too, and consequently class standing was somewhat jeopardized. Then you, by His will, came into my life, and how much you have changed every detail! I now welcome the hard knocks and am eager for work--to compete against these various departments and come out way ahead is joy indeed, for all belongs to you. Upon graduation mother receives my diploma, because she made it possible, and you receive me and everything that I am or ever hope to be, because I love you, because I will always love you with all the love my life and being is capable of producing. You too have made it possible for me to graduate--you with your loving-kindness, sweet and tender patience, always joyful and happy, and so willing to aid. I've indeed mounted the ladder many rungs because of you, and some day you will say that your faith has been rewarded. At present I cannot offer you the things you justly deserve, but I will work hard, and someday you'll have them all.

I'm so proud of you as the leading lady of "The Good Ship, Lecova," and I don't wonder at all for their choice. Songs and dialogue--I can imagine you in every role, and again I'm envious of the leading man. I'm a little worried that the wedding won't be a "fake." You see, these leading men have to be watched, and since I'm so far away, I'm afraid things will happen unbeknown to me. Of course, I don't wish him to lose the money, but can't he marry one of the chorus girls? All joking aside, I know you'll make good in your new part, and perhaps you will be playing on Broadway before so very long. Just when is the play to be given, and who are the directors? That is, who sponsors the production? You see, I'm awfully inquisitive.

Very soon you will have a snapshot of dear subchaser, and perhaps I'll include the entire fleet of them. They all have been very kind to us and have given me some happy moments. This week Mr. Bentley and myself will go on a kodaking expedition and see what we can find for you. Oh, by the way, last night Mr. Bentley made my bed, and when I attempted to retire, I found myself "short-sheeted." On further investigation the blankets were also found to be doubled and redoubled in such a manner that an entire new making was necessary in order to get to bed. A shower, very cold, at two o'clock did not appeal to him, and he seeks your protection on the grounds of unfairness on my part. <u>What do you think?</u>

Thirty-four days is so terribly long, my dearest one, but I'll wait and wait, because I love you, I do, I do, I do.

Millard (over)

Dear Jackie,
Greetings!

I have been studying with Mr. Klein, and he has given me permission to add this. How can I throw an oceanload of feelings into one sentence? Across the miles of whatnot between us I send my good wishes and the many, many other things which go to make up a warm friendship.

Very, very cordially yours,

J.C.B.

U.S. Naval Academy

31 March, 1931

Jackie, Dearest,

The third academic month of the second and last term is underway, and the days until graduation are slowly but surely passing away. I'm hoping all my marks for the past month, when combined with those of the first month, will warrant no further worry on my part concerning the outcome of the term. It's always such an excellent feeling to know that you have plenty of the so-called "velvet" and no further worries.

Our Admiral, beloved by all midshipmen, leaves us tomorrow, and he leaves a sad Academy behind. His tour of duty ends with his retirement tomorrow, and the Commandant will act as the Superintendent until his successor is named. Admiral [S.S.] Robison, by his always cheerful word and quiet demeanor, quickly won his way into the hearts of all midshipmen, and we hate to lose our most loved Supt. Tonight the entire regiment surrounded his house and demanded a word of farewell for our goodbye. The dear old man came out and said only a few words. "Boys," he said, "Tomorrow I go ashore for good, and I wish you all the happiness and success in the world." His emotions overcame him then, and he couldn't go on, but we all knew how he felt, and the Navy 4N with his name on the end will live in his memory for a very long time.

I'm having an awful time trying to type this paper of mine. I certainly am not an artist, and I've already spent hours trying to finish it. I've almost given up with the intentions of finding someone in town to write it for me. At the present rate, I fear that it won't be completed by the date of 15 March.

This morning I was vaccinated for typhoid fever again, and thanks to the Exec. Dept., I didn't have to go to class either today nor tomorrow. I've felt terrible all day, and I couldn't even pass the hours by sleeping. Perhaps after a good night's sleep, I'll be fine again tomorrow.

I'm going to miss you so this week-end, my darling. It seems now so long since you were here, and I'm only living for you to come again. Jackie, my own, can I say I love you, I love you, I do? I wish I could say how much.

I'll feel grand tomorrow, and a long letter will be coming.

Millard

U.S. Naval Academy

1 April, 1931

Dearest,

I've been so lonely today. It's been so terribly gloomy and rainy all day, and somehow I've missed you even more than usual. Perhaps it's because the week-end is coming with its activities, and I realize that I'm to be all alone. Gaasterland came in a few minutes ago with a happy smile to say that Marian would be here. I tried to smile too, but I fear it wasn't a success when I told him that he was surely a lucky boy to have Marian so close.

I'm so sorry that dear Mrs. Caskie is ill. Please give her my regards and hopes for a speedy recovery. I'm sure she must have enjoyed her trip south so much, and it must have been so unpleasant to return to our bad weather. Here's hoping she's well again very soon.

I went shopping again this afternoon and, on counting up the expenditures, found that $300 was gone. Not bad for one afternoon, but I fear I couldn't stand that very long. I think that I now have most everything purchased, and I'm quite ready to graduate. At any rate, I've about consumed all the funds the midshipmen's pay officer has for me, so I'll have to stop anyway. I believe that I have sufficient uniforms and swords and gold to last for some years, and I've almost decided I'm to be an Admiral instead of a lowly Ensign.

Happy days are coming, my dear Navy girl. I just know they are. A great smiling moon is shining outside my window, and he's telling me such wonderful things of you and those happy future days. Oh Jackie, I want you so. Everyday seems an eternity waiting for you, but I try so hard to smile, as you would do, and carry on. It's only a short time till the preparation will be completed, and then I'll really be doing those things which will bring the day when you are to be mine nearer and nearer. At present it seems that I am accomplishing so little for you, and I want to do so much. I want to work for you and give you many things and prepare that little nest of ours. It's going to be so wonderful doing just that, and I'm in such a hurry to begin. These slow dragging days make me impatient because I want just you. When you are near me, when I can see you smile and laugh, and when I can say to you--I love you--then my days will be the happiest possible, and life and fate and God will have indeed been kind to me. I'll be appreciative by trying to make you the happiest woman in all the world, and we'll always just be sweethearts and remember the days in dear old Crabtown and moments on the subchaser when we wished that we could drift away. How very sacred and wonderful is every moment I have spent with you since we met! Each moment recalls a thousand glorious memories, and these memories are all I have when you are away. They are kind to me and help to make my days as they should be lived, and because of you, I could never go wrong. But, my darling, I want just you--the only woman in the world who was meant for me, and I can never know real happiness until the day when I can fold you in my arms and realize that you are mine until death do us part. The most peculiar feeling comes around my heart when I think of that day, and I know that I'll love you always and always. Perhaps if Elizabeth Barrett [Browning] were here, she would tell me the words whereby I might tell you, but it's all in my eyes, in my actions, and in all my life.

Capt. [C.P.] Snyder, the Commandant, addressed the first class tonight on subjects which pertain to our graduation, and he caused us to realize that it can't be long now. He gave us hints concerning our actions upon first arriving on board ship and our duties for the first few days. They seem to expect quite a great deal, and with so much authority I'll perhaps need a day or so to find out what it's all about.

I'm holding you to the statement in which you said that you and Mrs. Caskie were driving up sometime real soon. We'll have lots of fun, and I think Mrs. Coleman should come also. Won't you persuade her to come along with you? We'll see everything, even the subchasers!

I'll be missing you so this week-end, dearest one in all the world, and you'll still receive your Saturday night letter. That will show you that my heart is beating just for you alone. The week-end will only mean to me that it's still shorter until

I see you again. I'm waiting for that day when you are mine alone.

I love you, dearest, I do.

Millard

U.S. Naval Academy

Annapolis, Maryland

Saturday Night

4 April, 1931

Dearest,

I'm feeling my old self again, and your surprise Easter box made my Easter the happiest ever.

I'm so glad that I recovered from the vaccination before the "chow" came, and I've enjoyed it so much. Oscar jr. is sitting in front of me, and we've become quite pals since his arrival. I give him a friendly punch ever once in a while, and he sways from side to side just to let me know he's there. The card attached to Oscar's neck saying, "Easter Greetings to a good boy," caused some dissention in the ranks. Mr. Bentley says, "That's him," and attempted to take the cake. He said you couldn't have possibly meant me, and that he was a good boy. However, I'll wager that he gets more than his share, even though I didn't allow him to confiscate the cake. I know you cooked this one, and it's so good. Again, Mattie, Jones, and Ray and Mike send their thanks. I'm afraid you're too good to us, and such dainties are bound to spoil us soon.

So the leading lady has entered into a new role! I should think the proper thing to do would be to secure a new leading man. However, I feel pretty good and am quite content to have you do the "tango" instead of engaging in loves scenes. If

I were only the leading man, I really believe I could act a real part, and my words would come from the heart. If I were Bob I would feel awfully bad, and I imagine he realizes how very unfortunate he is. Instead of being unflattering, I think it is quite flattering, because I know you to be the dearest armful in all the world, and I'm quite happy that you don't fit elsewhere. Isn't that conceited? Please say no.

I'm missing you so tonight! I've been on duty all day, and how glorious it would be to have you here to attend the dance. I could close my eyes and be in heaven, and with my arms about you, drift and dream forever. Life is cruel on these week-ends when you are so far away, and I need you so much. My only joy is the companionship I gain from these Saturday night letters. They tell you that I'm thinking of you and loving you with all my heart. When the week's work is completed, and a little time for diversion arrives, that's when I want just you, to tell you that I'm just that much nearer the goal and to say, I do love you so.

Thanks so much for the offer to type my paper, but fortunately I discovered a "plebe" who is very adept in handling a typewriter, and he consented to do the job. He did it very well, and the results of my efforts are ready for official presentation. I'll turn it in to the department this coming Saturday, and we'll await the decision. The more I think of it the less I consider the worth of my paper. However, I've gained some valuable information from my research work, and it's been fun to try. I discovered today that the rating midshipman of the Regiment is submitting a paper whose title is: "The Influence of Sea Power on World History." That's a potent subject and much room for discussion. I imagine he will be the most serious rival when the papers are read by the judges.

Gaasterland has a boil on his neck and is not supposed to attend the "hop" tonight, as he is a member of what is known as the excused squad. However, he's going to be in bed by ten o'clock and then come to the hop after the inspection of rooms has been made. He's asked me to escort Marian to the "hop" at nine-thirty, and then when he arrives about ten-thirty to take charge (Gaasterland, not me). It's nine now, so I'll dress and pretend I'm going to find you and have a wonderful evening. See you tomorrow night.

Sunday Night

Another week-end completed and the old humdrum world starts as usual tomorrow. The first round of the golf tournament occurred this afternoon, and surprises of surprises, I succeeded in winning the first match by two holes, and I was plenty lucky, while my opponent was unfortunate on several occasions. However, my next opponent is the "mighty" Hoye himself, so I'll very probably go down in defeat. He's the boy that started me along the golf road, and he states that he hates to beat his protege. However, under the circumstances he will be forced to do just that.

"Dope" finally has arrived from the Navy Department concerning the disposition of the Class of 1931. 35 of the men who are physically qualified for aviation will be sent to Hampton Roads on 9 June for flight training. 35 more will be sent to Pensacola on 11 June, and 20 to San Diego for the same purpose to report on 25 June. 70 Men will report aboard destroyers, East and West Coast, on 11 July, and the remainder of the class aboard battleships and cruisers on 14 July. Just how these men will be chosen is unknown, so it's uncertain just what will happen to me. The men who are qualified as aviators, and who are not in the 90 who will receive training first, are to report to ships and receive their training a year later. So it's possible I may be taking flight training real soon, or be aboard ship. From the above, you will notice that those who will be flying are to report almost at once after graduation, which means "no leave." I don't like that at all, so I'm wishing for a ship. I just must see you a little when midshipman days are over, before I go far away.

These beautiful spring days are hardly adequate for study, and those who have "velvet" have more or less "secured" on the various academic departments. The birds singing, the trees budding, and the grass growing green are evident signs that beautiful spring is here. I've just been imagining just where I'll be this time next year. If things go as I have planned, you will be preparing to come to me. Oh, my darling Jackie--that wonderful day when I can write you that all is ready for you, that I've prepared for your happiness, and we are to be together the rest of our days. Then and only then will I be happy, because I want only you for always and always.

Dearest One, I'll never tire of saying that my life is yours to do for you forever, and that I love you, I do.

Millard

WESTERN UNION TELEGRAM

ANNAPOLIS, MD.

MISS JACKIE COLEMAN, RICHMOND, VIR.

ON EASTER DAY MY LOVE AND WISHES FOR YOUR

HAPPINESS COME TO YOU OVER THE MILES.

MILLARD

U.S. Naval Academy
Annapolis, Maryland
7 April, 1931

Dearest,

Your ever wonderful letter was such a joy this morning, and blue Monday quickly assumed a different aspect, and a successful week began at once. I seem to enjoy every one a little better than the preceding one, and all are so very dear. I hardly know what I would do without them. In fact, without you, I couldn't.

I've requested as my three choices of duty, the U.S.S. *Tennessee, Maryland,* and *Saratoga.* All three are units of the battle fleet with home port at San Diego and which operate in the Pacific. Our present Commandant, Capt. Snyder, will assume command of the *Tennessee* in July, so if my first request is granted, I'll be shipmates with an old "pal" as "skipper." In perhaps two weeks we'll know just where we are to go, and after that definite plans can be made.

Gee, I would have liked to have been present at the supper Sunday night. The "bunch" is so very jolly, and I can imagine the gathering amidst all the shouts of laughter. Quite unfortunate for the Navy that the fleet wasn't in, but perhaps it won't be long until there will be an anchor dropped in the heart of a dear Navy girl. When that happens it will never be raised, and the Navy will be happy forever and a day.

I'm also quite anxious for you to meet my mother. Of course, she will love you dearly, because I love you so. In fact I think she knows you quite well at present, for I have told her very many things about you, and at Xmas you were always "propped" on my pillow, because that's the spot mother chose for your picture. I thought it such a good selection that you remained there all of leave.

Just a note tonight to say I'm sending my love and kisses by a multitude of stars. Watch for them tomorrow night. They promise to give them to you.

Millard

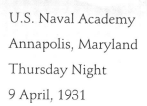

U.S. Naval Academy

Annapolis, Maryland

Thursday Night

9 April, 1931

Dearest,

The days appear to pass so slowly, and the numbers over my door proclaim twenty-three days yet to go until I'm happy again. Just below these figures others say fifty-six days until graduation. It seems that I spend most of my time counting the days until certain happy days or events are to transpire, and they do change so slowly. I'm wondering if the time is to come when I won't find it necessary to count the days until you come, but the prospect seems good to the contrary. That old "devil" sea will undoubtedly be keeping me away from you, and I'll have the days until port is made painted on some convenient hatch or stanchion. It isn't at all pleasant to think that all my life I'll be computing the number of days until my ship sights our little home with you waiting at the gate. It seems unfair to you to wait long lonely days for a sailor. But, my darling, your love and faith will accompany me to the ends of the earth, and because of them I'll always be brave and will carry on!--to give my best efforts to my country and to make my profession of "war" a success. Just in preparation, let me say that, although I may be called to the ends of the earth, your own sweet self will accompany me forever, and I'll be loving you as no man has ever yet loved a woman. Jackie, my own, I love you so, and I need you so. When I think that in only a short time I am to go so far away, my whole being revolts, for I want only you. If you will just let me love you all my life, you will do so much for my life and career. It is my life, and it has come to be a part of my soul, too.

I've been feeling sad tonight--perhaps because the long road of life has suddenly presented itself to me, and it has assumed proportions which until now have not seemed so large. After all, we don't consider the responsibilities until they confront us. Happy school days are most over, and a new phase of life is to soon be encountered.

I'm not afraid, however, and I even welcome the chance to go forth and begin the life for which I've been preparing so long. It's something else which makes me sad, and the nearer the time draws near, the harder it becomes to say I can and will.

Our orders were published today, at least generally, and life for the Class of 1931 for the next two years has been clearly defined. As I told you in a recent letter, 100 members of the class were to be assigned to destroyers, the remainder to battleships, cruisers, and aviation training. I requested a battleship with deferred aviation training, since the latter provided no leave after graduation. Destroyer duty is not generally recommended for a young Ensign, due to the responsibility involved upon such a ship. An Ensign reporting to a destroyer is assigned the position of Engineer Officer,

Navigator, Supply Officer, or First Lieut. and frequently has two of these jobs. No one requested these destroyer assignments, so it became necessary to draw lots for this duty. To make a long story short, I lost and have been assigned to the 6th Destroyer Division. I'm not unhappy, because I feel equal to the task, and I'll give my all to make a go of it. If I succeed, at the end of my tour of duty with these ships, I will have a knowledge of the Navy and experience which will be invaluable and which could not have been obtained aboard a battleship with limited responsibilities. If I fail, by running a destroyer aground or wrecking a turbine, a general Court Martial results, and a career is gone. The above two cases are the means by which officers fail, because a destroyer develops as much power as a battleship, and their extreme speeds are difficult to handle.

I've still not touched on the cause of my sadness. I welcome all the above and am not afraid. The Battle Force Division of destroyers operates between the West Coast, the Philippines, Hawaii, and the China station. Hence, duty on these ships means 6,000 or 7,000 miles away from you instead of 3,000, and every mile will appear to be half the earth. Jackie, darling, I only ask that you love me and always have that faith in me which has already done so much for me. If you will, I'll succeed. I'll soon pave the way for you, and when I've spent that year at sea, I'll be ready to send for you and say, "I'm ready to make you happy the rest of my life."

Wherever I go, wherever I be, I'll love you as I have since that day when I first told you those "three little words," which have come to be my all.

Millard

POSTAL TELEGRAPH

ANNAPOLIS, MD. APR. 12, 1931

MISS JACKIE COLEMAN, RICHMOND, VIR.

THIS IS JUST TO REPLACE MY SATURDAY

NIGHT LETTER. EXTRA DUTY KINDA

INCONVENIENCED THIS WEEKEND SINCE I

WAS A BAD BOY. I THOUGHT OF YOU ALL

THE TIME, AND, WITH ONLY NINETEEN DAYS

IN BECOMING HAPPY AGAIN, THE SAILING'S

FINE. NAVY GIRL, PLEASE HURRY CAUSE

I NEED YOU SO

MILLARD

U.S. Naval Academy
Annapolis, Maryland
13 April, 1931

Dearest,

Gee, the sailing is great these days. This afternoon four of us went for a short trip down the bay, and a stiff breeze made the afternoon extremely interesting. I can hardly wait for you to come so we can take a spin. It's such great sport, and I want to sail away with you forever. We'll take our "vic" along and have a wonderful time. How many days? Twenty. It is so very long, but I'll try so hard to wait.

Exciting days these last few ones. Since the assignment to ships has been published, all first classmen have been so excited. The general hail is: "What ship have you?" And each one has to tell all about his individual ship or destroyer. I'm becoming quite satisfied with my destroyer, and from information by various officers, the duty is very pleasant. I also learned of an additional duty which is to be mine. Since a destroyer carries no chaplain, the Ensign assigned will conduct the Chapel services every Sunday morning. I imagine me conducting a service and preaching for an hour! I've certainly been taking a "running" the last few days about all this, and we've had so much fun.

Your confidence in our golf match should now increase considerably. This afternoon I was shamefully eliminated in the semifinals by one "Red" Irons. I was terrible, and he was "shooting" fine golf. At the end of the match, I was down four holes, and my golf aspirations took a downward decline. I'm still in training for you, however, and I'll be the rest of my life.

I completed the final touches on my paper this afternoon, and it's all ready to be turned in tomorrow. I'm almost afraid to submit same, for fear that it isn't as good as it should be. However, I believe it the best I can do, so we'll await the verdict.

Faith! What a wonderful thing faith really is. Dr. Abernathy of Washington, D.C. gave an address Sunday on the above subject, and I enjoyed it so much. It is indeed something we use every day, and your faith and confidence in me aids me so very much. Your faith and love are the greatest things in my life, and I could never, never betray either. Every day I strive to be worthy of this faith you have in me, and someday you will realize just how much value it has been to me since our first happy days together. It would be impossible for me to have anything but courage and confidence in myself, because it is so essential for success, and I must at least be well up the ladder before saying, "I am ready for you." It does seem so long and so cruel that I can't have you until a year is passed, but the best thoughts for you say to wait that long.

You didn't mention how the play is progressing, nor your advancement along the radio lines. Are you attending the radio meetings every week? When you come, I'll be expecting quite a lot of improvement, and you should be able to receive five words per minute. Now that rifle is taking my afternoons, I haven't had the opportunity to do much "key twiddling," and consequently I've missed talking with W3FJ and sending you messages.

As soon as the last class is completed, I have to catch the boat across the bay to the rifle range. Practice consumes over two hours daily, as well as all of Saturday afternoon and part of Sunday. I'm doing fair and tonight missed the black one time in twenty rounds. The training table starts next week, and we'll begin receiving some real "chow." Rifle isn't strenuous physically, but it's so temperamental a game that we have to have special "chow" too. I noticed Floyd Jones over today, and he tells me he is going to try out. He says now that you've given him a taste of real food, he'd like to make the training table and continue to enjoy himself.

Exams again the last of this week, and some more real work for ten days. I'm glad they will be over by the time you arrive, and with only six rivers to go at that time, I'll really be happy when I greet you again to the Naval Academy. And then next time, I can sing "No More Rivers," and we will be ready to enjoy a week of heaven, to be climaxed on Thursday, 4 June. I can hardly wait for you to meet mother and granddad. They are both wonderful, and they will love you too. Granddad wrote me he was coming if he had to crawl.

Our stars will always shine, by day or night, all over the world. They will always shine for me, wherever I be, and in a measure be so comforting. Six thousand miles away your stars won't be my same stars, but they can represent your messages as always. Always send me a kiss and a gentle smile by them, for I'll always be waiting to receive them. Dearest, I'm trying so hard to wait, but can't you hurry just a little? I love you and I'm needing you so every day. Oh, that happy day on 2 May.

Millard

U.S. Naval Academy

Annapolis, Maryland

Sunday Morning

19 April, 1931

Dearest,

Please forgive me for not writing often this week. It's not because I haven't thought of you, for I have a thousand times a day, and I've missed our companionship thru our letters so much. However, these are busy days, and I'm trying to end the term with a blaze of glory. Rifle practice consumes all my afternoons, and at night it's prepare for the examinations. You've been so good about writing me, and if you only knew the joy your letters bring--the added energy and vigor which they give to me, you will never fail to write when we are apart.

The pictures are so lovely, and I thank you for sending them. I'm going to keep my promise too, just as soon as I can, and you will have memories of subchasers and everything to remember us by.

Duty kept me from writing you last night, and I paced the lonely third deck until 12:30, before the O.O.D. allowed us to secure. With the "Duke" on watch, I didn't dare to write a line, so I paced up and down and dreamed. Every so often I would go to a window and send a kiss soaring aloft to a smiling, twinkling star, which promised so readily to transmit it to you without delay. I hope they all arrived safely, because I was longing for you so. Jackie, I love you so. I'm needing you every day of my life, and the days which pass make me realize more and more that someday you must be mine--mine to hold in my arms, and to always call you my sweetheart and whisper that I love you, I do, I do. During these past 30 days since you've been away, I've dreamed a thousand dreams of you, and when I again see you two weeks from today, on a lovely spring morning, you and I will be sitting side by side in a quaint little church which I've grown to love. (I hope my boys miss me this morning.) I'll be so happy too, and everyone will know it too, for I'll be sitting so straight with my head high in the air and so very proud to be so near to you. That's one of the reasons I need you always by my side. It makes me proud of you and of myself. It gives me joy in life itself, and happy that I am privileged to live and do things for you and your happiness. Your presence strikes down all barriers that might bar my way, and your patient, cheerful smile gives me a determination which will not be stopped.

Your picture under the blossoms smiling so happily is going to be my constant companion. It's been cut down slightly to fit my pocketbook, and on many occasions it will give me courage. Perhaps it will be on a dark night at sea on the bridge of my destroyer. Ship will be darkened in battle maneuvers, and we'll be dashing along at 35 knots. Perhaps for a moment I will pause in my vigil ahead for danger to flash a tiny light on this picture in a secluded corner, just to catch a glimpse of your smile. Then, perhaps I'll signal for five additional knots, and on, on, in search of the enemy.

Last Friday the Regiment of midshipmen had the first full dress parade in honor of Prince???? of Japan, brother of the present Emperor. He received a 21 gun salute upon arrival, and officers in their full gold uniforms quite eclipsed anything the Japanese had to offer. We had quite a snappy parade, and I believe we impressed the honored guest very much. I hope more so than the West Pointers. He came here after reviewing the "Kaydets" last week.

It's been so terribly long since you left. I just must hear your voice again. So, tonight I'm going to call, and here's hoping you're home. It will aid so much in making these 13 days pass more swiftly. I'm sure they will, however, and then a little sailor boy will be happy, happy, happy.

Please just a word or so next week, until Thursday. It will give me courage during all these exams.

A year from today, perhaps we'll be getting ready. Perhaps I'll be preparing for that most glorious day of all my life.

Millard

WESTERN UNION TELEGRAM

ANNAPOLIS, MD. 1931 APR. 21 P.M. 8:43

MISS JACKIE COLEMAN, RICHMOND, VIR.

NO TELEPHONES TONIGHT, BUT I SEND MY LOVE

BY THE STARS

MILLARD

WESTERN UNION TELEGRAM

ANNAPOLIS, MD. 1931 APR. 25 P.M. 4:31

MISS JACKIE COLEMAN, RICHMOND, VIR.

I'LL TRY TO WAIT ONE WEEK FOR A LITTLE

HEAVEN

MILLARD

U.S. Naval Academy
Annapolis, Maryland
Saturday Night
26 April, 1931

Darling,

'Tis real happiness to be alone with you once again on a Saturday night, especially when I realize that next Saturday I'll have you near me. After these long, dreary 40 days since you were here, I will again enjoy happiness supreme-- happiness which only you are capable of giving me--happiness which I have grown to cherish above all else, and which I desire all the rest of my life. I attempt to be absorbed in my work and make golden moments from all available time. I succeed in part, but your memory is continually with me in all my actions and thoughts. Some things go wrong, at times, and it's then my heart yearns for you so. At other times, I am more or less resigned to our being separated, but beautiful hopes and dreams of the future are always present.

The week of exams, just completed, was a difficult one, and it's with joy in my heart that I realize only six more rivers to cross. I dampened my feet a trifle this past week, and I'm quite content to stay on dry land, as far as rivers are concerned. Salt water is different, but rivers are bad things to tackle once a month, when so many are encountered consecutively.

So tonight I'm resting. I've been a good boy, and these glorious moments, when you seem so near, cause all the difficult days to vanish, and in their place wonderful cheery days of the future come to my mind. It is a bright future, and I want them to come so quickly. I want you so, my darling. Sometimes I think I just can't wait for you. I want to take you in my arms and have you promise that you will remain there, forever and a day. Only then will I be happy, only when you are always near, and I can say always, I love you with all my heart and soul.

I'm so glad your play is progressing nicely. I'd give much to see your dance, and I know it's going to be a great success. Is the partner a great improvement over the first one? I couldn't possibly do the dance, but I'm sure envious of him. Congratulate him for me on having you for a dancing partner.

Monday morning the last academic month of the year begins. As June 4 draws nearer and nearer, I am appreciating more and more that "days I am going to miss" are passing, never to come again. I'm afraid there's to be a lump in my throat when I depart the evening of 4 June. In four years a place can become endeared to us in such a way that we don't realize until the time comes to say goodbye. Then, we look back and wish that we had taken advantage of the opportunities which were presented in a more capable manner than we did. Even now I can think of many things I would like to correct. However, the opportunities come only once in the Navy, and it's up to us to realize their significance and importance, and accept them. Then too, this past year has brought happy days of which I had only dreamed of before. Certain spots of the Academy have become endeared because of you, and when I am many thousand miles away, I will have just "memories." 'Tis true they will be wonderful memories, but there will be a yearning in my heart to be there myself just with you--perhaps on our way to a "hop," a sail, or a stroll. Perhaps I'm thinking a trifle too far ahead, but it's a habit of mine to plan the future and determine just what is to be expected. I can see now that it's going to tear my heart strings to say goodbye and take departure for lands so far distant. Your memory will be with me eternally until that day when you are mine, all mine.

I'm waiting, my darling. I'll always just be waiting until you come to always be by my side.

Millard

WESTERN UNION TELEGRAM

ANNAPOLIS, MD. 1931 MAY 1 P.M. 1:11

MISS JACKIE COLEMAN, RICHMOND, VIR.

WE'RE WAITING, NAVY GIRL

MILLARD

THE SHIP SQUAD

U.S.S. REINA MERCEDES
ANNAPOLIS, MD.

5 May 1931

Dearest,

The convict himself! I reported to my new home yesterday afternoon, and by this time am well settled in this entirely new environment. It is a change, but not quite as pleasant as Bancroft Hall. Beans and prunes three times a day — no butter or sugar is indeed food for bad boys. To begin things right, I fell out of my hammock last night — five feet to a very hard deck around two o'clock — it was some few moments before I realized just what had happened. At any rate I didn't trust myself so high again, and spent the remainder of the night on the deck. I really wished for my bed in 3220, before 0530 came, when "Rise and Shine" was brayed along the deck of this battle scarred old Cruiser. However, its all in the game and we have fun too. There are six convicts in all and being

Dearest,

The convict himself! I reported to my new home yesterday afternoon, and by this time am well settled in this entirely new environment. It is a change, but not quite as pleasant as Bancroft Hall. Beans and prunes three times a day--no butter or sugar is indeed food for bad boys. To begin things right, I fell out of my hammock last night--five feet to a very hard deck around two o'clock. It was some few moments before I realized just what had happened. At any rate, I didn't trust myself so high again and spent the remainder of the night on the deck. I really wished for my bed in 3220 before 0530 came, when "Rise and Shine" was passed along the deck of this battle-scarred old cruiser. However, it's all in the game, and we have fun too. There are six convicts in all, and being shipmates we are all pals regardless of classes. There is one first classman beside myself, reported for the same offense as I, one second classman, one youngster, and two "plebes." Tomorrow ten more first classmen report for duty also for the offense, "smoking unauthorized." We'll have quite a family gathering before long.

I'm writing this from the "forecastle" of this historic old battlewagon. Supper is just over, and I'm seeking a little companionship with you. The bay is beautiful this evening. The Navy's colors are prominent far down the bay caused by the setting sun over beyond the Chapel. The sea gulls are happy too and are noisily winging their way around my vessel, now and then dipping down to catch a floating bit of food. It is good to be alive, even if one has been bad. It is glorious to close your eyes and dream. Since that's my favorite pastime, I have ample opportunity here, and so I've been dreaming and living over again moments which are so wonderful in my life. The future hasn't been neglected either, and I've planned again those happy days which I hope are to be mine and yours. I am a foolish boy, but when I'm lonely it serves to, in a way, calm my soul and keep my courage intact.

Your letter awaiting me with the O.O.D. this morning was wonderful. Whenever you depart from "Crabtown," I am always a little anxious until I receive word that you have arrived safely again in Richmond. To have you travelling alone worries me, and I'm quite relieved when I receive your first letter. Of course, you weren't travelling alone this time, but perhaps that only serves to make my worries assume larger proportions.

I am ashamed, and I do wish to apologize. Several times during the past week-end I acted very, very childish and

harbored rather unpleasant thoughts. Jealousy is indeed such an undesirable trait, and I realize that it is capable of wrecking more havoc than perhaps any other factor. I never realized that I possessed such a characteristic until recently. It is something which I must learn to push away, whenever I feel it present, before it works harm. I am proud of you so very much and am happy and pleased that other men like you and admire the characteristics which I do. A few of my friends here have rather distorted ideas about their engagement, according to my own doctrines. For example, Gaasterland forbids Marian to go out with other men, and I have a vague idea that it's these same friends who instilled that little jealous thought, which lurked in a corner of my brain, while you were here. I certainly do not ask you to give up any friends because of me. On the contrary, I think such a demand would instantly result in creating forces which would not tend toward future happiness. Love is God's gift to mankind. With it comes glorious faith and trust, and without it, what would life be? When faith and trust die, so dies love! The two are so closely related, they can be interchanged freely, but not separated. So, my darling, I have attempted to face this squarely and apply the principles which my own mind dictates, and which I believe to be right, and which I hope with all my soul will lead to happiness divine. Success in life to me means attaining such a position through which life's long road may be made happy for your loved ones. Therefore, in the future you will find me free from those subtle remarks, which I this last week-end uttered, and which were so uncalled for--just because someone was being nice to the girl I love. Instead, I should have been happy and proud that someone was attempting to make my aim a little easier.

My Navy Girl, I love you, I do. I'll always be able to say those words regardless of anything. I want you for my very own, to be able to always hold you close in my arms and know that you are mine, all mine. That's why I want to foresee anything which might tend to create anything which would prove undesirable.

Until the happy day when you are mine, I'll be loving you as only a man can, who has found the girl of his dreams.

Millard

U.S. Naval Academy

Annapolis, Maryland

Saturday Evening

May 11, 1931 *Reina Mercedes*

at Sea Lat. 38 degrees 50' N Long. 74 degrees-38' W.

Dearest,

All six of us are congregated in our special convict room. "Danny," another smoking victim, is over in one corner cheerfully entertaining us on the mouth organ, and the other four are engaged in a poker game. Smoke is so thick that it could easily be cut, and "Danny" keeps us amused all the time. The poker game is gradually assuming huge proportions, and I'm quite glad I dropped out, when my financial condition had been reduced one penny. Above on deck a radio can be heard, and "By My Side" drifts down between the strains of Danny's organ. We've quite a happy family here. Everyone's pals. No one studies, and we pass the hours in various ways.

Tonight we completed our negotiations for a real "chow" on "Mother's Day." Fortunately I made a friend in the person of a Chief Petty Officer on this ship. Someone suggested how bad beans would be on Sunday dinner, especially on Mother's Day. Then someone suggested that if we could arrange for a cook to prepare us a steak, we could order one from town and really have a good dinner. I trotted up to see my Chief, and he soon had confidentially arranged with one of the galley men to prepare us a nice steak for

Sunday dinner. He even ordered one of the Philipino boys to go out in town and purchase same, and add some vegetables too. After this past week--Oh boy, our mouths are watering.

Your package was delayed in some manner and didn't arrive until this morning. If you could have heard the shout of joy that went up when the enlisted man came down the ladder and announced, "Package for Midshipman Klein." Six chairs hit the deck simultaneously, and six books landed elsewhere in this compartment. I can't ever remember when anything has tasted so good. This food they give us is awful. Our Philipino boy, who waits on our table, is a good kid, and educated too. His name is Marco, and he's always trying to "swipe" us better chow from the galley. I hunted him up and gave him some of your chow too. It made me happy just to watch him, when he started eating cookies. I don't imagine he ever had any before, and his smile with many "muchas gracias" made my heart so glad. And us convicts, we smiled and laughed with our dark companion. We were just all human beings so happy to get "chow" from home, and I, because the dearest One in all the world had thought of me. Thanks so much. You've made for us a happy week-end just through our stomachs.

And then when I returned from drill at 11:00 and came down our ladder, I quickly espied that familiar long envelope with its beloved handwriting. Gee, it's such a wonderful letter--every word so sacred to my heart, and I've read every word over and over. My heart seemed starved for your words, and, oh, the joy to read them over and over.

Dearest, I'm going to tell just why I wrote the last letter as I did. My love for you, trust and faith, has steadily grown day by day. That's why I can say over and over I will always and always love you, want you, and desire to make you the happiest woman in this world. <u>Nothing exists</u> which could destroy this love and faith which I have in you, and it has become part of my life, accepted as God's gift, in answer to my dreams and prayers. It is a characteristic of your mother, and in you, to always be cheerful and happy, no matter what comes. Making other people happy is joy for you, and it's joy for me too. That's why I love your smile, and why I miss it so when we are apart, because it makes me so happy and contented. The Naval Academy is divided into many small groups. These groups constitute our fraternities, and among these groups, due to our constant contact, lasting friendship is born. It seems that all human beings confide with their friends their joys and sorrows, and so it is with the boys who "chum" together in these small groups. All the groups are friends, but in the group itself every man knows the other man's joys and sorrows. All are quick to aid in time of trouble and give advice in time of need. You have met all the boys who are my close friends--Gaasterland, Jones, Hoye, "Mattie," Raysbrook, McKay, and Carr. They all knew when you came into my life; they knew I was in love with you, and that we were engaged to be married. The first "kidding" came when you sent Floyd a box simultaneously with mine. They found out before I and immediately began to "run" me all during the day. I didn't mind at all, because I understood and did not even offer an explanation to them. Floyd and I were friends. I came to know him through John, and he frequently came in to see me. Then the night came when Lt. Duval met you in Washington. It became known to the boys when I told them that I was glad he had, because it meant company for you all alone in Washington, and I didn't like to have you be there all alone. They immediately saw another view, and after that, every day the Lt. was mentioned. Out of this grew those foolish remarks of mine, after Mr. Duval had seen you at the "hop." I realized just how foolish they were and was so ashamed. They came out just unconsciously and can you ever forgive me? I swear my faith had never waned in you, and it never will. Last Sunday night after you left, I told every "pal" I had just why I loved you. Besides making me happy, you had other characteristics which I've never known in other girls, and which I quickly found out, after I had visited Richmond and you the Naval Academy. And so, I want you to send Floyd or anyone else--anything. "Chow" makes a midshipman happy, and I know that it's appreciated. And we are happy too, when we do things to make others happy. What would life be if we did not do this? At any rate every friend I have has apologized to me and to you, and they know and are envious that you have characteristics which they cannot boast of in the girl which they "drag."

Sometimes I just can't realize that I have found you, that God has really answered my prayers, and you are to be mine, all mine, to love and cherish forever and a day. To see your smile and to hold you in my arms makes me realize that it isn't still a dream--that it's really true that we are to have that little home. We will be so happy, and we'll make others happy, thereby gaining still more joy just in living. You've taught me just that.

I return to the Hall Monday morning, so my former address will then be resumed. I'll be careful, smoke your cigarettes, and stay off the "frap" [conduct report].

Next Friday the last set of exams to go. Six more rivers, then June Week, graduation, and you.

Gee, I'm just proud to be alive tonight. I have a wonderful mother and the sweetest and best little girl in the world. With these I am blessed, and I'll repay by bringing joy into their lives.

I'm going up to "pal" with Willie Winkle. Maybe he'll have something for me! Then I'll swing and dream.

Millard
Don't forget to tell me all about the play.

U.S. Naval Academy
Annapolis, Maryland
13 May, 1931

Dearest,

Bancroft Hall is a real home when one has been away, especially when you have been subjected to beans and hammocks for a week. At any rate I've learned not to smoke in the corridors or after taps anymore.

I appreciated the program so much. I know it was a big success, and I would have given much to have been present to see your art. I can imagine the encores you received, and I would have liked to join in. At any rate, perhaps you will do the act for me when you again come to see me.

Our last exams start tomorrow and extend thru one week. "No more rivers" is going to be the sweetest sounding phrase I've heard since you told me those three little words. I'll be thinking of you, dear One, and I'm, as usual, just counting the days and hours until you arrive.

The enclosed clipping gives you the result of the Van Dyke prize. I didn't win the watch, and since there is no second prize, all I get is a letter. I'm sorry, but I should have written a better theme.

I'm giving Willie Winkle a big load tonight. Will you take it all?

Millard

Postcard

Annapolis, Md.

May 19, 1931

Dearest,

"Three More Rivers," nine days and then you.

I, too, would like for Helena to be here for the June Ball. Would Von like to come with her? If so, they are both invited. If not, I'll look around and see who I can find and let you know later.

I'll write Thursday night.

Millard

POSTAL TELEGRAPH

ANNAPOLIS, MD. 1931 MAY 22, P.M. 5:29

MISS JACKIE COLEMAN, RICHMOND, VIR.

NO MORE RIVERS AND JUST WAITING

FOR YOU

MILLARD

POSTAL TELEGRAPH

ANNAPOLIS, MD. MAY 24, 1931

MISS JACKIE COLEMAN, RICHMOND, VIR.

PLEASE FORGIVE ME FOR NOT WRITING.

THESE ARE TERRIBLY BUSY DAYS WITH SO

MUCH TO ATTEND TO. I'M THINKING OF YOU

EVERY MINUTE AND WAITING FOR THE

COMING WONDERFUL DAYS WITH YOU. I CAN

HARDLY WAIT, AND WE MUST MAKE EVERY

HOUR COUNT. I DO LOVE YOU SO.

MILLARD

U.S. Naval Academy

Annapolis, Maryland

26 May, 1931

Dearest,

It's been so long since I've written you a real letter that this will be a real pleasure for me. I had the mistaken idea that when exams were over--the last river crossed--that there would be lots of time in which one could do nothing. However, since that time a thousand things have come up which hardly seems to leave a spare moment.

I've scattered orders for uniforms all over Annapolis, and it's been necessary to have fittings on them all--bills to pay, as well as our competitive drills and lectures during the day. Our orders arrived from the Navy Department day before yesterday, and ten extra copies have to be made--endorsements made by all the offices here, as well as making arrangements for our transportation ticket and first month's pay. These are a few of the things which have kept me busy and prevented me from writing you. I've wanted to so badly, and I've thought of you every day and the wonderful time we are going to have. We must include, utilize every golden moment, for all too soon they will be gone forever.

Already I'm beginning to feel the weight of responsibility which is going to be placed upon a young officer. No longer are we told just how and when a certain thing should be done, but a certain amount of initiative is now expected. It's going to require a lot of work to make good in the destroyer service, but with your faith behind me, I feel capable. Without it, I would have my serious doubts. So, won't you please always have that glorious faith, which I have come to cherish so highly, and which has mounted me to heights not ever before attained.

I've secured a "drag" for Helena, and if she doesn't come now, there will be two disappointed young men at the Academy. I attempted to find a classmate who was not "dragging" to the June Ball, but it seemed impossible, so I had to revert to the present 4th class, or should I say rapidly approaching "youngsters?" He isn't so terribly handsome, but he's a fine lad, and I believe Helena will like him. So tell her we are expecting her for the June Ball. In case she cannot come, please let me know so I can tell this "plebe," and he, perhaps, can make other arrangements. Here's hoping she can come!

Mother and granddad arrive Saturday afternoon, so I'll have them all settled when you arrive on Sunday. They are quite anxious to meet you, and both are going to love you for the fine young lady you are. It's a glorious June Week we are going to have!

Did I point out the *Robert Center* to you during your visits to the Academy? It's the large sailing yacht here and may be used by midshipmen who obtain permission from the Commandant. I requested use of this yacht for Monday, 1

June and have obtained permission for its use. Gaasterland and Hoye will have their parents and "drags," so we will have around twenty-five or thirty for the trip. We will start soon after noon and have the Commissary Department arrange to have us plenty of "chow." I'm going over to Carvel tomorrow afternoon and see Lt. Duval. I thought perhaps he would like to go and perhaps would be useful in handling the boat. Mr. Bentley is anxious to go, so Monday afternoon, weather permitting, we should have a delightful time.

I'm enclosing the program of exercises for June Week, as you requested. Also I'm saving the cap you desired until graduation, when it will be yours.

The "chow" arrived today, and it's lovely. I can easily imagine what a success your party was. I'm afraid that I wouldn't have contributed a bit if I had been there, except to my own enjoyment in being with you. Once again, I and the "gang" send their thanks and compliments for your good cooking. It's awfully nice for you to send us so much good "chow," and we all appreciate it so much.

It all seems a wonderful dream that graduation day is soon to be here. It also seems a wonderful dream that you are to be here, and that I am to have the privilege of glorious hours again with you. Your comings are so far apart that I sometimes wonder if it wasn't a dream when your last visit was made. I'm trying not to think of the time when we are going to part for such a very long time. It's going to be the most painful moment of my life, and it seems impossible for me not to think of it. I love you, Jackie, darling, more than my life, my all, and I don't see how I'm going to do it. I'll try to go away with a strong heart, knowing that it will only hasten the days when you will be mine--all mine to love and cherish and protect the rest of my life.

Let me know just when you will arrive, and I'll be there and, Oh, so happy!

Millard

II
DUTY IN PACIFIC WATERS 1931–38

M.J. "MIKE" KLEIN

JACQUELINE COLEMAN

WESTERN UNION TELEGRAM

KNOXVILLE, TENN. 1931 JUN. 9 P.M. 5:48
MISS JACKIE COLEMAN, RICHMOND, VIR.
I'M MISSING YOU TERRIBLY, NAVY GIRL
MILLARD

WESTERN UNION TELEGRAM

KNOXVILLE, TENN. 1931 JUN. 12 A.M. 1:47
MOTHER AND HOME SHOULD MAKE ME VERY
HAPPY, BUT I'M NEEDING AND WANTING ONLY
YOU. CAN'T THERE BE SOME WAY TO SEE YOU
BEFORE I LEAVE? I'M TRYING TO SMILE
ALWAYS, BUT I'M WANTING YOU BY MY SIDE
MILLARD

Ruston, La.

[on the way to West Coast]

27 June, 1931

Dearest,

This extreme hot southern climate is not proving to be just the best thing for me, and I am developing into the laziest person you ever saw. We spend our time with a fan and glass of ice water, in a vain attempt to keep cool. However, I am gaining a much needed rest from academic work and am enjoying myself just doing nothing.

Mattie and myself arrived in Ruston [Mattie's hometown] a week ago today, hot and weary, after three days driving. The car did very well, considering the temperature, and we believe that it will ultimately gain our destination for us, with careful attention on our part.

Ruston is a sleepy little southern town, and the people certainly live up to their reputation. No diversion except golf, and it's too hot for that. Consequently, I help Mrs. Hall milk the cows, churn, and do a little plowing on the side. It's great fun, and I gain my reward at mealtime by consuming about twice as much as anyone else. We all go to bed not later than eight, and everyone is up at five, except Mattie and myself. We count 50,000 several times, and finally arise about seven.

I spent an enjoyable week in Knoxville. I never quite recovered from the disappointment of your not being there, but your letter and telegram caused me to carry on. They always do give me faith, and courage, and strong convictions. I spent most of my time with mother and Mrs. Peck. Two days we spent in the mountains together, and I enjoyed being just with them. The remainder of the week kept me busy seeing remainder of the relatives and having a meal with them all. I had one date. Mattie and Martha, another friend of Martha's (Florence Maxwell) and myself, all had dinner together one night and played bridge afterward.

I've told the events of the last two weeks in inverse order, but it tells you just what I've been doing.

Just a word about mother. She loves you just as I do. She hasn't told me so, because she's always had the attitude not to like any young lady I've been with. However, I can tell in many of her actions--by the way she carried your picture around, finding the best place for it to rest. Also, after your letter came, I left it on my desk. That night I was looking for it to read again, and mother was carrying it around in her pocketbook. Mrs. Peck also told me that she wanted to meet you so much, because mother had spoken of you so proudly. So I know, and I wanted you to know. I hoped and prayed she would, and I knew it could be no other way. And granddad-- he thinks there's no finer girl in all the world than Jackie. Whenever I went to see him, the subject, largely, was about you. So you see, young lady, you've not only captured my heart and soul, but those of my closest family as well.

The days are now happy. Somehow those words of yours, "For us time is not," "Carry on," have been so

comforting, the most comforting I have ever known. During the day when I'm missing you so and at night when I'm dreaming too, I just think of those words and imagine seeing your dear sweet self telling them to me. Then my soul is quiet, and I am resolved to indeed carry on as best I can, even though we are separated by such a distance. It is only for a short time, and what glorious happiness when you are mine!

I dream over and over of those brief, glorious moments we spent on the beach together that beautiful day. The world just seemed to stop, and I was alone with the one girl who is life itself to me. I was, Oh, so very happy, just to be with you by our beautiful water. Just a while longer and I'm beginning that search in San Diego for a suitable site for our tiny home, and what a joy it will be building and planning every detail we have spoken of.

I also think of that moment when on your porch I pledged to be true always. With your sweet memory with me at all times, I <u>could</u> not be otherwise, and the words, "For us time is not," make me conscious of what I have to do--prepare for you, the most wonderful woman in the world. And so, I swear again to cherish and safeguard your memory until we meet again.

As yet, I haven't even thanked you for my stay in Richmond, even if I was given my hat. (Now I'm just joking.) I told mother why you sent me home, and she's very grateful. Your home is grand, and your father and mother too. I've grown to think of Taylor Avenue as my home too, and there

I've spent such sacred moments. Your present too is the most useful article I have. It's just another gift of yours I'll keep always.

We leave in the morning for Denver and will be there for three days. Write me: in care of Mrs. W.W. Watts, 1000 Logan St., Denver, Colorado. After that the address will be U.S.S. *Roper,* San Diego, Calif.

Until that glorious day next spring. "For us time is not." That phrase will carry me through.

Millard

Denver, Colorado

1 July, 1931

Dearest,

We arrived in Denver last night at 8:30, after three days riding through Texas, New Mexico, and Colorado. The car is doing quite well, up to date, and should serve us until we reach San Diego.

The West is wonderful! We left the rolling plains of Texas behind our second day from Ruston, La. and entered the mountains at Raton, N. Mexico. From there on the drive was beautiful, and I'm learning to love these wonderful mountains already. Out here the spirit of the country just possesses you, and you feel free and big and strong. The mountains hem you in on all sides, and the snow-covered peaks gleam beautifully in the sunlight.

I was a bit disappointed not to find your familiar letter when I arrived last night. During the last two hundred miles, I had dreamed of you nearly all the way, and I did want a letter so much. I know you've hardly had time as yet to answer, but I was wanting one anyway. Perhaps it will come tomorrow!

Today I've been homesick for the first time since I first went away to the Academy four years ago. I suppose it's because I realize I'm so far away from you and home. But I'm happy in the knowledge that I'm on my way to make a new home--a home for you and me by the sea. The mountains are beautiful, but we must be by the sea--to see and hear those waves we love so well. Perhaps we can have the mountains to the rear, but the sea must be in front.

I suppose you will be taking Stuart for his visit to the Academy very soon. It's hard to think of you in Annapolis without me there too. I know Stuart will enjoy it so much. I hope he will like the Academy and learn to love it as his future home for four years. When you go, please write me a card form old Crabtown. I guess I'm just a trifle homesick!

A card was awaiting me here from Mr. and Mrs. C.L. Gaasterland. I imagine you heard from Marian. They were married on 20 June, and their card was from Atlantic City. I know they are quite happy. I'll have to offer my congratulations after reaching San Diego.

I also heard from granddad. He says he received a long letter from you and was answering <u>immediately</u>. He's a grand old man, and he loves you 'cause you are Jackie. I love you 'cause you are Jackie too and because you are the girl of my dreams--the girl I am to make happy.

Our stars are wonderful out here! Since I left Richmond and started my journey West, they are becoming more and more my pals. I suppose it's because I'm needing them more now than ever before, because I'm wanting those messages so much. Please send lots by Willie!

Ten more days will find me aboard the U.S.S. *Roper* and underway upon my career as an officer. I'm quite anxious for the time to arrive and for work to come. Then, perhaps, will time pass swiftly, and those happy days of the future quickly arrive.

We are now separated farther than ever before, but our love can make it very close. I must, for I love you, I do, I do.

Millard

WESTERN UNION TELEGRAM

SAN DIEGO, CALIF. 1931 JUL. 9 A.M. 4:09
MISS JACKIE COLEMAN, RICHMOND, VIR.
I'M HERE AND HOPING THIS YEAR PROVES
"TIME IS NOT."
M.J. KLEIN

Excerpt from Jackie's Diary:

July 11, 1931--I've decided to not try to write my thoughts. Now that my love grows stronger every day (miraculous though it be), I find it impossible to express it. No human can express with man-made words that which God instills in his heart. It's something one feels and lives but can't define or express. I should have kept accounts of June Week and all its happenings, but whenever I start to write, I lapse into dreaming and enjoy it even more. And so I'll let my life be a month to month story--with only the happy moments and the victories told. I have promised to become Millard's wife. And may God make me the kind of wife he deserves. May He watch over us and keep us and bring us into His heavenly joy!

JRC

U.S.S. *Roper*
San Diego, Calif.
15 July, 1931

Dearest,

The remainder of our trip from Denver was uneventful, and we arrived in San Diego the afternoon of 8 July. Mattie and I were very tired, so after sending your telegram and one to mother, we turned in for nearly two days.

My career as a naval officer began Saturday morning at 7:30, when I came over the side, saluted the colors, and instructed the messenger on duty to inform the executive officer that Ensign Klein was reporting for duty. I went below to the wardroom, and there met the eight officers at breakfast. I was greeted very cordially, and everyone seemed to try and make me feel at home.

However, it's all new. I'm the junior officer, and for a while I'm going to have a hard time. I expected work, however, and I'm quite ready.

The Captain, Lt. Comdr. Gates, is one of the finest men I've ever seen in the Navy. He is superb at destroyer handling, and the great horsepower at his command is well used. He gave me a long talk and told me my lot would not be easy. For the first month I am to have no assigned work. I am to investigate the entire ship and learn all that I am able, become known to the men, and learn their names. It seems to produce much better results when you can call a man by his name, in giving him an order.

My quarters are nice. I have a small stateroom past forward of the wardroom on the port side. A writing desk, wardrobe, washstand, and bunk comprise its furnishings. A Filipino boy cleans my room every morning, blacks my shoes, and keeps my clothes brushed. It's great to have all the crew say, "Sir," salute every morning, and always ready to obey every command. As far as commands go, I'm not giving many just yet. I'm asking questions mostly, and the orders will come later.

So far I've been over all the ship. A destroyer is not large, but develops as much horsepower as a battleship. She is a swift, light vessel, designed to protect the capital ships. The U.S.S. *Roper* has a tonnage of 1,400 tons, a speed of 36.4 knots, and draws 15 feet of water. We went to sea yesterday for the day, and let me say this boat rolls. Along about noon, I began to feel a trifle bad, when the ship began to roll so much that the lifeboat almost went under every time. I went below, and for a time wished I were dead. I kept out of sight until I felt better, and nobody was the wiser.

A glorious letter awaited me here when I reported Saturday morning, and another came today. They were both grand, and, of course, I'm going to sail on and on. I need you though, my dearest, like never before. During the past few days, I've kind of been lonely. Being the junior officer I don't feel the urge to "pal around" with any of the officers. Only officially do we meet, and I'm discovering how much a "pal" is worth. A classmate aboard would be great. They are all nice, but there's always that insurmountable wall of higher rank to face.

I'm going to work hard this first year, and also take your advice about saving money. According to the officers, with Tia Juana and Agua Caliente so near, it's impossible to save, but I am, and I'm going to stay away from those places.

Here's how I was greeted aboard ship. After breakfast last Saturday, the executive officer, Mr. Grube, invited me out to his house for a party. It seems that a friend of his was leaving, so all of the officers aboard ship and the wives had been invited. I'm the only bachelor aboard the U.S.S. *Roper*. At any rate, I left the ship at 3:00 Saturday afternoon and went to Mr. Grube's residence. There I met the wives of all the officers aboard. I was a little late, the party was already well underway. I might add that this was strictly a cocktail party and nothing else. I accepted two and then refused after that. By six o'clock the wives were to the toe dancing point, so I excused myself and went aboard the *Roper* to think. This party was just a little disappointing to me, especially my first day, and I hope I offended no one by "shoving off" early like I did. The next morning when all the officers came aboard, it was mentioned that I was not a drinking man, but would soon learn out here. I'm not going to learn, however, even if every officer in the Navy and his wife are accustomed to these parties. And next year, you and I will serve a drink or two to the friends who come in and no more. Don't you think I'm right? I know you do, and so we are going to do things just a little different from the rest of the Navy.

I want you so, darling. I want to wire every day that I need you so, and for you to come to me just as soon as you can. I almost did Saturday night, for I did need you so, just then. But I must wait. I must make good. Just watch the bank account grow. She's empty now, but not for long. And every dollar will just shout for joy, because it's for you. I love you, Jackie. Perhaps, if I'm brave, I can wait for you awhile, but not for so long can I keep you from my side.

It's wonderful of you to say you would like to wait until I could accompany you to the Academy before going again. However, that's just up to you. If you want to go, I'm sure you would have a great time, and I know Stuart would like it. I used to be jealous (and still am just a wee bit), but you are not to sit at home, of course, but have a good time at things you want to do. In the meantime, I'm going to have a great time just getting ready for you. This week-end I'm going to start the search for the site for this "tiny home." It will be such fun looking and choosing just the place. I've already inquired the section of town to look, and Mr. Schaede, the Engineer Officer, remarked that it wouldn't be long until this ship had a full quota of married officers.

Sail on! And on! For us time is not. When I think of those words, it's not hard, and I'm not a bit homesick. I'm just getting ready for the girl I love more than life itself.

Millard

UNITED STATES FLEET
DESTROYER DIVISION FIVE, BATTLE FORCE
U. S. S. ROPER (147), Flagship

Long Beach, Calif.

12 October, 1931

Dearest,

I imagine you will think you are receiving a letter from a total stranger. In a sense you are, since I haven't written in such a long time. Please forgive me?

The picture was wonderful! I can't tell you how my heart reached out to you when I opened the package and found you. However, please don't ask me to destroy the other. It has too tender a place in my heart for that.

There's so much to tell you, I hardly know where to begin. For the past three months I've been so terribly busy. For two months, excluding four days, we operated at sea, and now we have started another cruise which is to last for six weeks. For active duty, destroyers cannot be surpassed by any other type of vessel. Weeks of training for our battle practices before the actual firing consumes much of our time. Since I came aboard we have fired our depth charge practice, short range battle, torpedo "C," long range and torpedo "B." The above sentence gives in a very few words what I've been doing since coming aboard the *Roper*. Our next six weeks will be employed in assisting the airplane carriers and battleships with their practices. That's the main disadvantage of destroyer duty. When her own practices are completed, she still must service the larger vessels. Of course, you never hear of a battleship serving us small fellows. It's all in the game, however, and I'm obtaining a world of experience, which my classmates aboard the battleships are not. In that respect I've passed them far behind.

Mother arrived in San Diego on August 10. It was a surprise, as I wasn't expecting her for some time. However, she became ill and wanted to be near me. Since she came, she has been under treatment at the Naval Hospital in San Diego and staying with my aunt, who lives in San Diego with her married daughter. This aunt is the wife of Uncle Jud. It seems that mother, after my graduation, just broke down and had to resign her position. The doctors at the hospital say that she has stood on her feet so long that she just gave out. I've been terribly worried, and more so because I'm ashore so little. Mother, indeed, has worked these many years just for me and richly deserves a long rest, and no more work on a ready-to-wear floor. I am quite happy that I can see her when I am ashore and can contribute something to her happiness.

I have rented a small apartment at 3366½ Grier Avenue in San Diego, and at the present time mother is there. She is feeling some better than when she arrived. Three visits to the hospital every week for treatment has improved her a lot, and I'm hoping that she will soon be entirely well again. I believe that it's rest she must have more than anything else.

So, my dearest, these last three months haven't been such happy ones for me. I've worked so hard to get a good start aboard ship, and mother's condition made it doubly hard. Then, too, I've been so homesick for you. Time and time again I've wanted to wire you to come to me, and at the same time realized that it was impossible because of finances. When I first came to the *Roper,* I wanted to start saving, but since mother came it has been impossible, and I've just managed to get along. Treatment and examination at the hospital is free, but the medicine bill has been huge, and, of course, rent and food must be provided.

I've really been very cruel in not giving you some information about what has been going on. But my plans were all crushed, and I've had to adopt other plans which haven't been easy to follow. I've been busy, worried, and homesick--all three causing me to wait in hopes I'd have better news to write when I did.

We are now anchored outside San Pedro. We are on duty with the airplane carrier, *Lexington,* until this Saturday, when we return to the San Diego area. Last night we received word that the *California* was coming into port. The *California* is the ship Jones is on, so as soon as she anchored, I went on a visit to see him. It was good to see him again, and he had lots of news for me. He is getting married on 16 November, of course, to Martha. She is leaving Baltimore on 5 November, and they are to be married in Long Beach. He certainly surprised me, as I wasn't expecting it until next year.

However, he, like myself, has been so lonesome and homesick, and there is really no reason why they should wait. Mrs. Jones is very opposed to the marriage and has forbidden him to marry, but that isn't stopping Jones. I envy him in getting married. I wish I were too. It's impossible for me to get leave, so I miss out on the best man proposition, as well as even attending the wedding. I'm sure they will be very happy.

Mattie is now in Bremerton, Washington, where his ship is undergoing an overhaul. The *Roper* goes there for overhaul on 12 December, so I'll be there during Xmas--all alone. Mattie returns to San Diego on 19 October, very soon now, and he can give me the "dope" on the place where I'll be for two months.

We abandoned our partnership on the Hudson when he left for Bremerton. We traded the Hudson in on a 1929 Ford Coupe, which I now have in San Diego. Mother isn't able to drive, so the Ford is idle at Grier Avenue much of the time.

All the foregoing brings us up to date and gives you an idea of what's been happening these last three months. So now let's talk of the present and the future.

I imagine you've been lonely too, since your family has moved from Richmond. You must send me their address. However, Mrs. Caskie, I know, is a joy to you, and that would help so much. Give her my love and kindest remembrances.

It seems that out here even the stars aren't the same. Somehow they don't twinkle like they did when I used to receive messages from you via every one in the sky. Just to

check up, I investigated and found out that the stars which shine in Richmond don't appear in San Diego, except a very few. It's so hard just to imagine you're near and not so far away. Jackie, dearest, I love you with all my heart. I always will no matter what happens. It's only possible for a man to have one dream girl, and that's you as far as I'm concerned. You must understand my neglect in letter writing. In my heart there has been no neglect. I haven't forgotten, nor will I ever, ever forget. It seems only yesterday, and yet a million years, when I whispered to you on the porch there in Richmond, that I would be true, and I always will. Then, too, that marvelous time on the beach with you that last week-end in Richmond. We were so close then. You just penetrated my whole being and soul. I cannot...................Gee, it's hard to remember those sweet moments. Times when I do, it seems that I cannot carry on. It's you who are the true Navy girl. With you by my side, I could be brave in the face of everything. Without you, sometimes I'm a coward, and right now I'm a coward, because I'm wanting you so, need you so, when I'm not able to have you. And then, I remember your dear sweet smile, so patient and true--the little curve of your hair over your temple--and in a measure I am comforted, with the resolve to carry on, and surely God will make a way for the day to come when you are mine, all mine. I love you so, I do, I do, I do.

I'm dying to hear from you. Will you wait long?

Millard

San Diego, California

26 November, 1931

Dearest,

Thanksgiving Day! I've just been thinking of the things I am thankful for, as well as those of which I cannot be thankful.

It's a lovely night--the sky just full of lovely stars and a great California moon. "Goodnight, Sweetheart" just came over the radio, and here I find myself attempting this letter after a dozen vain attempts.

As soon as I received the "<u>package</u>" and letter, I immediately wrote a letter, but it did not express myself, so I never mailed it. Since then I've been just a little dazed vainly trying to grasp something which is just beyond my grasp. So strange, too, that since "that time" everything has gone wrong!

I've been vainly trying to understand. You returned something which I had given you for life--a ring which was to always bind our souls together as one. If your letter had said that you no longer cared, perhaps there would now be no battle in my heart--just an eternal wound which would never heal. However, your letter read that you loved me, and there would never be another. Those words are the reason why this has been so hard to write.

I have here over my heart a tiny ring. I can feel it through my coat. It causes a terrible pain in my heart, but I carry it there because you requested that it be there. That pain will always be there unless this ring returns to its proper place.

My dear, surely you realize that I love you, that I have asked you to be mine for always. You can't have forgotten that. As for being a hindrance to my advancement, you have been the cause and inspiration for what progress I have made. If that inspiration fails, I hardly dare to predict what the future holds.

You do look at everything so very noble. Perhaps it is asking too much to require you to live on my pay with mother here too. However, I was going to leave that entirely up to you. But, if it cannot be, and we must wait until my first promotion, why send the ring back? That one question has been before me every hour of the day and night. Sometimes it seems that I cannot bear it, I'm wanting you so. I love you, I do, with all my life and soul.

I cannot help but feel that my neglect in writing influenced you. I'm sorry, but I want to say that our love was not neglected. Every minute I was striving for that "service reputation" which will be so valuable to us in later years. My first fitness report to Washington was an excellent one. Those weeks when you received no letters was utilized for our happiness alone. For happiness for you and I is all that I've been striving for.

So, my dearest girl, I'm asking that you accept this ring again and all that it means, until death do us part. If you will not, then you must say that I can never contribute toward your happiness. Then I will go my way, happy in the knowledge that I've kept my promise--<u>I've been true</u>--and I will always, even if I am not to have you. Will you accept this ring again? <u>I cannot, I cannot</u> for long wear it next to my heart, because it is slowly breaking that which beats only for you.

Your place is here with mother and me. Your picture is here before me in all its loveliness. The radio is playing again that beautiful melody, "Goodnight, Sweetheart." Mother is asleep on the couch. She knows my heart is breaking for you, and she will sacrifice anything [so] that we can be together. Won't you drop her a card: 33661/2 Grier Ave., San Diego, Calif.?

The *Roper* gets underway again in the morning at 5:30. As soon as I finish this, I'm leaving for the ship. We came in late Wednesday night for the holiday. On 15 Dec. we leave for the Bremerton, Washington Navy Yard. We will be there until 1 February, when the fleet concentrates for the annual cruise--this year to Hawaii. After 15 Dec. I will be away from San Diego until April 10, or thereabouts.

Jones was married over a week ago in Long Beach. I was unable to be there, as we were at sea. I know they will be very happy. Gaasterland and Marian were in San Diego for a month, while Gaasterland was taking elimination flight training. I had dinner with them twice before they went back to San Pedro. Marian is becoming a fine cook, and they were so happy [but] I was so very envious.

I'd like to hear from you before we sail on 15 Dec. Will you hurry and again make me happy and full of confidence to go ahead. At present I'm not advancing at all--just waiting--in the knowledge that I love you dearly.

Millard

Christmas Card

Millard J. Klein

Ensign, U.S. Navy

"Kindest thoughts and best wishes for the happiest Christmas that has ever come your way."

U.S.S. *Roper*

Bremerton, Washington

28 December, 1931

Dearest,

You've made a very happy Xmas for a lonely sailor boy. Thanks so much for the box--the pipe, tobacco, candy, and that fine plum pudding. I gave your formulae to our cook, and we had some very good sauce. All the officers of the *Roper* send their thanks to the best maker of plum pudding in the world.

We arrived in Bremerton on 20 December after seven stormy days at sea. We are here in dry dock for overhaul until 19 February when we shove off for Honolulu on the spring cruise.

Bremerton is a small country town which probably wouldn't exist without the Navy Yard. Most of its inhabitants are employed in the Navy Yard, which is quite a large place and quite beautiful. The surrounding country is beautiful too--pine forests and distant snow-covered peaks. I imagine it is wonderful here in the summer, but at this time of year the weather is terrible. Rain every day and very unpleasant. The natives say they have two seasons here--August and the rainy season.

Seattle is an hour's run by ferry boat across the bay. Most of the officers spend their time off over there, as there is nothing of interest in Bremerton.

My official designation aboard ship has been Ass't Communication and Ass't Gunnery Officer with various additional duties. Two days ago the Communication Officer was ordered to attend the torpedo school for officers, which begins Jan. 16 at North Island, San Diego. This officer leaves on 9 Jan. to attend this school. The dope is that I am to succeed to the head of the Communication Department. Quite a break for me, since my class is supposed to be under instruction until 1 June, 1932. Since this news came, I've been studying hard in order to feel capable of assuming new additional duties. Confidence must be there to make good.

I've so much to say it's difficult to find a starting place. You are such a dear, so wonderful and true, the finest girl in all this world. Long over a year ago I've realized this. That's just why I've wanted you all for my own--that and because I love you more than my life.

During the past few months since my arrival out here, I've endeavored to make a good record. In outward appearance I've been industrious and a hard worker, and I believe I've done well. In my heart I've been unhappy, for it seems that fate is denying me that which I want most of all--you.

The problem as you know is mother. Mother is all alone in the world except me. I love her very, very dearly, and I realize that after all these years during which she sacrificed so much for me, I owe her all that I can contribute during the rest of her life. This happiness which I owe her is my duty, and one which I am happy and proud to assume.

After you sent my ring back, I was heartbroken. I took the ring home that night and told mother that we had had a misunderstanding and for her to wear the ring. The next day I wrote you the letter asking you to again accept the ring which I wanted to bind our souls together forever.

And then your letter came which told me to return the ring, and you would always and always keep it. I was, Oh, so happy. I hadn't felt so good in a long time. That was Saturday morning. Before I left the ship, Mattie made arrangements with me to play golf that afternoon. I thought your letter very, very wonderful, and the attitude you had taken toward mother just what Jackie would do.

So Mattie and I stopped by home for my golf clubs, and I left your letter for mother to read, telling her that here was the best letter ever.

When Mattie and I returned about five o'clock, mother was ill and in bed, with the lady downstairs with her. I was never so scared in all my life, for mother was numb and crying, and I couldn't find out what was the matter, because when I left a few hours previous she was feeling fine.

Mattie went over and brought over my aunt (Uncle Jud's wife), and we had a doctor to come up from the Naval Hospital. He stated that it was a nervous spell, and that she must be kept quiet. It was nearly a week before mother was up again.

From my aunt I found out that mother is just afraid that I will marry and leave her all alone. It isn't you, Jackie.

You are too fine and noble for anyone to object to. Perhaps I don't understand a mother's feelings. Maybe you do and will help me. I've always, since we met, imagined us three very, very happy together, and I can't believe that it could be otherwise. I let my aunt read your letter, and she too thought it very wonderful. All my family who have met you have approved of you very highly--granddad and Uncle Jud. Aunt Bartol tried to explain to me how mother felt. Auntie said that she felt the same way when her son married, but that she had other children, so it was much harder to lose the only child.

I do hope you will understand, dearest Jackie. Sometimes I cannot help but cry when at night I dream of you and wake up in the night realizing I love you so. I will not, I cannot give you up ever. I'm praying every night that God will show the way and solve this problem which is making me so miserable. You pray too, and I know that there will be a way.

It was impossible for me to send you only a card and my love this Xmas. I sent my all to you by those darling stars on Xmas Eve night. I hope you were happy on that day.

Please write me very soon, 'cause I'm yours and I love you.

Millard

Navy Department
Bureau of Navigation
Washington, D.C.
20 August, 1932

Dear Jackie,

Do pardon the long delay in answering your questions. It was not because I have been either too busy or too forgetful, but simply because it was not too urgent.

Your friend is still on the *Roper*. Incidentally, he is doing fine and has made an enviable record for himself. I know this will please you, for it will fortify your confidence in your own judgement of human character. Perhaps some day he may serve on my ship, and I assure you that I shall be glad to have him.

With best wishes I am
Sincerely yours,
Miles Duval

Baldwin Hotel

321 Grant Avenue, Near Sutter

San Francisco

Sunday Morning

25 September, 1932

Dear Jackie,

I hardly know where to begin. I imagine that you rather I wouldn't, but I beg of you to read on.

I'm terribly ashamed of myself for the way I've treated you. I've reread this morning your last letter begging me to be fair with you and to tell you the truth. As I read those words again, I felt about as low as anyone could be. I answered only with silence during the past long months, and I don't blame you the terrible thoughts you <u>must</u> think of me. I really have no good excuse, so even at this late hour I will offer none--nor ask your forgiveness, because I'm not worth it.

This letter is mainly to give you some news of myself. I know that you cannot possibly be very interested, but I cannot forget the moments when you've told me that you were proud of me. Those thoughts are undoubtedly dead now, but I cannot refrain from writing.

During the past year I've worked terribly hard. I realized very seriously how terribly important it was to attain that service reputation during my initial year at sea. For that aim I have struggled now for over a year, and I must admit that I neglected everything else, although I didn't forget. That's hard to understand, I know. Two months ago I became the Chief Engineer of my ship, much to my great surprise, and I have done my job fairly well. At the present time the *Roper* stands one in the Engineering Competition among the destroyers of the Battle Force, and if this efficiency is maintained will win the highest of all engineering honors--the white "E." I believe that I have a good start toward a successful career in the Navy--and well--somehow I wanted you to know.

I have just a few statements I desire to make and then I'm through. Perhaps I will never hear from you again or ever see you. That's why I want to make them.

I've treated you terribly by not writing, by not telling you something of why I did not. That alone is unforgivable. However, that is all I am ashamed of. During the past year I've struggled to get along, to some day to be worthy of your once saying that you were proud of me. I've been true to your memory just as I promised I would be. In my heart there is an image of you that will never, never depart and is the finest and sweetest thing I can ever possibly possess. It has caused me to ever desire to forge ahead--to gain the heights--to be worthy of those dear words you once told me. I know that those words--those thoughts <u>must</u> be dead now, but I wanted you to know that whatever good I ever attain in this world--you alone are responsible.

During the past year I have been happily busy. But during the past few months I have slowly begun to realize what I have done to my heart. When I am on my ship I feel a sense of power as I listen to the throb of the machinery, 30,000 horsepower strong. But at times there comes a sense of loneliness as of something lost. The hum of the machinery seems to taunt me and say that I have gained nothing, but lost the greatest influence in my life. I may have lost you, Jackie, but I cannot have lost your influence. It was too sweet and fine and powerful for me to ever lose. This loneliness will continue to come up throughout my life, but your influence in my heart will always be there to steady me when the crisis arises which calls for a steady nerve and a strong heart.

I know you heard of dear old granddad's death. It was a terrible shock to me, and I haven't quite gotten over it yet. Somehow, when I left him last summer I thought I would never see him again. He also was a strong influence in my life--and he too realized your worth. He considered you the grandest girl ever.

We are in San Francisco for a two weeks visit before returning to San Diego on 5 October. I came ashore last night to be free from the monotony of the ship for a short while. I went to a show last night, and as I emerged, I nearly bumped into Jones and Martha. It was the first time I had seen them in many months. We came up to the hotel and talked for a long while. They both asked of you. They will soon be married a year and are very happy. I envy them greatly.

The Baldwin Hotel is a small quiet hotel just on the edge of Chinatown. Whenever we come to San Francisco, I always slip away on a week-end and come here just to be quiet and alone. It's a relief to get away for a short while and just to be alone with memories. It's so crowded on the ship, with senior officers always present, I like to get away. They often ask, when I come strolling in on Monday morning, where I've been, but they will never know.

May I ask something of you, which I did not grant you? It would make me very, very happy to have at least just one more letter from you. It would be a comfort if you would write and tell me that you are happy. I can't say with truthfulness that I would be happy if you wrote that you had quite forgotten me. But please, at least one more letter. We leave San Francisco on 3 October, to arrive San Diego 5 October. Could I expect an airmail letter to reach me before we leave on 3 October? I don't deserve one word from you, but I'm on my knees for just a line.

Millard
U.S.S. *Roper*
Oakland, Calif.

U.S.S. *Roper*

San Diego, Calif.

9 October, 1932

Dear Jackie,

Your letter arrived just an hour before we heaved in the anchor at San Francisco and proceeded to San Diego. I had looked for it just days before it <u>could</u> have arrived. You cannot possibly realize how hungry I was for that letter, and I've been so very, very happy since I read every word very many times. Your words filled in something that was missing in my heart and which has been missing for so long. I cannot remember when I've been so happy since those glorious days we spent together that week-end last year.

I realize now how terrible I've been, and how much you have suffered. I do ask your forgiveness, and I'll spend the rest of my days asking your forgiveness and try to make up for any sorrow that I've caused you. I didn't realize what I was doing. I was concentrating every effort at my command to gain something worthwhile, so that you would justly be proud of me. Really, I haven't been selfish about anything, for you and mother are the only two persons that matter in my quest of that worthwhile. You have been in my heart since that first day I told you "I loved you" in that little house on King George St. I'll never, never forget that afternoon and how happy I was when we left a few minutes later. Remember?

I am happy to know that you have been happy, and I hope that it is to be God's will that you will be supremely happy. I'm happy that you have been making delightful trips, and I hope you have learned much about life. I, too, have learned much about life in the year that I have been here. I have learned much about the hard knocks life can offer. I have learned that one must deliver results and work hard to stave off defeat. I have learned that even in defeat you must smile and carry on and do better the next time, because there cannot be a second failure. I've learned how lasting, how permanent a love for a wonderful woman can be, how wonderful it is to work for her and resist temptation, just for her no matter how difficult. And then, I suddenly realized what I had done, that I had lost the only real love in my life, the only thing that really mattered. Success and love--they must go together. I stressed too much on success and neglected love.

I would give much to be able to see you and talk with you tonight. There are a thousand things I would like to tell you of the West Coast, my life on a destroyer. What a fine ship and what fine officers the *Roper* has. We are so very close together and get along so fine. There is only one criticism which I have of the life I have observed since I came to the West Coast. There is a terrible lot of drinking among the Navy set, and general unfaithfulness on the part of many officers' wives. I appreciate the situation that the officers are gone a great deal, but still it doesn't seem just right. I am not adverse to a certain amount of reserved drinking, but I don't like

parties in which the sole aim is to become terribly drunk. These parties occur very frequently when we are in port, and I've made several people angry by not accepting on various occasions. I suppose I'm old fashioned along many lines, but that's the way I feel. I hope this hasn't bored you. I was only giving you an idea of the only objection I have to the Navy and its officers and wives.

I am very glad you have that admirable characteristic--that of forgetting unpleasant things. I sincerely hope that you have remembered all the pleasant things about you and I. I'll be sorry all the rest of my life for any unpleasantness which I have caused you. An eighty year probation is rather a long time, don't you think? Couldn't you possibly reduce it by a few years. I am only concerned about one thing--that you believe me when I say that "I love you," that I have always loved you, and never for an instant, during the time I've been away from you, have I forgotten the vows and promises I made before we parted. I made them because I knew I could carry them out, and because I loved you with all my heart. I realize that you could not possibly know all this when I am silent for some 12 months. My hope is that perhaps you have not succeeded in forgetting me, that we can again be just as we were, so gloriously in love and so happy. At this late hour it appears to be more than I could possibly expect or hope for. If we could wipe the slate clean of that long silence of mine and be back where we were, I would be the happiest man in the world. Can we do that, dear Jackie? I'm praying you will say yes. Can't we go on with those glorious plans for the future? Do you still have <u>our</u> pictures? I've collected some more to add to them.

Please tell me news of yourself, of your work and your family. When have you seen your mother? I wonder what she thinks of me? Has Mrs. Caskie forgotten me? I could ask a thousand more, but tell me everything. I'm starved for news especially of you and especially if there's any hope for a bad sailor boy.

<u>Mike</u>

WESTERN UNION TELEGRAM

SAN DIEGO, CALIF. 1933 MAR. 20 A.M. 11:29
MISS JACKIE COLEMAN, RICHMOND, VIR.
RETURNED FROM TEN DAYS MANEUVERS THIS
MORNING TO FIND YOUR TELEGRAM. AM WELL
AND FINE. SAN DIEGO. NOT DAMAGED SHIP HAS
BEEN AIDING IN LONG BEACH. WRITE SOON.
LOVE
MILLARD

Dear Jackie,

Have you given me up for dead, or have you just ceased to think of me altogether? I hope neither one, although I justly deserve either one.

I reported to my new ship last Sunday, 11 June, and so far I haven't succeeded in getting my bearings aboard a big ship. It's quite different from a destroyer, and I almost feel as if I were just starting out anew with no experience whatsoever behind me. However, I suppose I'll soon find out what is required of me and do it to the best of my ability.

The *Roper* is no more, at least as far as the officers are concerned. We all were ordered away this June, and a fine ship is no more. I hardly believe that no finer body of officers and men will ever be together again on one ship. The Captain cried when he left, and all of us left with a big lump in our throats. I wish you could have known them. The Captain was especially fine, and we all love him very much, not only as the Skipper, but as a man and a friend.

Mother and I are now living in Long Beach at 1727 E. Broadway. I was allowed four days from the time I was detached from the *Roper* until I reported aboard the *New York*. This allowed us time to find a house and get all our belongings moved from San Diego.

The results of the recent earthquake are still much in evidence, although much construction work is going on. Mother is a little nervous about future ones, but I selected a frame house which was untouched by the last earthquake. Most all damage and loss of life was due to brick buildings not steel reenforced.

I did not like to leave San Diego, as mother liked the city and home, and I liked my ship. These battleships seem so cold and formal, while my destroyer was cheerful and non regulation. Perhaps after I know everyone better, I'll have a better opinion. I hope so at any rate.

The *New York* sails 23 June. Here is our itinerary for the summer. Remember the one I sent you before.

23-30 June	At anchor Santa Barbara
1-2 July	En route San Francisco
2-5 July	At San Francisco
6-11 July	En route Seattle and Puget Sound area
12 July- 8 Aug.	In Puget Sound
9-12 Aug.	En route San Francisco
13-20 Aug.	At San Francisco
21-22 Aug.	En route San Pedro-Long Beach

I've been talking quite at length about my own selfish self. Suppose we shift the conversation to something more interesting. For example: yourself.

I have just completed reading the last letter I received from you. I have a very complete file which I keep in a large cubbyhole of my desk. Every so often I obtain new life and courage by referring to the contents of a favored few. I realize that I am an abdominable[1] (Is this word spelled correctly, and does it express what a bad boy I am?) person not to write you, but believe me when I say I think of you very often, and that I have never met anyone who has taken your place in my heart.

Would you write a sailor boy very soon? I'd like to have some news of you, of Mrs. Caskie, of your father and mother and Stuart. Does Stuart still remember me? I still have and prize greatly the ship model he presented me.

Next spring I take my promotion exams, and I intend to begin study early this fall. If I succeed in passing them and gain the increase in pay which usually goes with promotion, I hope to be able to make a trip back to the East and claim something which I will always believe was intended for me. Perhaps I'll not pass, but happy thoughts of the future have always been so pleasant for me. Don't you think so?

I was trying to think of the place[2] where we spent such a happy week-end just after my graduation. I think I can pronounce it but never spell it. What was it please?

Can I let my hopes soar for an early reply, or can I expect my own medicine and look for a letter in 1934 or 1935? The <u>same</u> person you knew ages ago.

Millard

---

1. He means "abominable."
2. Shoansy-on-the-Piankatank in Virginia.

U.S.S. *New York*

Seattle, Wash.

24 July, 1933

Dear Jackie,

Your letter arrived at a most convenient time. I had about decided that you didn't intend to write, and during the past week I've been in more or less of a lethargy which required only your letter to change the aspect of everything. Really, I was tremendously happy to hear from you. I even took the first paragraph smiling and reread it again before proceeding. I actually enjoyed it and, after it was all over, felt much better than I have in a long time. I suppose that's because I devoured every word, the dollar signs, stars, @,#, included.

So you think I have you on tap for further use if needed? Just what do you mean by those words? Your statement, that you were just the sort of home brew that is very apt to have a spontaneous combustion when kept on tap too long, amused me greatly, and I've laughed and laughed. That saved the whole first paragraph (that long one) of your letter, and I couldn't get mad at all. As a matter of fact have we ever quarreled? I don't remember any.

You dated your letter July 20, 1935. I wonder what we are doing and where we'll be at that time?

My new job aboard the *New York* is Radio Officer. I like it fairly well, although not near as well as being on the *Roper*.

It almost broke my heart to leave her and the officers. A finer bunch of men and officers could never possibly be assembled again. A battleship is, of course, more regulation, and I do not have as much authority as I did on the *Roper*. I have 150 men and a lot of equipment under me--much more than on the *Roper,* but at the same time someone is always butting in and won't let me run the show like I want to. I suppose I'll have to instigate my changes one by one, and I have a lot of them as far as the Radio Officer is concerned with the Radio Department. Of course, I'm boss of the Radio Department, but I'm responsible to too many people. You know, you can't please many people at the same time. They have ideas too--some do at any rate, others don't. I'll organize 'em on a *Roper* standard, and the *New York* will soon be at the top instead of way down the list.

Since we left Long Beach 20 June, I haven't left the ship, so you see I've been doing a little work. I planned to "hit the beach," as my new roommate says, tonight and attempt to shake off this dull feeling I have, but I couldn't resist pouring out my heart to you. After all, I'm beginning to realize that I've poured too much of my energy into the Navy and not enough of my heart to you. In other words you've been on tap long enough, and I want to be there if any explosion occurs. I'm just about ready to explode myself, so maybe between the two of us there would be a grand detonation.

My new roommate, Dave Roscoe, [is] a classmate, although I didn't know him very well until recently. He and I

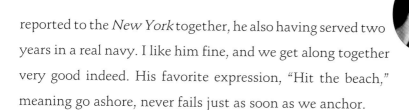

reported to the *New York* together, he also having served two years in a real navy. I like him fine, and we get along together very good indeed. His favorite expression, "Hit the beach," meaning go ashore, never fails just as soon as we anchor.

"Mattie" Hall was married last November. He married Miss Frances King from Colorado Springs. Miss King is the sister-in-law of Lt. Schaede of the *Roper*. She was visiting the Schaedes last winter, and "Mattie" met her in San Diego. They lived only a block from us in San Diego. They are very happy apparently, and I believe Frances will be a good wife. "Mattie" is now on the *Oklahoma,* and Frances is visiting at her home. As soon as we return to Long Beach 22 August, Frances will be there, and they'll find a home. I think it was rather a shock to Martha Sanford, and it even surprised me. Martha and "Mattie" just drifted apart, and she sent the ring back, and thus a grand romance ended.

Referring once again to your first paragraph. (You know a lot of information and statements are contained in that paragraph.) "I'm in love with you, and it's a disease acutely, not chronically." I've pondered that statement, and I haven't gotten a great deal from it. If acutely and chronically means with your whole heart and being, then your statement is correct. It's an interesting, but unhappy thought, to think back over the past two years and trace the trend of things as they have worked out. Two years ago I thought that very soon we would be together, inseparable the rest of our lives, in the little house with the green shades, sun dial, and our pictures on the wall. And then, after assuming responsibilities which I then did not realize, I came to know that, for the time, it was impossible for us to be together. I've never, never ceased a moment to love you with as complete sincerity as that first moment when I told you and all the subsequent happy days. I've realized, however, that we were separated by such a great distance, and existing circumstances made it a matter of years, before I would be in a position to plan further for happiness. I know that sun and water are needed for the hardiest of flowers, and I know too that your love was not of the hothouse type. Therein lies my greatest error. However, I have one glorious thought in my heart. If we ever are reunited and find that we love each other as we did during that glorious first class year, it will be a grand test of real love and devotion and self sacrifice.

You are right when you say that it's not well to plan for the future. Soon I must start study for my exams next spring. Perhaps I shall fail. That would blast all my plans. But, someday I know I will be dropping in on you, and it will be a surprise. You won't know I'm coming, and we'll see if we can be as we were. I know that now it's not a matter of years. Two have already faded into the past, and perhaps soon the light will show in that day of eternal happiness for you and me.

Today has been a happy one for me--the first in a long time. I completely forgot the ship and the Navy and lived just in your letter. I was back with you at the Academy, in

Richmond, and I was meeting you on the stairs for a good morning kiss--Oh, so completely happy!

Millard

I'm 25 years old tomorrow, and your letter over my heart insures a happy day.

U. S. S. NEW YORK

Dearest,

29 October, 1933.

Doesn't time fly? The days, the weeks, and the months just appear to have flat wings and speed by before one can take the opportunity each day brings. I often wonder if I am taking full opportunity of each day and living it as I should to obtain the maximum benefit. Lately I don't seem to be able to accomplish much, and as each day passes to come no more, I wonder again if the time is being utilized properly. I usually am able to find many mistakes in how I do things, and when I think of the valuable time lost, it is very discouraging. Each day there is so much to accomplish, and the days just aren't long enough, and the results appear to be so small.

I've just finished reading your last letter dated 13 August. I could hardly believe that I am over two months in answering. I'm very happy that you don't treat me as I do you and wait two months or more to answer. Please don't ever do that, will you?

The past two months have brought many things, and as above so little has been accomplished. Six weeks ago mother, while riding with "Mattie" Hall's wife, suffered a severe accident. The automobile door suddenly flew open, and mother fell out, the car going at 45 miles an hour. I've been marveling ever since that she wasn't killed. She suffered a

broken elbow, severe cuts and bruises all over her body, and severe scalp lacerations. Being very nervous, she has had a hard time being in the hospital over two weeks. She is much improved now, although her arm will always be stiff. The elbow bone was knocked off, and the elbow itself suffered a compound fracture. I was terribly worried about her for a long time.

Then too, things haven't been going so well on the ship. The past eight weeks I have had the hardest job I've yet tackled. The ship's direction finder is under my care and supervision. I had some experience with radio direction finding on the *Roper* but not near enough. The *New York* was recently overhauled, and her masts and rigging radically changed. This very materially affects the characteristics of the direction finder. This meant that it had to be calibrated again completely. Ordinarily this is a hard enough job, but not too complex. Results obtained so far are very discouraging, and the Captain isn't at all pleased with my efforts. Calibration curves have been run day after day on various frequencies and excellent results obtained on that particular day. However, the very next day it has been impossible to obtain the same results as the day before, which is very important for accurate direction finding. Some outside influence is affecting the instrument which I have been unable to find. I've worked on it day and night, read every book and pamphlet on the subject, and so far have arrived at no definite conclusion. Help me out will you, and give me an idea?

I've been hoping maybe you wouldn't wait for my letter and write anyway. It would have been such a help. I miss you terribly at times. I'm glad I have something which keeps me busy from the minute I get up until I take a few hours out for sleep. Otherwise I might not be able to carry on without you. Most every night I dream of you and lie awake and wonder at the strangeness of fate and this old world of ours. Particularly, I do this after observing some smiling young wife and her adoring young husband.

I'm beginning to collect data for my approaching promotion exams next spring. What a job that is going to be, and I'll soon be buried up to my neck with studying again. I'm afraid I've forgotten how to study, but maybe it will return easily.

John wrote me of his trip to Chicago and seeing you there. I was very envious. I'm happy you had the opportunity to go and accepted it. I know you had a glorious time. It would have been "swelegant" to have met you there, but it just could not be.

Thank Stuart for his note. I enjoyed it so very much. I wish I could show him my radio plant. Maybe he can give me an idea about direction finding operation.

My dreams of you are sweet, grand, and very, very real. I picked out a bright star tonight and sent you a kiss. If I could take you in my arms tonight and tell you over and over and over that I love you with my whole heart and being, I would be completely, sublimely happy.

"Mike"

UNITED STATES NAVAL MESSAGE

U.S.S. NEW YORK

LONG BEACH, CALIF. DEC. 16, 1933

WHEN DIRECTED BY COMMANDING OFFICER

ABOUT TWENTY EIGHT DECEMBER ENSIGN

MILLARD J. KLEIN DETACHED PROCEED MARE

ISLAND CALIFORNIA REPORT COMMANDANT NAVY

YARD TEMPORARY DUTY CONNECTION FITTING

OUT U.S.S SAN FRANCISCO AND DUTY ON

BOARD WHEN COMMISSIONED.

(What do you think of this?

Love you, darling.

Millard)

Dearest,

Here I am in a strange land among strange people and longing for you something terrible. I don't think I will ever become hardened to being transferred away from friends to strange places, as apparently many do.

I departed from Long Beach 30 December on the S.S. *Yale*. (I had always wanted to make a sea trip on which I could rest easy, have a drink, and do no work.) The trip was nice and instead of one drink, I had one too many, but was feeling grand when we arrived at San Francisco the following morning at 11 A.M. I spent a quiet New Year's Eve by going to a show and afterwards observing the merrymakers along Market Street. I departed New Year's Day and arrived Mare Island late that evening.

I reported for duty early Tuesday, 2 Jan., and was immediately informed that I was the Radio Officer of the new cruiser *San Francisco*. I was surprised but pleased, because the cruiser is equipped with the most modern equipment and up-to-date system of communication. I have inspected the *San Francisco* from stem to stern, and she will be the last word in naval warship construction. She will have the power of a battleship and the speed of a destroyer. The Captain and Commander both seem very pleasant, as well as the other

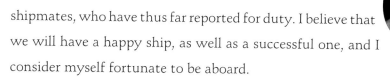

shipmates, who have thus far reported for duty. I believe that we will have a happy ship, as well as a successful one, and I consider myself fortunate to be aboard.

The orders were very much of a surprise to myself as well as the *New York*. I expected to have duty aboard her for at least two or three years. When my orders were received, the ship, due to the fact that no one was available to relieve me as radio officer, sent a dispatch requesting my orders to be revoked, due to the fact that I did not desire transfer and due to the above condition. I thought that this request would be granted, and I was a little sorry, for I did consider it an excellent opportunity. However, the Bureau replied that it was not practicable to revoke my orders, and here I am. I did regret leaving the *New York*. I had just become firmly established and known, and results were beginning to show in the department. However, I feel that after the new ship is completed, I will like it even better.

You are such a dear. Always so thoughtful, true and kind. Your letter, received the very morning I reported for duty, was so very welcome. I spent a lonesome, sleepless night the night before, and I was really feeling low. I read your letter through twice before I called on the Captain, and it made me feel a 100% better. Thanks for your thought in writing just then.

As for my Xmas you made it a completely happy day as usual. I was like a kid digging out each object from that sock. I have your tobacco pouch right here, and it will bring memories of you the many times I use it each day. (I'm still using the lighter you gave me.) And now to scold you for that awful trick you played on me. I spotted the bottle almost before I had removed the first few things. I excused myself from mother in time to hide it in the next room before she saw. After all the other presents were opened, and mother was in the kitchen, I eased out to have a drink of real old Canadian rye, 50% alcohol. I opened up and was hit squarely in the forehead. Don't you feel ashamed to disappoint me so much? That afternoon I went over to Mattie's and offered him a drink. He was so greedy he was hit in the nose. I've had lots of fun, and I'll forgive you this time. However, I do think you should send a thimbleful of real rye to make up for the disappointment. Thanks again for a truly marvelous Xmas.

The new ship still is not fully completed, and I am living temporarily aboard the destroyer *Lawrence.* The ship expects to be commissioned 11 February. Then follows weeks at sea in which all of her trials must be successfully completed. Then a two weeks stay in our namesake city, followed by a six weeks shakedown cruise, destination as yet unknown. It is estimated that all this will last until the middle of May. The Fleet leaves for the East Coast early in April. It is not known whether the *San Francisco,* the middle of May, will proceed to the East Coast to join the fleet or remain here until the fleet returns. If we do not go, I will never forgive myself for being transferred. (As if I could have helped it anyway.) However, we'll hope for the best.

I have started my study for my promotion, and with my new duties, I am going to be terribly busy. However, I still have that ache in my heart which has been there ever since I've been on this Coast. It's an ache only you can cure. I love you, dear heart, and perhaps soon we can count the days until you are in my arms again. It's been so long, the very thought seems like heaven divine.

Always and forever,
    Millard

Commemorative Postcard

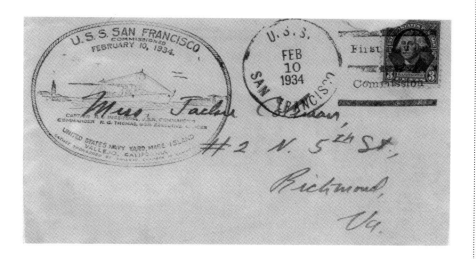

(The postmark is just a souvenir I thought you would like to have. Awfully busy these days, but think of you always. Love, Millard)

Vallejo, Calif.

5 April, 1934

Dearest,

Your letter arrived in the midst of my examinations and thus was doubly welcome.

Many fine memories were returned to mind when I read of your visit to Annapolis. I'm happy that you had the opportunity to go and that you enjoyed yourself so much. I am exceedingly jealous.

This afternoon completed eleven hard days of examinations, and I feel that I could sleep for a week. However, tomorrow morning, I'm being operated on for tonsillitis at 9:00 A.M.

This is just a note and not an answer to your very fine letter. I just wanted to be sure you would write while I am in the hospital and to let you know I'm in love with you.

The *San Francisco* sails for South America 28 April for a 3 month cruise. Write me, when and how we can see each other. I agree with your ideas and think that you should look me over once again. I wonder if you will find me much changed. I hope not.

I believe that I passed my exams. Give a little prayer that I did. We'll probably know in a month or so.

Always I've loved you. Please write as soon as you receive this.

Millard

U.S. Naval Hospital

Mare Island, Calif.

Napa, Calif.
Monday Night
9 April, 1934

Dearest,

I came home from the hospital today, and with the exception of a very sore throat, feeling in great shape and much rested after those eleven days of examinations. I would submit to a knife most any day, rather than go through those eleven days again.

During the time I was taking the exams, the ship went to sea for trials, to last two weeks. She does not return until Monday, 16 April, so I have practically a week's leave, which however doesn't count as leave. It is the first vacation I've had in three years, so today I've been quite lost here, hardly knowing what to do. I've gazed at your picture, most of the time, and thought that life has been cruel to keep us apart as long as this.

I read in tonight's paper of the sailing of the fleet from San Pedro and San Diego, and a wave of regret swept over me, because I was not on my way to you. Once again, fate or something has prolonged our meeting once more. There must be a limit to everything, and I'm just at my rope's end, for want of seeing you.

Seems like today I've missed you more than at any time during the past three years. Three years! That is a long time, isn't it? Too long for someone to be parted from someone, who loves the first someone more than anything else on earth. I imagine it's because I've been free of any worry today. When I'm aboard ship, I think of and miss you, but I can always bury myself in something, and then it's a lot easier.

I've just completed reading your letter once again, and you certainly did have news for me, didn't you. I am very happy you enjoyed your trip to Annapolis, and while I am both jealous (very) and envious, I do not begrudge you the trip at all and happy you enjoyed yourself. It revived many old memories and called to mind others I could never forget.

I can hardly think of J.B. as a first classman and about to graduate. I still remember him as a plebe, of course, and it's hard to shift the scene. Guess I'm getting old.

Your trip to Europe sounded very exciting and apparently is an excellent opportunity for you. Since it is definite that the *San Francisco* is not coming East, I suggest that, if possible, you take advantage of your opportunity. I know you would have a grand time, and such opportunities should be accepted, if possible.

To learn that John had joined the Navy was a surprise. Was it his intention to attempt to enter the Academy preparatory class and enter Annapolis that way, or did he just crave to see the world? Perhaps we'll be on the same ship some day!

My new job aboard the *San Francisco* is in the Gunnery Department Turret 3. I was first slated to be Radio Officer, but the Captain considered I was smart enough in Radio and needed to branch out. So instead of "twiddling the key," I've shifted to shooting.

I'm just a little tired, so I'll close for this time. Hope you'll write me soon and give me your additional news and your plans for the near future.

Sweetheart, I love you, I do.

Millard

U. S. S. SAN FRANCISCO

Hilo, T.H.

25 May, 1934

Dearest,

A special cachet has been designed for letters being catapulted from our ship and sent to Honolulu by our planes, for further relay to you by steamer and rail. I thought you might like to save this one too.

Thought I would have a letter here from you, after 12 days at sea, but I was disappointed. We arrive Vancouver, B.C. 4 June.

Please write.

Love,

Millard

Plane leaves in 10 minutes.

WESTERN UNION TELEGRAM

VALLEJO, CALIF. 1934 JUL. 17 A.M. 3:39

MISS JACKIE COLEMAN, RICHMOND, VIR.

ARRIVED MARE ISLAND TODAY FROM PANAMA TO
FIND YOUR LETTER. VERY MUCH THRILLED OVER
YOUR PROPOSED TRIP TO CALIFORNIA. CAN
ONLY SAY THE SOONER THE BETTER. EXPECT TO
BE NEAR MARE ISLAND SEVERAL MONTHS, SO
THINK I CAN GET A FEW DAYS LEAVE WHEN YOU
ARRIVE. MY NEW TITLE IS LIEUTENANT JG.

LOVE,

MILLARD

Vallejo, California

26 July, 1934

Dearest Sweetheart,

As usual, you have made me very happy by always remembering to remember those dates we should. Your lovely gift arrived this morning, and I appreciate it so much, because I love you so. You are far too good to me, and I'm not so deserving as to warrant all the lovely gifts you send me. I have them all and will keep them always. I only use your lighter on special occasions, and it's still good as new.

I'm so thrilled over your coming to California that I wake up at night and think about it for so long, and the thoughts are so lovely, I'm unable to continue sleeping. If you don't hurry, I'll be all worn out from no sleep.

Your proposed date of 15 August appears to be just fine, and I'm almost certain to be able to get off for a few days. We finish our official trials on 9 August and at present are scheduled to be in dock here at the Yard after that time. I'm planning on driving to Los Angeles and meeting you upon your arrival. When your plans are complete, please let me know when you are to leave, and the exact time you arrive in Los Angeles. I shall want to request my leave as far ahead of the time as possible, as it is more often approved when not requested at the last moment.

I shall probably be so excited that I won't ever get to L.A., and when you step off the train, I'm afraid to even think just how I'll feel. It's been so terribly long, and we'll have so much to do, see, and talk about.

A little busy these days, so I won't write any more this time. Here's hoping to hold you in my arms in less than a month and tell you how dear you are to me and I love you, oh, so much.

Millard

WESTERN UNION TELEGRAM

VALLEJO, CALIF. 1934 JUL. 29 A.M. 2:11
MISS JACKIE COLEMAN, RICHMOND, VIR.
VERY DISAPPOINTED. MAILED LETTER
YESTERDAY TO EFFECT WOULD EXPECT YOU
FIFTEENTH. LEAVE CERTAIN THEN. WANT YOU
TERRIBLY. HOWEVER, IN FAIRNESS TO US BOTH
BELIEVE YOU SHOULD ARRANGE VISIT FIRST TO
DETERMINE IF THREE LONG YEARS HAS
MATTERED. CAN YOU ARRANGE VACATION LATER
IN FALL? LOVE YOU MUCH.
MILLARD

San Francisco, Calif.

8 August, 1934

At Sea

Dearest,

Your dear letter of 1 August reached me yesterday in 'Frisco, where we anchored for one night. I haven't quite woke up to the fact that I will not soon be on my way to Los Angeles to meet you. We have been parted so long that I could not conceive of anything happening which would prevent your coming. Perhaps I was too optimistic, but it was nice to be so, and now that I know you aren't coming, I realize just how much I wanted to see you.

Do you think we can go on like the past three years-- always being apart and just dreaming dreams that don't come true? I really think, in fairness to you, that we should soon find out if we love each other as we think we do. This endless dragging on of an engagement, which is really not one, but an understanding that seems so futile if we are to be eternally separated. Perhaps, I'm just feeling low, as an aftermath of your letter, but don't you think I'm right? What it really amounts to is a trip to California for you in the near future, as it is practically impossible for me to get leave long enough to come East, and I still have four years out here before I will be ordered to Annapolis. The prospect of 4 years, like the past 3, is not very pleasant, and I don't want you to go through with them, to perhaps be disappointed when we did meet.

I wish I could honestly tell you to chuck that terrible job of yours and catch the first train. I do want you to do that, but in both our hearts we know that would be wrong. In case something has happened to us in these three years, and we would not feel toward each other as of old, it would be a terrible mistake that perhaps could never be corrected.

Why is it that you cannot arrange to come later on when you do get your vacation? Surely you are not to be denied your vacation altogether, and at present our schedule calls for us to be at Mare Island several more months. If that is true, I think I can get a week or ten days most anytime between now and Xmas. After that it would be very uncertain, as we will be with the fleet operating, and another fleet problem will be close by.

Please write me real soon, and I'll be hoping we can reach a solution.

I think and dream of you so often. You are beginning to appear as something which isn't real, or which is always just out of my reach.

All my love, dearest,
Millard

WESTERN UNION TELEGRAM

VALLEJO, CALIF. AUG. 25, 1934

MISS JACKIE COLEMAN,

DUNDEE COTTAGE, VIRGINIA BEACH, VIR.

ABLE OBTAIN TWO WEEKS LEAVE ANY TIME IN
SEPTEMBER. IS THIS INSUFFICIENT TIME TO
DRIVE EAST? SUGGEST MEETING YOU ANY CITY
APPROXIMATELY HALF WAY WHICH WILL ENABLE
TO VISIT FEW DAYS AND MAKE PLANS FOR
FUTURE. DIDN'T LIKE EXPRESSION QUOTE
DANGLE UNDER MY NOSE UNQUOTE, BUT LOVE
YOU ANY WAY.

MILLARD

Vallejo, Calif.

1 September, 1934

Dearest,

What a surprise was in store for me when your letter arrived! You may have met me more than halfway, but please give me more warning when you change your mind again about such things.

I am completely thrilled and happy over the joyful prospect of seeing you in barely two weeks. After three years it hardly seems real, and I still read your letter over and over to be sure I'm not dreaming.

I expect to leave Mare Island Saturday, 15 September for Los Angeles, and I'll be there when you arrive. So be sure and let me know the train you will take and at what hour (PST) you arrive in L.A. I bet you won't know me. Shall I wear a red or white flower? I'll probably have on a whole bouquet in honor of such an occasion.

The days I know will drag terribly, but I'll try to keep busy, and perhaps it won't be long until I hold you in my arms once again.

Life is indeed beautiful, if you only love me like I love you.

Millard

[After consulting with Uncle Jud in San Diego, Mike and Jackie went over the border to Tia Juana and were married by a Mexican judge on September 22, 1934.][3]

Thursday Night
[last of September, 1934]

My Dearest,

What a thrill I will get when I address this letter to Mrs. Millard Klein! I have wondered all day if it is really true--that you are my wife forever and forever.

I left Los Angeles two hours after your departure and drove straight to Oakland, where I remained the remainder of the night. I have never felt so terribly lonely and blue, and the drive seemed endless. However, I made the ride in 10 hours, arriving in Oakland at 12 midnight. I arose early and drove the remaining 28 miles to Vallejo, arriving at nine A.M.

I am looking forward to your safe arrival message and hope you and mother [Jackie's] will have had a pleasant journey.

Conditions were a little different in Vallejo than I had expected, and we will have to alter our plans somewhat. First,

3. Mike's mother received a telegram from her son five days before his elopement. She placed it in her scrapbook and on the back wrote: "Last Message from My Boy."

338

I should have brought you to Vallejo with me, and I now regret that I did not do so, if you possibly [could] have done so.

Mother took the news just a little harder than I expected, and she has been rather ill the past few days. She says that she had been expecting us for three days and did not send us a message, because she did not know that we were returning to Hotel Commodore after our marriage, but expected that we would be in Vallejo at any time. Mother, in her excitement over our news, rushed over to several of the neighbors, among them several of the officers of the ship. Consequently, everyone knows that we are married, and so you can imagine what I've been through today. My arrival this morning spread rapidly, and I've already explained at least a thousand times as to why I only had a three day honeymoon, and my wife returned to Virginia. I am glad now that everyone does know, for it means that you must return here as soon as you possibly can arrange your affairs. At any rate, I know that I could not stand to be separated from you any one or two months, so you needn't even unpack your bags. (Lord and Master now speaking.)

Most everyone on the ship have called or sent their congratulations today, and I feel terribly lost without you. Of course, I am the one who should have the congratulations, as you could not be congratulated on having a husband such as I, but I prefer to have you by my side and those <u>big</u> slippers near.

I've talked to mother at great length this morning, and I'm sure everything is going to be O.K., and we can all be very, very happy. I think she will give in even more when she sees how we love each other, and time will do the rest. She still is rather upset and nervous, but by the time you arrive, that [should] have worn away, and in that respect it was perhaps best that you return. She was prepared, however, to receive us, and our room was all ready to receive us.

I will attempt to find us a larger place this week, but in case we cannot, I am sure we can make out until we depart for Long Beach either in December or January. In any case, please return as soon as you possibly can, for I need you terribly, and the sooner we start this home I think we will all be better off.

Sweetheart, I am sure no one person can possibly love any other person as much as I love you. In the years to come we are to be separated many times, and now when it is not necessary, it must not be. Besides, shortly after the first of the year, we depart on the three months fleet problem, and we must have our home life firmly established as soon as possible.

Mr. Milliken came down yesterday afternoon, and I enjoyed telling him "our" story, and how much we love each other. He wants to meet you very much and says that you should have come home with me. He's right too, because I've just been miserable since you left, and I'll be that way until you return. So I'm going to expect a letter, just as soon as you

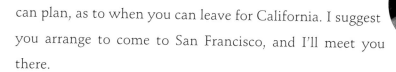

can plan, as to when you can leave for California. I suggest you arrange to come to San Francisco, and I'll meet you there.

My leave is not up until Monday, but I think I will return tomorrow, as I must have something to do. I'll try to work hard, darling, and pray that you will soon return to one that loves you more than life.

Millard

U.S.S. *San Francisco*

San Pedro, California

Sunday, 27 March, 1938

My Dearest,

How the time drags, and how much I miss you! Each succeeding year that I depart on our annual cruise, finds me missing you and longing for your arms around me more than the last year. I lay awake at night, listening to the water outside, and wondering what you are doing, and longing so for your head beside me and my arms tight around you. I love you, dearest, more each year that we are together, and each year I learn to appreciate you more and more. My life would be empty and forlorn without you, and no one could ever be that in my life that you have been. I thought I loved you when we were married, but I did not know that you were becoming a part of me that I could not live without. I think I first began to realize this fact last year while I was gone. The only thing that really matters in the world to me is that you love me--please do always--I couldn't do without it. Everything else is secondary.

I believe the time passes so slowly just because I am looking forward so to the beginning of our shore duty, 30 April. I think you and I deserve an honest-to-goodness honeymoon, and I mean just that, even if we do have the two sweetest children [Kay and Cissy] in the world. I intend to utilize the opportunity of this shore duty just to love you and have you for my very own every day and night for two years, and we begin just as soon as I return. I'm sad, because 30 April seems so terribly far away, as if it could never arrive. You must write me and tell me you love me over and over again--that you are awaiting my return, and that I too am a part of you that you love, and you couldn't do without me. Maybe, with those words close to my heart and singing in my mind, the eternity of this next month will be easier to bear.

You deserve a lot of credit for sticking by me through thick and thin, and at least it has served to bring me even closer to you. I have always looked at the situation from the point of view that our love could be no greater, and that all obstacles coming up against the stone wall of that love would be thrown aside. But, vacation time is near, and I'm crazy to go on a honeymoon with the only girl in the world for me--who I love, love, love, more dearly than I can possibly express with mere words--and who I shall always adore until the last breath leaves my body.

We are now engaged in the second phase of our maneuvers--the attack and the establishment of a base on the island of Oahu. (Somehow, my mind isn't on make believe war. I can only think of you every hour and minute and how much I love you.) We probably will anchor at Lahaina Roads about Wednesday or Thursday the 30th or 31st. We remain there for a few days, put to sea again and exercise for another week in putting landing forces ashore. We should arrive at

Pearl Harbor about the 8th. After that, it's a matter of wasting ten days for the start back across the Pacific to you.

The weather is stifling hot. The long watches seem to never end, and it's impossible to sleep below decks. I am looking forward to anchoring so that a good night's rest can be had with the sweetest of dreams of you.

How about our honeymoon, taking in Boulder Dam, Grand Canyon, and the Carlsbad Caverns? You can break out your maps and have it all figured out. Anywhere suits me as long as I have you and the chicks around when nightfall comes, so I can take you in my arms and kiss you sweet and tell you over and over and over again that I love you.

Mike

[M.J. Klein had two years of shore duty in the Office of Chief of Naval Operations, Navy Department, Washington, D.C. from May 1938 to May 1940.]

III
DUTY IN ICELANDIC AND NORTH AFRICAN WATERS 1941-42

Richmond, Virginia

February 27, 1941 [postmark]

Tuesday

My Darling,

Now that you are actually gone, I miss you horribly already. I have had the radio on all morning and have scanned the newspapers diligently, hoping for some news on what is up. A commentator this morning predicted the lend-lease bill would not be passed by the 1st of the month, as the opposition was growing stronger, and there is a filibuster planned. Also the President left Hyde Park for Washington last night. I got home about seven, as I waited at the Monroe Hotel until 4:30 hoping for some word....

The weekend with you was lovely. I love just being with you and looking at you and talking. I hope getting things sort of off our chests will help. I know how you feel, as I feel just the same way in a milder degree--milder, because every time I look at that debit side of our lives, I compare our credit side, and I may be a damned old Pollyanna, but the credit side certainly outweighs the debit. The biggest credit is that you are mine, and we have each other and the children and good health. And though I wonder where you are and wish frightfully that you were here, I do not fear for you like so many British, German, and Italian women in the same walk of life are fearing for the men they love. Certainly, I'd love a home and things others have, but material wealth is rather paltry when compared with the wealth of love and comradeship I have in my life with you. I'm just made that way--it's like my taste for clothes, etc., is far inferior than my taste for friendship and consideration and such. So I can wait for our own little home--and have it, we shall. If it's only a tumbled down cottage, we'll have such joy fixing it up. It's something to look forward to and dream about. I'm writing a bit every day to you, and when I know where you are will send it on.

Wednesday

Am still watching newspaper and radios and no clew [clue] as to your whereabouts--and am still missing you frightfully. Mamma suggested calling in some girls for bridge tonight to help pass the time for me....

Know, my dearest one, that I love you more than I can express. Go everywhere you go with God; I pray His everlasting arms to stay beneath you.[1]

Devotedly,
Your Jacque

---

1. Deuteronomy 33:27: "The eternal God is thy refuge, and underneath are the everlasting arms."

In March Hitler had extended U-boat activities by proclaiming that Iceland and its surrounding waters were now in the war zone. ... On April 9, 1941 the United States, at Denmark's behest, agreed to assume responsibility for the protection of Greenland until Denmark was free of the Nazi yoke. The Navy projected a Greenland patrol (and laid plans for Iceland). Theodore Roscoe, *United States Destroyer Operations in World War II* (Annapolis: United States Naval Institute, 1953) 28.

U.S.S. *Benson*

Port Everglades, Florida

29 March, 1941

Dearest,

We arrived back here at Port Everglades last night at 1 A.M. and expect to be here over the weekend. The President speaks tonight and probably will depart tomorrow. The Captain hopes to remain over Monday so as to possibly get our pay list so we can get paid. We are all flat broke.

Your letter meant much to me, received this morning and written by you on the 25th. I never seem to get tired of you telling me you love me, and each time seems sweeter than the last; for I love you too, in the same way.

Our cruise was uneventful. We only were distant from Port Everglades by about six hours. We sailed in and around the islands of the Bahamas during the day, while the President and party trolled and anchored early offshore in the afternoon for them to take to the boats. One day was spoiled by bad weather. The President did not come aboard the *Benson*. I met in one way or another: Gen. [Edwin M.] Watson, Aid; Tommy Qualters, bodyguard; Harry Hopkins [Presidential aide]; Attorney General [Robert H.] Jackson. All of them came aboard one afternoon to see the ship. [Interior] Sec. [Harold L.] Ickes, they say, is a poor sailor and stayed close aboard the *Potomac* [presidential yacht]. I guess Alex Ball is the only one who had any contact with the President. The President went out one afternoon in one of our small boats, and Alex was boat officer.

Apparently, the President did not want to get far away from port, so the cruise itself did not amount to much. All the big boys I met seem very nice. Hopkins looks like a sick man.[2] We had 3 secret service men and 3 newspaper men representing the three big coverages, and they are all very nice--but hard drinkers and gamblers.

The Captain expects orders as soon as the President departs. He believes that we will do the following. Leave here either Monday or Tuesday--Stop at Charleston to strip ship of all unnecessary gear which will take two or three days, and then proceed to Norfolk. That schedule will probably land us in Norfolk about the first of the week beginning 7 April. A week or ten days in the yard stripping the ramps, etc., from our decks.

All the ships of our division which went on to Guantanamo without us have returned and are basing at Newport. So as soon as we finish at Norfolk, we undoubtedly will proceed to Newport. All destroyers on this Coast are being concentrated on the Northern Coast of U.S., and it seems evident that there will soon be convoy duty in extreme Northern latitudes (Greenland & Iceland), since we have received more heavy clothing and charts of those places. Of course keep this to yourself, as there is no need to spread the

2. Hopkins suffered a complexity of nutritional diseases.

word around, but we must face the fact that it is coming, now that the lease-lend bill is through and the money available.[3]

I only want to spend every available moment with you, and I am so thankful that we have over six years of married life behind us. I would not change anything, and I am truly thankful for the happiness we have shared together and hope that there are many more ahead. If it should not be thus, I will try and be content in the knowledge that I found the one girl in the world for me, and that no one could ever love her more than I.

As soon as I get the "word" about what we do, I will let you know, but I think you can expect us in Norfolk in approximately a week, providing we stop in Charleston, which I think we will.

My arms are aching to be around you and will hope to see you waiting on the dock at the Navy yard when we arrive.

Yours forever,

Michael

You might write Newport later on and see if you can locate us a place.

---

3. Lend-Lease Bill provided American aid to Britain.

On March 19, shortly after the passage of Lend Lease, Roosevelt and Hopkins had gone on the yacht, *Potomac,* for a cruise in the Bahamas. This, as it happened, was the last of the "carefree" fishing trips for either of them. There was no pretense of inspecting bases this time and the yacht never ventured more than a few hours' sail from the Florida Coast.... The *Potomac* then returned to Port Everglades, Florida [March 28]. There was a German ship, the *Arauca,* tied up at Port Everglades. She had been chased in there by a British cruiser in December 1939, and had remained ever since, flying one of the last Nazi flags visible from American soil. Early in the morning of the last day of Roosevelt's holiday, word came to the *Potomac* that the F.B.I. had uncovered a plan for the wholesale sabotage of Axis ships by their crews, so the President ordered them seized immediately. Later that day, Sunday, March 30, Coast Guardsmen boarded the *Arauca,* removed her crew "for safekeeping," and hauled down the Nazi flag. This episode gave Roosevelt and Hopkins considerable pleasure: at least, it was action of a sort. Robert E. Sherwood, *Roosevelt and Hopkins, An Intimate History* (New York: Harper & Brothers, 1948) 277-78.

Brighton, Mass.

September 9, 1941 [postmark]

Monday Night

My dearest,

    I'm sitting here missing you frightfully and so will talk to you the best way I can. I keep busy during the day and that helps, but when night comes I miss you so very, very much! What I wouldn't give to see you sprawled out on the sofa with your shoes off (and a mouse in your sock) or propped up in the bed with the evening paper. Last night for supper I had a fresh peach pie--perfect according to the standards of Fannie Farmer, but tasteless and cloying to the throat to me, because you weren't here to eat it with me....

    I took the children to the doctor today to let him look Kay over before she goes to school. I have to have a vaccination certificate to get her in. Her school starts Thursday the 11th, and she is so excited--so much so that she says she isn't going to suck her thumb any more. Cissy is unconcerned about book learning--one can't eat that! Your mother is still piddling around in her room unpacking, using reams of shelf paper and newspapers to "protect" her "buggits." I knew I couldn't keep her from the radio or newspapers any longer, so yesterday at breakfast I casually said the radio had some story about another encounter of a sub and destroyer like we heard about this summer. Fortunately Sunday's papers had quieted down, and headlines were smaller. She seemed concerned, but didn't "relapse" and discussed it calmly. So you never know how things will set. Since my heart constricts every time I think of it, I was afraid it would put her in the bed.... I suppose you get news there as quickly as you do my letters, but in case not--the most important is the *Greer* incident and the death of the President's mother due to "collapse of the circulatory system due to age." I imagine she just went to sleep. How wonderful to be in command of all your faculties until the summons comes and then go to sleep. He was to speak tonight on a "major importance" theme, but has postponed his talk until Thursday night. I feel he has always and will always do what he believes in his heart to be right--and what more can a man do--but, Oh God, may he believe right! Good night, my love; into God's keeping I commend you.

Devotedly,

Jacque

President Roosevelt's answer to Hitler's Icelandic war zone ultimatum [March, 1941] was a quiet directive to Admiral Stark ordering the Navy to reconnoiter the approaches to Iceland.... In the Ocean southeast of Cape Farewell one merchantman after another had since been blown to the bottom by sharpshooting U-boats. "Torpedo Junction" the seamen called it--an apt name for North Atlantic waters where wolfpacks waited to meet the east-bound Allied convoys.

The United States destroyer *Greer* was not steaming with a convoy when she neared "Torpedo Junction" on the morning of September 4, 1941.... The *Greer* was proceeding independently... with mail and supplies for the American Icelandic base....

[A German submarine fired two torpedoes at the *Greer*. The torpedoes missed. The *Greer* did not return fire until after the torpedo attack began.]

Three days after the *Greer* episode, the American merchantman *Steel Seafarer* was bombed and sunk in the Red Sea by Nazi aircraft. On September 11, President Roosevelt made an historic radio address. Broadcasting to the world from the White House, he declared: "Upon our naval and air patrol--now operating in large numbers over a vast expanse of the Atlantic Ocean--falls the duty of maintaining the American policy of Freedom of the Seas. That means ... our patrolling vessels and planes will protect all merchant ships, not only American ships, but ships of any flag, engaged in commerce in our defense waters. From now on, if

German or Italian vessels enter the waters, the protection of which is necessary for American defense, they do so at their own peril. The orders which I have given as Commander-in-Chief of the United States Army and Navy are to carry out that policy at once."

Spoken one week after *Greer's* brush with the U-boat, this was the famous "shoot on sight" order which untied the hands of the United States forces defending Western Hemisphere waters. From that hour on the United States was involved in a *de facto* naval war with Nazi Germany. The war was undeclared, but the term *de facto* means actual, or patently existing. Roscoe 29, 33-34.

Brighton, Mass.

September 11, 1941

Thursday

Darling,

I wish you could have been here today to see your first-born go off to school. She woke me at the break of dawn and was so excited. We left at a quarter to nine amid the howls of Cissy, who wanted to go too, and went on down the street with Kay, book-bag on shoulder, grinning like a Cheshire cat. They took her unhesitatingly into the first grade. She has her own desk, and they started them right in on a full day's work. They have an hour for lunch at 12:15 and get out for the day at 3:30 P.M. She was so proud of her first "work" as she got a gold star on it and wanted me to send it to you. And so another milepost passes in our life, Daddy. We are all getting along fine and are as comfortable and satisfied as we can be in our apartment, but still miss you more than tongue can tell.... Life is so sweet and perfect and full when you live it with me and so void of meaning without you near. It's just a succession of days and nights that have to be lived through until you come home again, and then it becomes so wonderful--yet fleeting. It's rather dull at present and no news other than Kay's school, but I like to prattle to you anyway in the only medium possible at present. It helps the loneliness for you some.... The radio is playing "When Day is Done," and it's so my sentiments right now that I'm bawling, so I can hardly see what I'm writing. Your mother has gone walking, and the children are out playing, so I'm indulging in doing what I feel like--bawling for you. I feel better already just getting it off my chest. Yet I feel a bit ashamed, since I've yet so much to be thankful for--they aren't <u>really</u> shooting <u>yet.</u> The President speaks tonight. May God guide his words!

Know that He is watching over you, and we both are loving you with all our hearts.

Your devoted Jacque

Brighton, Mass.

September 14, 1941

Saturday Night

My Dearest,

The words I waited for and feared were spoken by the President in his speech. I suppose it was all one could say, and my heart has been in such turmoil it won't let my head think it out clearly. I simply don't know whether it's right or wrong. I think you should be ordered to protect yourselves, and you can't wait until fired upon to see if you are going to be attacked--you must shoot first--but the question in my mind is should our ships be so far away in Iceland, so near the combat zone. It relieves Britain of the task of preventing Germany to surround her at sea, but Britain asks too much in her request for aid. If we give her supplies, she ought to get them to England. As far as I'm concerned, Thursday's orders is war--war for the Navy, and if we're going that far, we ought to go the whole hog and send the whole works--Army and Navy over to give the knockout blow and be done with it. There's still one hope I cling to with all the tenacity of my being--that Germany will heed the warning now that Russia is becoming more than she bargained for. But whether right or wrong--we <u>are</u> in Iceland, and what's done is done. I still say I may not always agree with the President, but I do believe he does what he sees right sincerely, and that's all one can ask of a man. Knowing you were in the Navy should have prepared and hardened me, but it hasn't. The thing that keeps me up is my religion--puny and weak as it is in my case; it sustains me in such a crisis. When I lie awake in the night thinking of all the chaos and turmoil in this world, panic begins to grip my heart and throat--and then a still, small voice or thought surges up in my panic saying--"Peace, I am still God."[4] And, Oh Michael dearest, I know He will watch over you. I don't deserve His special care, but that's why He is such a wonderful God; He rewards us not according to our deserts, either large or small, but according to His great mercy. And all I ask is my loved ones near--healthy and happy. It gives me more courage just to write my thoughts. I know He will watch over you and bring you safely back to me. And I pray it will be soon. We all went downtown today to get Kay some school clothes. We stopped by the Common and took some pictures for you. I hope we did it right this time.... Mother Klein is knitting you another pair of socks, and I want to start you some mittens as soon as I can get the right thread. But I'm hoping I'll not have to send them to you, but that you will be coming home soon to get them.

Be of good courage, my love--and come back soon to my waiting arms. I love you more than I shall ever be able to show you, could I live a thousand years. And I know He will keep you neath the shadow of His wings.[5]

Your devoted Jacque

---

4. Jackie is probably thinking of Psalm 46:10: "Be still, and know that I am God."
5. Psalm 91:1,4: "He that dwelleth in the secret place of the most High shall abide under the shadow of the Almighty. . . . He shall cover thee with his feathers, and under his wings shalt thou trust."

Censored by U.S.N.

U. S. S. BENSON (421)

16 September, 1941

Tuesday

My darling,

It seems so long ago since I left you after our wonderful two weeks together. Each succeeding time that I leave you grows more difficult, as it must, since my love grows more and more for you each day.

We arrived early this morning. As this letter is to be censored, I cannot divulge our location, but I'm sure you will know. I hope that our plans will not be changed, and that in another week I'll be on my way back to you and those arms that I long so for to be around me and those two little bits of you and I.

I hope you all are settled by now and have a nice place that you like. I have worried about you, because I'm afraid moving around so much hasn't been so easy. Pryor said that Mrs. Pryor thought you looked tired, and it has worried me. I didn't think so, but I know you have a tendency to work too hard, lift more than is good for you, and in general do too much. I want you to get out while I am gone and see people your own age and get away from the kids some. If necessary you can get someone to come in during the afternoons and take them off your hands for a while. I think it will repay us a thousandfold and especially if we are thinking of having another child...., so

I'm expecting you to be careful. To get away from the children and Grandma for a while when you feel the need I know must be important, and I want you to plan to do it and don't mind the cost of having someone to take care of the children. You must avoid mental strain as well as physical strain. Now, don't say you will and then go on and do as you generally do.

I love you so, want you so, and need you so that you must not only take care of yourself for the children, but for me. Someday, I hope not too far distant, I'll be coming home every night to have your arms around me, and to me that is all I want from life--you and your love. I didn't realize it while we were in Washington, but I do now, and I only pray I have the opportunity to make up to you for my mistakes there. In return, take care of yourself for me and ours. If fate should not be kind to us, it would make me very happy for you to realize and know that I love you and you alone, and I am thankful for the happiness you have brought me thus far.

Yours forever,
Michael

I haven't forgotten our 7th anniversary, and I have written to have you some flowers delivered on the 22nd. In case the letter is delayed and your flowers are late, I'll be thinking of you on that day when, seven years ago, I took unto myself the only girl in this world for me and who I have grown to love more than anything else. I knew I loved you then, but I did not realize how much or what a lucky man I was to get you. I hope we have many, many more anniversaries and that each one will mean just a little more in love and understanding. When I get back, I'm going to dress you up and take you out and show the world what I have to be proud of.

Until then with all my love,
Michael

Brighton, Mass.
September 17, 1941 [Postmark]
Wednesday

My Dearest,

I hardly dare think you may be back soon, so will write on anyway in case you aren't. There isn't any news, but I grow so lonesome for you that it helps a little to prattle on by pen anyway. ... Knight called his wife the night before you all left and said he'd see her in about two weeks. Of course, the President's speech may have altered those orders, though I don't know whether I'd rather you stay in Iceland to be out of the dangerous waters between us, or run the gamut so that I might hold you in my arms. I know you shall be watched over and taken care of, but still I don't want you to run into danger. Mother writes that I must keep my chin up and remember it's tough on any Germans with you at the business end of a gun trained on them, and Dad writes to remember that God is in His heaven and doesn't let anything happen to good people, except it be for their good. So I know you'll come through. You are good, darling, the best man other than Dad I ever knew--so loyal and true and kind to us, your little family, and we are grateful. All I ask is that you may be kept safe and come soon back to us. I keep busy during the day and knit or crochet like a house afire in the evenings to keep from thinking. God bless the woman who figured out how to twist a string into intricate patterns. A mind which has to guide moving fingers and count stitches isn't employed enough to keep from enjoying the radio, but can't concentrate on such subjects as what is to become of the world. Kay still loves school and is learning fast. They are taught the sound of letters such as, "What does the tired dog say?" Answer: "h" (pronounced like a panting dog) instead of "aitch." And they also are taught to recognize words before they learn to spell, such as "have" or "my," etc. Kay recites all she has learned over the lunch table and each evening. Cissy ambles on thru life as contented as ever, as long as there is plenty to eat. Which reminds me that it is awful how much prices are rising. I do think there should be a maximum price law. Your mother is knitting you a second pair of socks. She is holding up very well and even listens regularly to all the alarming newscasts. Whenever she gets to looking on the darker side, I suggest we talk of something else. I miss you more every hour and am praying you will come home soon and safely. I love you with all my being and will always--dearest Michael--love.

Your devoted Jacque

Brighton, Mass.

September [?], 1941 [postmark]

Monday Night

Dearest,

I have been looking for some word from you all day, and now that it's past eight have just about given up until tomorrow. Though I try not to be disappointed ... , I can't help hoping and praying and watching for you.... I want to write how much I love and miss you anyway. It's the only way I have of talking to you. Looking for your return is what makes life worth living, and having you with me is worth all the loneliness and heartache of waiting. I just stop living when you're away and live twice as full a life when you come home, so I suppose it "divvies" up in the end. Life plods on its mediocre way with an occasional fire or such to make it exciting. Our little 5 & 10 at the corner had a big fire this week with no end of excitement when the engines rolled by. And I watched the big $1,000,000 Charlestown fire from the apartment house roof, but could only see great billows of smoke. Kay is getting along fine in school and learning fast, and Cissy still rolls merrily through life. Your mother is still knitting your socks and seems contented, especially since the little neighborhood theater has a Sunday Vaudeville. She and Kay went Sunday at 1:30 P.M. and got out at 6 P.M. They swore they didn't sit through anything twice--and all for 28 cents and a dime! Mother [Jackie's] writes that she may run up for a visit before she goes to Rocky Mount..., and

I hope she will. She is such a good tonic for the blues.... I keep busy so the time passes finally. When I'm not busy, I'm watching the comings and goings of my neighbors thru the parlor curtains. My bedroom is on the inner court, and one can hear everyone else breathe. I am very amused hearing the place wake up every morning. All is peaceful stillness, and I lie watching the patch of pink sky turn to blue through the brick sides of the buildings. When 7 A.M. comes, a radio is turned on full blast, and one of those "genial Jims" asks, "Is everybody happy this fine morning?" Everyone evidently is not, for he bellows out into the morning air, "Turn that radio off!" And someone else groans. Then a baby begins to cry, and someone cries, "Oh my Gawd!" It's a good way to start the day off with a laugh. I call it my "tenement symphony." I agree with Lew Lehr that "people are the craziest people" and funny too!

Good night, my dearest love. Know that God watches over you, and that I love you with all my being and am watching and waiting and praying for your safe return.

Devotedly,

Jacque

Censored by U.S.N.

U.S.S. *Benson*

Monday

22 September, 1941

Our 7th Anniversary

My Darling,

Today I'm thinking of you even more than on other days, and my thoughts fly back to this day, seven years ago, when we were bound to each other forever and ever in a funny, little old shack in Tia Juana by someone we couldn't even understand. I would like to go back and start all over again, from that moment, when in the Eyes of God we were man and wife, because in many ways I haven't been a very good husband, and I would like to live these seven years over again, so I could correct the mistakes. On the other hand, I wouldn't turn back the clock to that day, because we wouldn't have our beautiful little girls, and I wouldn't have the love for you that I do now. I have learned that two people, who were meant for each other, realize just how much the other means as the years roll by. Seven years ago, I knew I loved you and wanted you by my side always, but I didn't feel then that life would hold nothing for me if you didn't belong to me. Now it is different. You are the most important thing in my life, and I only live for the day when we can have our home and our children, and I can have you by my side always. Instead of hoping to be an Admiral, that is my ambition. Just a home in the country, you and our children. No one could ever take your place, so you must take care of yourself for me and those happy days to come.

We are still here, and still no word as to when we leave. We hope by the end of the week, the transports will be ready to depart, and that then we'll be on our way back--back to you--so I can fold you in my arms and tell you over and over again how much I love you.

I hope to have some mail from you this week, as the mail destroyer gets here Thursday or Friday.

My love to the children and to Mother. I hope to see you all the first week in October, if all goes well.

Yours forever and ever,
Mike

Brighton, Mass.

September 23, 1941 [postmark]

Saturday Nite

Darling,

The full realization that you are gone has swept over me like a wave and left me half drowned in loneliness for you. During the day when I'm busy it isn't so bad, but when evening comes along and you don't come with it, the hours drag and lay heavy on my heart. The last two glorious weeks with you flew by so quickly, but I am so thankful for having been able to have them with you. I'll live again when you come back. We got here about 6:30 P.M. and, found the two-bedroom apartment waiting for us. It is just what I wanted and would be perfect if you were here. And how I miss you at my home-cooked meals. They lose all savour to me when you aren't enjoying them with me. The apartment has a large entry hall that can be used as a dinette when company comes, living room facing on Washington St. as does Mother Klein's bedroom, large kitchen with table for eating, and pantry. In the children's and my room are twin beds. It's in good taste too. I am so grateful to you that you give me so many comforts and take care of us so well. It just isn't fair that you can't enjoy the fruits of your labor more yourself. The grammar school is only 2 blocks away, and school starts next Thursday. I asked about the $5.00 deposit I left last time, and they are "looking into it." I noticed they didn't ask me

for one this time though. Our suitcases and washer came this morning. That's good service. The children have been out playing all day, and thank heaven those bad boys are gone. Mother Klein is still unpacking, but seems very pleased with her room. We are on the 3rd floor front, and she is afraid to go in the elevator by herself. She hasn't heard about the *Greer* incident yet, and I hope she doesn't until the sensationalism of it dies down a bit. I couldn't go to sleep last night until 1 A.M., though I went to bed at 8:30 P.M., for thinking of you. The greatest comfort I have is the thought that God is still in His heaven even though all is not right with the world,[6] and He will watch over you day and night and bring you safely back to me. May He keep you always under the shadow of His wings--my dearest one. And hurry home safely to one whose love and arms await you eagerly. I love you, I do! I do!! I do!!!!

Your Jacque

---

6. Jackie is referring to two lines in Robert Browning's *Pippa Passes:* "God's in his heaven--All's right with the world."

Brighton, Mass.

October 21, 1941 [postmark]

Tuesday

Michael, darling,

You have come and gone, and it's only been a fleeting moment to me. And yet I am thankful for that, as, though only a moment, it gives me the strength and courage to go on. Each time you go it grows harder to send you off with a smile, but somehow I feel God will watch over you and bring you safely back to me. If I did not have that surety I would go mad, but I truly believe He is concerned with those who love and trust Him and who are as good as you are. Honestly, Mike, when I sit and think how good you are to everybody, I feel like dropping down on my knees and giving thanks that you are mine, and that I was the one so blessed to get you. My dearest one, how can I express the joy of being with you for one glorious week! I simply live for the times that you come home again. We left Portland about 10 A.M. Sunday and got home around 3 P.M., having stopped on the way for dinner. I found Mother Klein and Kay O.K. and getting ready to go to their Sunday movie. They seemed to have gotten along beautifully, though how they ate, went to movies, and bought what odds and ends they did on $2.50, I can't tell. I suspicion they did not eat much, but there were no complaints from either. I spent Sunday evening getting back into the old grind after a soaring trip to heaven and Monday pitched in to keep busy and thus keep from thinking. All the things from the storage house came, and though it crowds us a little, it's nice to have the things one has needed so many times since they were packed. Everything was O.K. except the old radio which evidently had been dropped and was practically all to pieces. I put it together as best I could, but knowing nihil of radios, I may have not gotten some little thing back, and then again I may have everything backwards. At any rate, it doesn't play. The big radio does though, so I gave your mother the portable. She is remarkably cheerful and pleasant though I dreaded returning at the time I heard of the *Kearny* incident. I just suggest we don't talk of it whenever she gets on the subject, and so keep her mind off the war and all the horrible things that could happen. The children are delighted to get their toys, and it's like Christmas here now. I went to the tea at the Schums this afternoon, and though I enjoy getting out and talking to people, I don't think it was any great success to get the Navy wives together. Mrs. Schum did all she could and had a lovely table, but the crowd dissolved into little groups of those who knew one another already and thus thwarted the effort to get everyone acquainted. However, I meandered around a bit and met two very attractive people--....

I am writing to L.L. Bean for a catalog, as I want you to have one of those duck hunting coats. I wish Wally or Blackie had let us know they were going up, as you should have it on this trip. Keep warmly wrapped, and if you should take cold, start in on soda every 3 hours at the <u>very beginning.</u> Take good care of yourself 'cause you belong to me. Remember I love you more every day I live and am living for that day when you will always be near, and remember God is everywhere and knows and cares for you, and remember to

> *Fear not the secret foe,*
> *For more o'er thee is watching*
> *Than human eyes can know.*

And may He watch between me and thee when we are absent one from another [Gen. 31:49].

Good night, my dearest love--
Jacque

On October 17, about 350 miles southwest of Iceland, a U-boat torpedo hit the U.S. destroyer *Kearny* and eleven of her crew were killed. The ship herself managed to limp into the harbor of Reykjavik [Iceland]. Sherwood 380.

German U-boats were a constant menace to the convoys in the North Atlantic. The wolfpack, or *Rudeltaktik,* was the idea of Admiral Karl Doenitz, commander of the German U-boat Force. The teams of submarines were moved to mid-ocean far beyond the reach of Allied aircraft bases. The packs of subs would stalk the escort vessels and lie in wait to attack. See Roscoe 25.

U.S.S. *Benson*

Argentia, Newfoundland

23 October, 1941

My Darling,

Just a note to let you know we are this far up the line. Arrived yesterday and we expect to depart tonight for the usual run. I just found out a mail ship comes in tomorrow, so wanted to get a note off before we leave.

I miss you so much. It's so hard to leave after I've been with you for such a short time, it takes me about a week to get the lump out of my throat. After that I just exist until the ship is pointed back to you. It was so grand being with you, but just one week was such a short time. I am just living for the day when I can take you in my arms every day in the week and not ever have to leave you anymore.

If this trip goes well it should take us ten days up, ten days there, and ten to return, which will be about the last week in November for us to get back. It seems so far away, and then when I do get to see you, the hours and minutes just fly away, and before I know it I'm saying goodbye again. I'm hoping we will have our three weeks at Boston on our return, and that will be wonderful at Xmas time especially, since the children will be able to appreciate Xmas more than ever this year.

Now keep yourself well and happy for me, and I'll be back soon to tell you I love you more and more every day I live. You have been a wonderful wife and mother, and every night I thank the Lord that I was so fortunate to get you. Give our children a kiss for me, and each night I'll dream you are at my side.

Yours always,
Michael

I'm enclosing $10 to help you along. I imagine your new allotment won't get to you until 1 December. In other words, they will start taking out for it on 15 November, and you will get the $150.00 on 1 December. So beginning on 15 November, I'll start drawing $37.50 less than I've been drawing, since they will take out $37.50 on 15 Nov. and the other $37.50 on 1 December, so that you will then get $150.00 instead of $75.00.

So on 15 November I won't be able to send you $50, but will send you all I can. I'll hope to get a letter off to you as soon as we arrive in Iceland, but you probably won't get it for some time.

All my love,
Mike

Newfoundland, a huge land mass with ragged coasts separated from the Canadian mainland by the Gulf of St. Lawrence and the Strait of Belle Isle, is North America's nearest approach to Europe. As such, it was the "jumping-off place" for Allied convoys bound for Britain. In 1940 the Navy selected the harbor of Argentia, deeply recessed in the Avalon Peninsula, as an advanced base for convoy escorts.... On July 15, 1941, the United States Naval Air Station and Naval Operating Base were formally commissioned... and thereafter the base was "headquarters" for the destroyers of the Support Force. The destroyermen found Argentia anything but Snug Harbor. Flailed by winter storms, the bay was a rough anchorage; the frost-bitten village provided little for the entertainment of weary blue-jackets. But Navy tenders were there to rejuvenate tired DD's. And Argentia would look like Paradise to destroyers after North Atlantic convoy hauls.... Upon concluding a convoy run at Argentia or Halifax, the DD would steam to Boston.... As it eventuated, the duty-worn destroyer was unusually lucky if she had five days of grooming at Boston. Roscoe 28-29.

Brighton, Mass.

October 25, 1941 [postmark]

Friday Evening

Michael, dearest,

All is quiet in "camp," and though I enjoy the restfulness,
I miss you even more at this hour. During the day I am so busy
that I have only time for the pleasant thoughts of you and the
beautiful past we have spent together, but when I sit down to
think of you and rest, the thoughts of anxiety crowd in, and I
feel I must run out of the house into the darkness and find you
and gather you safely into my arms, like a mother hen gathers
her brood under her wings. I want all my brood under my wing
when night comes. Yet I know a greater Protector than I has
you under the shadow of His wings, and I am comforted.
Whenever the anxious fears well up inside, I read the 91st
Psalm, and calmness gradually comes back to me. I have been
doing fall cleaning, and I can't find a better medicine for mental
ills than a big dose of elbow grease. I am not overdoing my
strength, but I find keeping busy the whole day keeps me from
thinking of all the horrible things that could happen and also
wears me down sufficiently to be able to sleep at night. My little
nest is so fresh and clean now. I do wish so frightfully you were
here to enjoy it with me. My idea of heaven is surely not that of
dressing in sheets and strumming harps--nor eating milk and
honey altogether. I'm not particularly fond of harp music, and
too much honey must cloy to the tongue. My idea is a warm,

comfortable little cottage in a garden with you puttering around all the time, and hot corn bread and fried chicken on the table, and the fall cleaning done. And we shall have that heaven some day--you and I--just wait and see. Kay's teacher sent word for me to come see her, and I did yesterday. The first thing I asked was if her behavior was all right. Miss Crowley said it was exceptionally good, but she wondered why Kay was so <u>shy</u>! Can you fathom that! She said she thought Kay knew the reading, but when she called upon her to read, she tucked her head and responded with a barely audible whisper. She asked if Kay was allowed to express herself at home. I was flabbergasted, since I think both children talk a lot and, in moving around so much, had much poise. She told me to take her books home and see if she knew the reading. I did, and Kay reads beautifully, practically the whole book. The only conclusion I can get is that she is shy before the other children. I can remember how my heart pounded in recitation at school when I thought the children might laugh at my mistakes. I did not gain confidence until I made the honor roll, and found I knew as much as some and more than some others. Perhaps I should talk to her more and explain things. When I am busy and tired, I sometimes brush her by with a "I don't know" or "Go look at a book." I have been coaching her at home to hold up her head and speak up when she reads. It is amazing how well she reads after only 6 weeks of school. There is no continuity of thought in the sentences, in order that they do not learn by memory or rote. They have to recognize the word itself to read it. I used to learn the page by having it read many times, while I looked at the picture and learned it like a nursery rhyme. There are no pictures in Kay's book. When she stumbles on a word like "read," I notice she says r-r-r e-e-e a-a-a da and gets it entirely phonetically. I certainly believe every generation progresses over the preceding one. I expect mother [Jackie's] up by the first of the week, and she will help to pass the weary time away waiting for you. She is like a tonic with her cheerfulness and philosophical outlook. Every letter she massages my backbone by reminding me of God's love and your prowess as a gunner. She reminds me to read the 91st Psalm and says she pities the German on whom your gun is aimed.... Your mother has been busy lining her sheepskin and as usual did a very neat job. She holds up surprisingly well and has been real chipper lately.... There's no more news--in fact, the foregoing could hardly be called news--but I grow so lonesome to see and talk to you that it helps some to prattle on paper to you. I love you so frightfully much, my dearest, that life is just living when you are gone and is a beautiful and joyous thing when you return. May it be soon, darling! And may all this chaotic world become sane soon again, so that we may live our life in peace and quiet love until eternity. Know my deepest love and most fervent prayers are with you always.

Your Jacque

Brighton, Mass.

October 27, 1941 [postmark]

Sunday Night

My Dearest,

I'm sitting here listening to the radio and missing you more every moment. I can't enjoy anything unless I am able to share it with you. All the good winter programs are back, and I miss you especially on Jack Benny's "Inner Sanctum" and Walter Winchell tonight, because I know you particularly enjoy them. And Pearson and Allen are on Sunday night too. They predicted tonight that legislation to outlaw strikes in defense industries and to make arbitration compulsory would be introduced in Congress this week. And I think it's time, as that renegade John L. Lewis is calling a coal strike this week, and it burns me up when I think of you and the Navy boys doing all that you are for the country, and he (one man) can induce so many men in important industries to be "slackers" and sit down on their behinds. If they're so dissatisfied with their lot, they should be out to work on a ship that's likely to be the target of an enemy submarine. Lewis is fighting for a closed shop this strike, which means only his henchmen can be employed. I am for the laborer in that I want all people to have a good standard of living, but I don't think John L. is prompted by any humanitarian compassion on his part. Oh well, no matter what I think or how much I holler, they simply won't let me run the world. And I don't only miss you when I'm enjoying programs or want to discuss news--it's all the time when anything is going on....

Goodnight, my darling, take care of yourself for me, and God bless and keep you always.

Devotedly,

Jacque

Brighton, Mass.

October 28, 1941 [postmark]

Tuesday Nite

My Darling!

What a lovely surprise I had this morning to find your letter in the box. I had resigned myself to the fact that I should not hear from you until you arrived at your destination and knew that could not be so soon. How wonderful it is to start a day off with a letter from you. It makes the world look rosier and lifts my heart up. And the news that you may be here sooner than we thought is enough to make me happy until you come. I could hug the whole world. And thank you for the money. I'm sure I shall make out very nicely until you come. Oh, the thought of you being here at Christmas is so very wonderful. It's hard enough to be without you every day, but at such a joyous season I am afraid I couldn't enter into the spirit of it with you away. I just feel like singing! And am praying the situation will not change and change the things I so hope for. The President spoke last night on the Navy Day program, and I thought it was the most militant speech yet. He called for not only arming ships, but said that our ships should have the right to go into any parts they chose, which I interpreted as complete repeal of the Neutrality Act. Well, I feel (even though I don't want war) that as long as we're half way in (and that half is mine), we should get all the way in and mop up the mess. Women may see a personal slant on every subject, but I feel as long as my dearest possession is in it, everybody and the whole country should get in and help you. I hope Russia holds, but if she falls I'm for going in--A.E.F. [Allied Expeditionary Force] and all....

Good night, my love, may the angels watch over you--and know I love you, love you, love you and while "tolling the silver iterance, being mindful to love you in silence with my soul."[7]

Your devoted Jacque

7. Jackie quotes a line from *Sonnets from the Portuguese,* XXI, by Elizabeth Barrett Browning.

On October 27, Roosevelt gave his annual Navy Day speech in the Grand Ballroom of the Mayflower Hotel in Washington. It was by far the strongest speech he had yet given. He said: "The shooting has started. And history has recorded who fired the first shot. In the long run, however, all that will matter is who fired the last shot.... I say that we do not propose to take this lying down.... Today, in the face of this newest and greatest challenge of them all, we Americans have cleared our decks and taken our battle stations. We stand ready in the defense of our nation and the faith of our fathers to do what God has given us the power to see as our full duty." Sherwood 382.

Brighton, Mass.

October 31, 1941 [postmark]

Friday

Michael, dearest,

The news of the *Reuben James* has just come in, and my heart bleeds for the wives and mothers of her men, but, Oh God, how thankful I am it was not your ship! I feel--and I must feel--that you will come thru safely. All I want in this world is to keep my little family together and in good health, and I believe God will grant me that one wish. We must remember the everlasting arms are beneath you, and His love is all around you. Just remember that, and that I am always waiting for your return, and nothing can keep us apart. I find by keeping busy or on the go and not talking of the awful mess the world is in helps me from running amuck. Mrs. Franz kept Kay yesterday after school so our mothers, Cissy, and I could spend the day downtown. We shopped until lunch and after lunch started in again. The grandmas gave out and went on to a movie, and Cissy and I finished and came on home. I was worn out, but the "girls" didn't get in until 8 P.M. I told them I was getting ready to call the police. They saw the new Fred Astaire picture and seemed to enjoy it immensely. I am letting the children have a Halloween party tomorrow, and they say they are clearing out again to get out of the noise. I have invited . . . in to lunch on Tuesday. Mother insisted I not have anything for her, so I had to confess to her I wasn't having them so much for her as I was having them while she was here, so she could help me and do some of her fine cooking. I'm having fried chicken, rolls, sweet potato puffs, grapefruit salad, and coconut cake. Does it make your mouth water? Well--bless your heart, you shall have the same as soon as you set your dear old feet under my table again. I am living for the last of November and praying you will be back then. Know I love you with my whole being--with the smiles, breath and tears of all my years and only better through eternity.[8] Good night, my love--

Jacque

---

8. Elizabeth Barrett Browning, *Sonnets from the Portuguese*, XLIII.

They called her *"The Rube"*--a nickname that expressed the affection of American destroyermen for a DD.... From Iceland she was dispatched to the States to engage in escort-of-convoy duty. And so came a day in the latter part of October when *Reuben James* headed out into the North Atlantic as one of a group of five destroyers (under Commander R.E. Webb in *Benson*) screening eastbound convoy HX-156--a ship-train freighting Lend-Lease goods to the British Isles.... There was tension in the ocean air. The escorts had heard of the *Kearny* incident; all hands were aware the convoy was in wolfpack water. But the voyage during that last week of October was proving uneventful. Routine steaming. Nothing to report. Nothing--until the morning of the 31st. On that date the convoy was in the "Momp" area [abbreviation for "Mid-ocean Meeting Point"].... The hint [of impending disaster] came on a gust of ocean wind, invisible, about 0525, when a guardship picked up a "foreign" radio transmission close aboard.... [The *Reuben James*] was... on the point of turning to investigate the direction-finder bearing when (time: 0539) she was struck by an unseen torpedo. The war head hit her on the port side near No. 1 stack. A sheet of fire flagged skyward. Blending with the torpedo explosion, a stupendous blast almost lifted the destroyer from the water.... A pillar of flame towered from the sea where the destroyer went under.... Rescuers were on the way at top speed.... As the convoy drew away from the scene of the torpedoing, *Benson* made three possible sonar contacts, and launched urgent attacks on the target…. The submarine bent its efforts on a getaway. Its hit-and-run tactics were only too successful…. Aroused by the thunder of torpedo-fire, Congress voted the following week to amend the Neutrality Act. Two amendments were passed. The first permitted the arming of American merchantmen so that they might defend themselves against attack. The second abolished the restriction which denied European waters to American shipping. The Navy could now convoy Lend-Lease goods to ports in the United Kingdom; the unrealistic postures of "isolationalism" and "belligerent neutrality" were virtually ended….

In the autumn of 1941, weeks before Pearl Harbor, American Navy men were fighting the Battle of the Atlantic. The destroyer *Reuben James* was the first United States warship lost in World War II. Roscoe 39-40.

Three days after Roosevelt spoke [Navy Day, October 27, 1941], another U.S. destroyer, the *Reuben James,* was torpedoed and sunk. One hundred fifteen members of the ship's company, including all the officers, were lost. Sherwood 382.

[Jackie wrote in the margin of page 382 of Sherwood's *Roosevelt and Hopkins:* "Mike saw this from the deck of the *Benson* and engaged in trying to track down the submarine afterwards."]

Brighton, Mass.

November 2, 1941 [postmark]

Saturday

Michael, dearest,

I am sitting here trying to concentrate on writing while the children are having a party in the kitchen. Mother and your mother cleared out, and, as it was raining, I took them down to a show and will go for them. The news over the radio says that 44 of the *Reuben James* have been rescued, and it is hoped some more were picked up by the convoy. I do hope so. It has been awfully cold here, and I am so glad to get our winter clothes. I was shopping with the sealskin gloves you brought me, and the salesgirls asked me where I had gotten them and crowded around to see them. They are so warm too. Now don't get anything this time, as you have already brought so much. I would like to have some more cards for Christmas presents if you see some, but nothing else, as I think things are expensive. Your mother said you might buy another sheepskin. Bring her one if you want, but please don't bring me one, as I've so much to pack now, and it will be moth-eaten before we get to use it in our own home. Besides, I don't particularly like them between you, me, and the gatepost. All the ladies seem delighted that I am having them to lunch on Tuesday. They all accepted with alacrity, and Mrs. Franz even bought a new outfit. It will help pass the time, and that's the main thing with me when you are away. I shall never grow used to having you away. I just don't begin to live until you come home again. The past seven years have been the happiest of my happy life, and the last year has been the happiest of those during the time you are home. I love you, I do, I do! And as I breathe, I pray for your safe return to my arms. We all send love and our prayers.

Your devoted Jacque

Brighton, Mass.

November 5, 1941 [postmark]

Wednesday

My Dearest,

Figuring by your last letter, I judge you have arrived at your destination by now, and my heart is quieter and immeasurably grateful. I have felt it constrict with fear for four times, when I saw the headlines of the *Greer, Kearny, Reuben James,* and *Salinas,*[9] and then, when I read the names of the ships, to beat again with thankfulness. I dread to open the neat roll of newspapers the boy leaves each afternoon, and yet I wait eagerly for the hour he comes with a morbid fascination. I must look at it--yet God only knows the gratitude I feel after I've looked and not seen the ship's name I dread to see. I feel like dropping on my knees right at the door. Yet struggling with the mortal fear is the divine knowledge that God is concerned with you and me and is keeping you neath the shadow of His wing, and in the struggle it beats down the frenzied fear, and calmness and courage return with gratefulness. All I ask of God is to give us health and to keep us together, and I feel He will grant me this one thing.

Yesterday the ladies came and seemed to enjoy the luncheon immensely. The food turned out beautifully if I do say

9. *Salinas* was a naval oiler torpedoed October 30 in mid-ocean, but survived.

so myself, though most of that credit should go to mother. I fried the chicken and helped with the fresh coconut cake, but mother did the rolls, and they were gems of perfection....

Know, my dearest, that I love you more than I shall ever be able to tell or show you, and that my prayers are continuous for your safe return to my arms. I am counting the hours until your next letter and living for the day you come back to your

Jacque

Brighton, Mass.

November 8, 1941 [postmark]

Friday

Michael, dearest,

The headlines tonight are so encouraging. They say that "Hitler is doomed" in large letters and smaller ones adding, "Stalin says." However, Goebbels in a speech today told the German people that they were fighting for their lives ,etc., and I hope the situation in Germany has become so bad that he has to tell them that to keep them fighting. How wonderful it would be to pick up a paper and see "armistice declared" as one day we did in 1918 and to know you would come home to stay! That is my prayer and all I want in this world. I miss you so frightfully and love you more every day. I do so much want you home, my darling.

Mother is still here, but is threatening to go every day. I am persuading her to stay just "one more day" each day. She has bolstered our morale so much. Your mother has genuinely seemed to enjoy her and has been so cordial to her. She has taken her to a show and bought her a lovely gift handkerchief (paid 60 cents for it!) and has tried to make her feel most welcome. I do appreciate it and told her so. She feels Dad will be looking for her this weekend and says she's going tomorrow.

I got a bulletin from All Saints' Church today, notifying me of a Navy Service Sunday night. When Mr. Hedgewick called on me, I asked him to say the prayers for the Navy and those going to sea and told him how at Annapolis the boys closed each service singing "Eternal Father, strong to save." And now he is having a whole service and announcing that hymn will be sung in accordance with the services at Annapolis. Mother Klein and I both are going and say our prayers for our dearest one.

We went to the movies today and saw pictures of the Navy in Newfoundland in the newsreels. A new destroyer was shown, number 420, and when I first saw it, my heart leapt. I thought it was yours.[10]

Good night, my love. God bless and keep you and bring you safely back to your devoted

Jacque

For Those In Peril On The Sea

Eternal Father, strong to save,

Whose arm hath bound the restless wave,

Who bidd'st the mighty ocean deep

Its own appointed limits keep;

Oh, hear us when we cry to Thee

For those in peril on the sea!

10. In 1941 M.J. Klein was Gunnery Officer on the *Benson* (DD-421). DD-420 was U.S.S. *Buck*, the destroyer which would be under his command in 1943.

O Christ! Whose voice the waters heard
And hushed their raging at Thy word,
Who walked'st on the foaming deep,
And calm amidst its rage didst sleep;
Oh, hear us when we cry to Thee
For those in peril on the sea!

Most Holy Spirit! Who didst brood
Upon the chaos dark and rude,
And bid its angry tumult cease,
And give, for wild confusion, peace;
Oh, hear us when we cry to Thee
For those in peril on the sea!

O Trinity of love and power!
Our brethren shield in danger's hour;
From rock and tempest, fire and foe,
Protect them wheresoe'er they go;
Thus evermore shall rise to Thee
Glad hymns of praise from land and sea.

Rev. William Whiting (1860)

[Every worship service at the United States Naval Academy is closed with the first stanza of the hymn, the entire congregation kneeling or seated with bowed heads.]

Brighton, Mass.

November 9, 1941 [postmark]

Sunday

My Dearest,

I am watching every day now for some word from you.
When you first leave, I resign myself to silence, since I know it
is impossible to hear from you, but as the time drags by, and in
my mind I place you at your destination, I become eager, even
impatient, for your letter. Your last was a pleasant surprise, but
it is old now. However, I console myself with the thought that
no news is good news. These long, quiet Sunday afternoons are
hardest with you gone, as when the ship is in, I look forward to
Sunday all week when I shall have you home the whole day.
And too, I am not as busy as on weekdays, and by keeping busy
I keep from thinking and worrying. Mother Klein, Mrs. Franz,
and I are going to the Navy Service at All Saints' Church
tonight, and I hope you may feel our thoughts and prayers
around you in spirit. Mother went back yesterday, and we all
miss her so. Whenever the blues got the best of us, she would
say something courageous or witty to pull us out of the abyss.
Your mother insisted on her staying as well as I, but she said she
had to go. I never saw your mother so cordial to anyone, and I
appreciate it. Mother wanted to take Cissy back with her, but
I wouldn't allow it, as with moving and getting settled, I was
afraid she would find Cissy a care. So she says she will run up
again and get her. I don't believe I could do without her though

for long. Though I pound on them and get out of patience with them, I simply could not do without them with you away. I still have them, and they give me a reason for living. What would I do without them and you too, I don't know. Sometimes, after nearly shaking their teeth loose and spanking their bottoms, I go into the bedroom and find them sleeping with undried tears still on their cheeks, and a flood of tenderness wells up in my heart and chokes me. But the next time they're bad I pound just as hard, so don't think I'm not disciplining them. I'm really very tough. I must stop losing my temper though when I discipline them. Yet I don't believe I could touch them unless I was mad. Kay is doing very well in school, and her teacher says she has improved so much in shyness. She said her behavior was excellent. Mother and I got them shoes the other day, and their feet look enormous. They do grow so fast, and we had to pay $4.00 a pair! I don't pay over that for my own. I ordered a tire for the car, and it came to $14.00 by ship's service--so it surely keeps your dear old nose to the grindstone to keep everything shod. I also had Prestone put in the car. It took $4.10 worth, but he says that will last all winter, and the other evaporates. We are having quite cold weather here now, and I was afraid I'd wake up one morning and find the buggy frozen up. We are all fixed comfortably up for winter in regard to clothes, and I am so thankful I have a good coat. Clothes are sky high and, I think, inferior this winter. Are you clad warmly enough? I got the catalogue from Bean's in Maine and wish you had one of the heavy coats like Wally's. If you come and go back you must have one, as January and February are the coldest months. I wish I could send you things. I never have anything good to eat that I don't wish you could be having some, too. However, I suppose it is senseless to send anything with the mails so infrequent. Yet I simply can't enjoy anything unless I share it with you. Even good movies make me long for you to see them. I suppose that is what is meant by marriage making two people one. My life is so wrapped up in yours that every thought or act I do has some concern for you. I knew I loved you the first time I kissed you that cold November day back in 1930 in Mrs. Lietch's front parlor, and that knowledge has never left me, yet it is only in separation that love knows its own depth. Now I know that, without your love, life would have no meaning. If I did not have your coming back to me to look forward to, I should not want to live. And so I feel God will bring you back, for it must be right to have one I love so much. Good night, my Michael, peaceful dreams.

Jacque

Brighton, Mass.

November 12, 1941 [postmark]

Wednesday Nov 12

My Dearest,

As the time draws nigh for you to be leaving according to my figuring and my hopes, I grow more impatient and have mingled emotions of joy and dread. Joy to think you are coming home and dread that you must go through dangerous waters. But I shall remember that underneath you are the everlasting arms and permit only the joy to remain in my heart. I have heard no word from you and am not certain that you are coming, but only surmise it in accordance with your other trips. I pray you will not have different orders this time. When you're away, life is just one dull, dreary wait until you come back again. I go out and try to keep up with the world, but all the savor of living is gone, and living is something mechanical. But when you do come, I live more abundantly than ever before, and perhaps it divvies up in the end. It would be easier though, if I could hear from you oftener. One imagines so many bugaboos--are you well?--are you happy?--are you warm enough? Silence and suspense makes one imagine fearful things. It has been very cold here the last two days and a slight sprinkle of snow this morning. We are all well, except for Kay and Cissy who had slight stomach upsets, but no temperature. So many children have had it that I believe it must be the lowness of the water in the reservoir, and some fungus is getting through. But otherwise we are all in exceptionally good health--just lonesome and longing for you. But I'm waiting for you and shall always be waiting--for I love you more every day I live, and were I able to turn back the clock to Sept. 22, 1934 [wedding day] again, I would not change my actions on that day one whit.

Devotedly,
Your Jacque

Brighton, Mass.

November 17, 1941 [postmark]

Sunday Night

Darling,

Another week of waiting has drawn to a close, and I am looking eagerly for tomorrow's mail in hopes of some word from you. It seems I never get used to your absence, but each week of waiting grows more difficult to go through. But I shouldn't and won't complain as long as you are safe, for which I give thanks with every breath I take. And I [have] much to be thankful for in the events of the day. It seems Germany is slipping, and I, personally, don't think she can win. Japan is in the front again, but I believe she's pulling the old bluff, and I don't believe we'll go to war with her, or if we do, it will be much more than a bombing expedition to Tokyo. Of course, I really don't know anything about it, but that's what I derive from what I read in the papers. But all I want is peace and you back home again in my arms. My eyes ache to see your dear face and my arms to hold you close. I'm afraid I was cut out to be a farmer's wife. I want to work by your side and rest by your side. Someday we shall have that little piece of good earth and be together always. That's what we have to look forward to and dream of. You must turn into a farmer, I suppose. Anyway, I'd rather be a Navy wife of yours than anybody else's wife. So all I ask is that you come back to me safely. We are all well now, though the children and your mother had a little upset this week. We suppose it was the low water, but they're all well now. I wonder if you are well and warm. Whenever I have something good to eat or hear the wind outside my cosy nest, I wonder about you and pray you are warm and well-fed too and am filled with gratitude that you face such dangers that we may be safe and well. I am grateful, my darling, and pray I may be worthy of your devotion. All I can offer in return is love, and I give you all my heart can hold, not only because I choose, but also because I can't help loving one so fine and good.

Devotedly,
   Jacque

[On the back of an earlier letter is a poem written in Jackie's hand:]

To One at Sea

Whenever a gale springs up at night,
And the blinking stars grow few,
I lie and stare at a nameless dread,
And pray that it's well with you.

I lie and shiver and softly say:
"I wonder if it's stormy where you are?"
Where the gray waters lift to the cloudy spray,
Oh, sailor, is it stormy where you are?

And I sit dreaming when the sun goes down,
(The same sun's sinking on you),
And the evening star in the opal West,
Oh, sailor, is it shining on you?

Where the gray fog blankets shift and roll,
And the lone destroyer's prow
Blindly gropes like a wondering soul,
Is it well with you, sailor, now?

You that face the heart of the howling storm
In the blinding, shrieking night,
Will never know my anguish before the dawn
Lifts into widening light.

I wait, wide-eyed, in the windy dark,
But somehow I think that I know
That the God of the sea and the Navy
Will keep you wherever you go.

Brighton, Mass.

November 21, 1941 [postmark]

Friday the 21st Nov.

My Dearest,

Thanksgiving Day came and went, and I am glad it is past. Not that I'm not aware that I have much to be grateful for, but because it brings back so many dear memories that bless and burn since you are away. I went to church and gave thanks that He is watching over you in all the danger you are going through, and my heart is truly grateful. But I could not restrain the tears when I thought how lovely our first Thanksgiving was. Do you remember that was my first hop at the [Naval] Academy with you, and how suddenly we found out we were in love. With that first kiss I knew it, and I have never since doubted that knowledge. In thumbing through my old scrapbook, I came on this poem that reminded me of that Thanksgiving, which I found when we were apart those three long years, and it comforted me now.

November Days

by Mary L. Lawless

Who said November days are drear and sad?
November days are merely gray and still.
October's fuss is over; leaves are down.
Most of the nuts have dropped. Upon the hill,

Trees, unashamed, display their naked grace
Against a background Nature has prepared,--
A soft gray sky that throws into relief
Each tiny twig and branch the winds have bared.

Who said November days are drear and sad?
Still, yes; but many lovely things are still;
In silence, often, come our <u>greatest things</u>,--
God's love; healed wounds; the sunrise o'er the hill.
November's gray makes apples redder seem;
Makes <u>fires seem brighter</u>, and adds to their cheer.
November days are lovely days, <u>to me</u>,--
Gray, still, and chill,-- <u>yet intimate and dear</u>.

How intimate and dear to me! I had to get out of the house yesterday, since you were not with me. We went out and had dinner at a restaurant and then to a movie. I console myself with the thought that, since you were not here for Thanksgiving, perhaps the delay will make it possible for you to be home for Christmas. I am praying for that. I am dogging the postman's steps, looking for some word from you. I keep telling myself that no news is good news, but how much easier it would be to see with my own eyes your dear handwriting, assuring me that you are safe and well. I am proud that you do not hesitate to lay down your life that your children may have freedom, but oh!, I am afraid that both they and I would be happier even in bondage with you than free without you. I don't

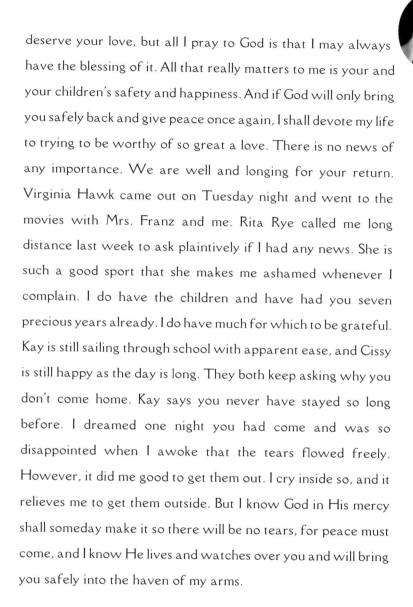

deserve your love, but all I pray to God is that I may always have the blessing of it. All that really matters to me is your and your children's safety and happiness. And if God will only bring you safely back and give peace once again, I shall devote my life to trying to be worthy of so great a love. There is no news of any importance. We are well and longing for your return. Virginia Hawk came out on Tuesday night and went to the movies with Mrs. Franz and me. Rita Rye called me long distance last week to ask plaintively if I had any news. She is such a good sport that she makes me ashamed whenever I complain. I do have the children and have had you seven precious years already. I do have much for which to be grateful. Kay is still sailing through school with apparent ease, and Cissy is still happy as the day is long. They both keep asking why you don't come home. Kay says you never have stayed so long before. I dreamed one night you had come and was so disappointed when I awoke that the tears flowed freely. However, it did me good to get them out. I cry inside so, and it relieves me to get them outside. But I know God in His mercy shall someday make it so there will be no tears, for peace must come, and I know He lives and watches over you and will bring you safely into the haven of my arms.

Good night, my dearest love.

Jacque

Censored by U.S.N.

U. S. S. BENSON (421)

November 24, 1941 [postmark]

5 Nov.

Dearest,

Your letter, written 21 Oct., has just reached me, and how good the world seems to hear you are O.K. and our loved ones too.

In connection with the winter coats, the ship was issued 10 coats just like the boys bought at Bean's for $15.00. So, I have one gratis from Uncle Sam, and there will be no need for you to buy me one. I have plenty of clothes now, so don't worry about that. When I get back, I may need some more woolen socks, but that's all at present. The ones you knit me are wonderfully warm, and I wear them all the time.

I hope your mother gets up to see you and stays as long as she can, as she can help pass the time away, and I know will cheer everyone up. Give her my best love and tell her she has the most wonderful daughter in this world.

The mail boat leaves soon so must close now. My heart is full of love and joy for you and just seems to grow stronger each day.

Until the last week in Nov.

All my love,

Michael

Iceland

5 November, 1941

[enclosed with above letter in same envelope, Nov. 24, 1941 postmark]

My Dearest One,

We arrived here safely yesterday at dawn, and for once this place even looked good. As usual our trip was a rough one, so it will be good to be in quiet waters for a few days. All the mountains are covered with snow and look like huge glaciers. We don't stick our noses out except when we have to, as it is really bitter outside.

Your picture is such a comfort to me. Anywhere I move in my room, your eyes follow me, and I know you are thinking of me, and I gain strength because of your love. I imagine there are many men in this war who only keep going because of the love of their women back home.

We were saddened to learn upon our arrival that a British ship, whose officers we had made friends with, our last time in Iceland, had gone down off England. The captain was the only officer saved. You may recall that the doctor from this ship was with me on my sheep hunting expedition. He was hoping to get back to Canada for Xmas, as he hadn't seen his family in over seven months.

We are tied up alongside the tender[11] for our stay here. The *Kearny* is here alongside with us.

I love you, oh, so much and am just existing until I find my way back to your loving arms. We expect to leave here about 10 Nov. for the long haul back, and, if so, we should be back about the 25th of November. The way back is not so long, since I know each day brings me closer to the one girl in all the world who is my life. Now, don't worry about me, as we will be twisting and dodging, and we won't be an easy target.

Love our girls for me and always remember how much I love you.

Michael

---

11. Tender: a vessel accompanying a group of vessels for effecting repairs, carrying stores, etc.

Brighton, Mass.
December 2, 1941
Tuesday

My Dearest,

Those six lovely days seem like some beautiful dream.
I've waked up again, and you seem not to have really been home
at all, for life is just a dreary plodding again. But I still have
January to look forward to again, and I'm living for the day I'll
have you again in my arms. It was more difficult than ever
before seeing you go this time, as I had set my heart on having
you three weeks anyway and with luck maybe for Christmas.
But I will not celebrate Christmas until you return, except to be
thankful that He has watched over you and will always bring
you safely back to me. I have been anxious about you since you
left, as I have felt bad and knew you were suffering from the
same ailment before you left. I was worse this morning and
have been boiling the water for the last two days. I'm O.K.
tonight though and hope you have not had the bother.... The
children miss you and said how nice it was for Daddy to come
home, and Kay adds, "bring us so much nice candy." We shall all
miss you so frightfully at Christmas when you used to enjoy
seeing them open their presents. If it were not for the fact that
the other children would be showing their toys, and ours would
feel left out, I would have them wait for you too. Virginia Hawk
came over Sunday night and said she was spending Christmas
Day with me. Edith had lunch here Sunday, and I took her to the

411

train. The expected baby seems to have done her so much good, as she was better composed and more cheerful about Wally's going than I ever saw her.... I'm a rich woman today. My new allotment came, and four Christmas cheques and mother's. The four were $42 each for you and $27 each for me. I suppose I'll have to wait for your signature before I can deposit yours. If so, will keep them in our insurance folder.

The Germans are being beaten back by the Russians in the southern sector, and that looks hopeful, but Japan is still cockily "threatening" us while still trying to subdue China. I'll bet they'd be sorry if we ever bombed Tokyo once. I watch the papers hopefully for any news which might signify peace to this crazy world once again and you home again for good. Heaven can be had here on earth if we know what we want it to be. And mine will be my loved ones near and happy. I pray God it may come soon....

God bless and keep you, my darling, and know I love you more than I can ever tell or show you.

Jacque

U. S. S. BENSON (421)

4 December, 1941

My Darling,

We have arrived on the first leg of our journey and expect to leave tonight on the leg which is the longest and hardest. I always dread the outgoing trip, because I know it is putting so much distance between us, whereas the return trip is much easier, because, then, I know each day brings me closer to you.

Our five days together in Boston were so wonderful that I cannot think too much of them, or else that lump comes up that is always present when I am leaving you. Those days passed so quickly they hardly seemed like five days at all. If I could have only been more grateful when I had you all to myself for our two years in Washington. However, I hope that the opportunity will come again.

I have reread all the letters you wrote me on our last trip, and they are such a treasure. The last one, written on Nov. 21 just after Thanksgiving, is such a lovely one that I want to keep it always. If I could only receive these letters while we are away, how comforting they would be! It's wonderful to know, however, that you are thinking of me, and makes things much easier. I love you so very much and am so fortunate that you are mine.

I know that at times it is difficult for you, and I am all the more grateful. I see no reason why you cannot go home if you so desire, and I am sure mother can get along for awhile by herself. However, you probably will need another tire if you make the trip by car, and, of course, the weather must be considered. I would investigate the train fares although, since you have to pay for Kay now, it probably would be much more expensive by train. As I see it, it's just what you prefer to do, and it's O.K. by me anyway you choose. If you do drive, you must take it easy and not drive at night, and have the car checked over thoroughly before you go. The only thing that worries me is the weather and bad roads, as it is quite a trip down to North Carolina. Consider that carefully before you attempt the trip.

In any case, my thoughts will be with you wherever you are, and I know God will be looking after you and ours. Don't worry about me and think only of those happy days ahead when we have our home and can live in peace and happiness.

You may not receive any more letters before Xmas, so I hope you and the children will be most happy on that day. My thoughts and spirit will be there with you.

I will love you always and always.

Michael

Brighton, Mass.

December 5, 1941 [postmark]

Friday

Michael, dearest,

Almost another week has dragged by and as usual seems like a year without you. The world is swinging into a holiday mood, but I can't seem to muster up much excitement over Christmas. The children do give me a spurt of "spirit" with their contagious enthusiasm over it, and so in another way I don't know what I would do without them. Tomorrow we are all going downtown to see the windows and Santy Claus. I shan't try to do any shopping then as it is impossible under those circumstances. I have already gotten them blackboards and little nurse's kits to doctor sick dolls and Kay some roller skates. Cissy wants a carriage, and I am going to try and get her a cheap one, as Kay lets her play with hers only under coercion and then with little peace. Mother sent me the money to buy our gifts from her this year, as she says it's so hard shopping in Rocky Mount [NC].... My Christmas doesn't come until you get back even if it's mid-July. I had the car greased yesterday and thought for Christmas I'd give it a new set of seat covers, but Sears had sold out of the $5.95 ones, and the next price was $7.95. I'm going to try and find some for about $5.00, as these we have were that, and more will last the lifetime of the car if they last like these....

This Christmas I shall spend being thankful--if not joyful--though I have much to be joyful for too. The very fact that I found the one man in all the world and have had so many glorious days with him is enough to be most joyful for, even if this Christmas Day finds us apart. And only God knows how thankful I am that He has watched over you and shall bring you safely back to one to whom you and your children are her whole life.

Devotedly,
Jacque

Autumn and winter escort work in the North Atlantic was arduous and exhausting for men and ships. That section of it covered by United States destroyers, between Newfoundland, Greenland and Iceland, is the roughest part of the western ocean in winter. Winds of gale force, mountainous seas, biting cold, body-piercing fog and blinding snow squalls were the rule rather than the exception. The continual rolling and pitching, coupled with the necessity for constant vigilance night and day--not only for enemy attack, but to guard against collisions with other escort vessels and the convoy--wore the men down....

The strain was not only physical but psychological. These officers and men were enduring all the danger and hardship of war; yet it was not called war. They were forbidden to talk of their experiences ashore, or even to tell where they had been and what they were doing, and so had none of the satisfaction derived from public recognition.... But our bluejackets had seen for themselves the new terror that the Nazis had added to the perils and dangers of the deep. Few realized better than they the threat to America in this German strike for sea supremacy. And the fact that morale in the destroyers remained high, throughout this period of bitter warfare that yet was not war, attests the intelligence, the discipline, and the fortitude of the United States Navy. Samuel Eliot Morison, *The Two-Ocean War: A Short History of the United States Navy in the Second World War* (Boston: Little, Brown and Company, 1963) 37-38.

Brighton, Mass.

December 7, 1941 [postmark]

Sunday

My Darling,

The awful news of Japan's attack came over the radio to me at 2:30 P.M. I was sitting here sewing, and I thought I must be hearing things. When I heard it again, I still could hardly believe it. But right away I felt, oh, so thankful that you are on this side. You are in great danger, but somehow I feel I'd rather you face this eastern enemy than the Japanese. Their suicidal attack of us shows their fatalist outlook, and their method shows their treachery, and I earnestly pray you never have to fight such a foe personally. The news just came over that the island of Oahu was attacked at 8 A.M., and a bomb hit on barracks at Hickam Field killed 304. The *West Virginia* is believed sunk and the *Oklahoma* on fire. However, a Japanese carrier has been sunk. It's all so strange--I feel I'm dreaming some horrible nightmare. So now it is a world war. It is terrible times we are living in, but I feel the world has gone through horrible times before and, with God's help, will go through the fire again and be more purified. I honestly believe that people are going to see the futility of war after this one is over and nobody is the real winner and will someday outlaw it. And that is something we can be proud to hand on to our children. But I still can't help but take a personal view and be glad that you are not in the worst theatre of war now. I thought you were up until today, but all the time since the news came over I have been thinking of the LeHardys and all our friends stationed in Hawaii. News is pouring in from the war, and I still feel I'm dreaming. May God always watch over you and bring you safely home to me. And remember that "A thousand may fall beside thee, and ten thousand at thy right hand; but it shall not come nigh thee, For He shall give His angels charge over thee, to keep thee in all thy ways" [Psalm 91:7, 11].

And know I love you more than my life.

Jacque

The morning was fair; visibility good. In Honolulu church bells were clanging. On board the ships in Pearl Harbor sailors were shining their shoes and sprucing up for morning service. At 0755 all thought of Sabbath observances came to a rude end. Over Hickam Field roared a squadron of some 18 Japanese dive-bombers. In a moment the Army aircraft parked in neat rows on the field went skyhigh in bursts of debris. About half of the Japanese bombers roared on past to blast the American battlewagons conveniently tied up two by two at Ford Island. Torpedo planes followed the bombers.... And Pearl Harbor was a charnel of wreckage, agony, and death.... On December 8, 1941, the United States Government declared war on Japan. On December 11, Germany and Italy declared war on the United States, and Congress promptly returned the compliment. This was it! But to the forces of DesLant [Destroyers, Atlantic Fleet], "it" was only so much anti-climax. The official declaration of war found the U.S. Navy's destroyermen already fighting the Atlantic Battle with their gloves off. In the war from that hour when a Nazi U-boat took a shot at *Greer,* they had long since dispensed with formalities. And after the *Kearny* and *Reuben James* torpedoings, the only gloves in evidence in the DesLant Force had been those on the hands of the "hot shell" men. Roscoe 46,42.

Brighton, Mass.
Thursday the 11th
[December, 1941]

Michael, dearest,

I can't tell you what your letters mean to me. They take the kink right out of my backbone when it begins to sag. And it has plenty to sag over now! However, I feel now we <u>know</u> what we have to do, and the suspense is over. I suppose it is our war after all, and the President saw far ahead enough to know it. My faith in his judgement waned a little at one time, and I thought he had too much love for the British, but I'm admitting he knew what he was doing now. I argued 3000 miles of water was a barrier against invasion, but I was wrong. And I feel my morale has been bolstered now that the whole country is behind you. It was mighty low when I saw a handful of ships warring in the Atlantic by themselves and my beloved on one of them. As long as we were partially in, I wanted to go all the way. No one can say Japan was provoked. I think we did too much appeasing there and should never have let her have the supplies she got and reserved from us. I've no doubt we shall beat the dickens out of the treacherous little yellow devils, but I dread the cost of doing so in American lives. I pray God to watch over you, and I have faith that He will, because I believe He watches over those that are as good as you. When I think how loyal and dutiful you've been to your mother and what you are facing now for me and our children, I feel like falling on my knees and

giving thanks for having such a wonderful husband. It's no wonder I love you so--you have compelled my love by your sacrifice and tenderness, and I can't help loving you. And I can assure you it is no task--it is the crowning happiness of my life--to love you and be loved by you. We shall ever strive for that heaven that is ours--to live in peace and quiet love together here and forever. I appreciate your agreeing to my going home for Christmas, but I had already told you I would not go. I want to, of course, but now my wants seem so insignificant. Mother wrote and said John Jr. [Jackie's brother] would not get home for Christmas now, as he has gone back to California to work with Douglas Aircraft again. He wants to be in the army there too if they call him. And she says to bring your mother down for Christmas, but I feel now that we had better sit tight, as, if things should get bad here, we might have to go later. We had one air raid alarm here, but everyone remained calm. I don't believe it is dangerous, but one never knows what will happen these days, and, should Boston be raided, I'd want to get your mother and the children away. I'd go to Richmond and get an apartment and come up whenever you came in to be with you. However, I'll sit tight until it seems more probable than it does now. Your mother still complains of her chest, so I called Dr. Doyle and asked him about it. He says the only thing he can do is take another X-ray, but he said, "I'm sorry to tell you, Mrs. Klein, but my honest opinion is that your mother is a hyponchodriac [hypochondriac]." I can't spell it, but he said when people get older, they want attention and sympathy and are just like children. He said he would take another X-ray to satisfy her, but it couldn't be broken, and the outside skin showed no mark. Of course, I can't tell her what he said, so will take her over to get another X-ray tomorrow. I'm not doing anything for Xmas much except for the children, but now I am not the only one. I think it is a year when people should be thankful for that which they have and pray for the strength to keep it. Mother sent me a cheque for $10.00 to get you and the children something and has given me a slip and shoes. Aunt Nona sent you $1.00, and Uncle Tom sent $5.00 for us all. I will get what we need with it and get the children defense stamps with theirs. Aunt Stella sent a box which we haven't opened. My Christmas comes every day that begins with a smile and a kiss from you, and I just had one in November and am looking forward to another in January. Dec. 25th is only a date. Christmas with its promise and its meaning can be everyday in our hearts. Know I am with you ever in spirit, loving you now and ever.

Your Jacque

Brighton, Mass.

December 14, 1941

Sunday

Michael, dearest,

How I do miss you! As Christmas draws nearer my longing for you grows deeper, for it is a time for joy and thankfulness, and I can't seem to feel much joy with you away. However, I feel better about your being on your duty now, since I feel the whole country is back of you. Before I felt only that handful of ships was bearing the whole burden, and, if we were going into the fracas, we might as well go whole hog. I didn't like to feel you and a few others were fighting alone. Now the whole country is aroused and unified. And where I complained because you, whom I love so, were fighting, now I feel you may not be in the most dangerous zone after all, and I am thankful, though I know you would not flinch to go into the thickest of the fray. We women can't help taking a personal view of things. I am proud that you are fighting for your country, but more I am thankful you have been spared, and I have faith that God will give you the victory and bring you safely back to the one who loves you more than mere words can tell. There isn't much news other than the war, and I sit glued to the radio day and night. We are all well, and I am getting Santa Claus ready for the children. Christmas must go on for them, and working at it helps me keep my sanity.... The children are counting the days until Christmas and say, "Won't Daddy be home for it too?" No one knows how much I wish you could be home for it too?" No one knows how much I wish you could be! But my Christmas will come the day you come home. We have had no more air raid alarms, and everything has settled back in apparent normalcy. I am going to a Red Cross class in First Aid though, starting this week.... William L. Shirer[12] is on the radio now and is saying the sinking of the ships at Honolulu (supposedly the *West Virginia* and the *Oklahoma*) and the *Repulse* and *Prince of Wales* in the Far East has proved "Somebody" Mitchell[13] was right and those who court-martialed him wrong, since it proves the vulnerability of warships to the torpedo plane. The losses seem to be great at Honolulu with at least 1,500 dead and 1,500 wounded. The ships had only Sunday morning skeleton crews, and the Japanese were practically unchallenged. I suppose Admiral [H.E.] Kimmel jumped on his cap plenty after that....

I've been downtown twice shopping.... For the children Santa will bring blackboards, dolls, a carriage for Cissy, and skates for Kay. After all, Christmas is a "spirit," and I'm afraid I can't work up much with you gone. To me it will be a season of thankfulness for your safety and prayers that it may continue. And when peace comes, as come it will--and must--you and I shall have our happiness together in that tiny home we have dreamed so long of. I know God is in His heaven and is with you, and I know we are fighting for the right this time. There is no

---

12. W.L. Shirer was foreign correspondent in Berlin.
13. Brigadier General William "Billy" Mitchell, U.S. Army--a vigorous advocate of air power in the 1920's.

doubt now, and He is with such as do what they believe to be right. Know I love you with all my heart and soul and will always be waiting for you.

Jacque

Churchill had recently sent substantial reinforcements to Singapore, particularly the battleship *Prince of Wales* and the battle cruiser *Repulse*…. The sinking of the *Prince of Wales* and *Repulse* off the Malayan coast and the quick capture of Hong Kong by the Japanese were the first of a series of irreparable blows to British imperial prestige in Asia. Sherwood 424, 442.

Brighton, Mass.

December 19, 1941 [postmark]

Friday Nite

Michael, darling,

As Christmas draws nearer I miss you more and more. The children are getting more excited every day and are counting the days on their fingers. I have been busy and thankful for what I had to do, as it makes the time pass less slowly and keeps my mind occupied. I think of you every minute of the day, but when I'm busy it's usually living over in my mind all the beautiful days we've spent together. When I indulge too much and sit down to think and dream without anything to do, that center of my brain that usually knits or sews seems to crowd in with fearful thoughts. And so I prefer to be busy. My first aid class takes two afternoons a week, and after I get Christmas all through, I am going to knit for the American Bluejackets. And the first "Bluejacket" is you. I want to make you a heavier pair of socks. Then I'll knit for the others. Your mother seems much better in her chest now and says she will knit something too. She got a letter from Aunt Stella, saying Aunt Mabel had gotten a cable from Tommy in Hawaii that he was all right. There's no other family news, and the world news is as usual--everybody fighting. Old Hitler is on the run in Russia and Libya, thank Heaven! But the Japs are keeping everybody busy in the East. It seems ironic that we can still celebrate the birth of the Prince of Peace in all this holocaust, but we must realize His birth has made the world better, and all this fighting proves His way is the only solution for a peaceful world. And so the day will be one of prayer and thanksgiving for me. Prayer to watch over you and give us peace, and thankfulness that He has watched over you and shown us how to have peace in our hearts. Know I love you more than life itself, and God bless you.

Your Jacque

Censored by U.S.N.

Brighton, Mass.

December 23, 1941 [postmark]

Christmas Eve 1941

Michael, dearest,

The children are tucked "all snug in their beds w[hile] visions of sugar-plums dance in their heads," while I am sitting here in the glow of the Christmas tree, thinking and longing for you. This is the first Christmas since we were married that we have been parted--and when the tears well up in my eyes at the thought of it, I feel ashamed, since I have so much for which to be thankful. The very fact that we are married is enough to keep me happy all the days of my life. Though I am impatient for our heaven together, I realize we are both fighting to have that heaven for ourselves and our children, and we shall cherish it the more for the fact that we had to fight and sacrifice to attain it. Of course, it is natural and human for me to miss you so frightfully and to be filled with anxiety for your safety, but when I begin to slip into the abyss of worry and despair, that still, small voice says to me, "Be still, and know that I am God" [Psalm 46:10]. My strength and courage comes back, and I am sure that you are safe and will come back to me. I can't help feeling it and knowing it. God looks after His own, and you are so fine and good that I know His love encompasses you round about, and no harm can come to you. After I had finished the trimming of the tree, and the children had admired it profusely, Kay turned to me and quite suddenly asked, "And won't Daddy be home for Christmas, Mamma?" When I answered, "No, darling," Cissy must have read my expression, as she came over and put her arms about me and asked, "Aren't you happy, Mamma?" It was hard to restrain the tears, but I said, "Of course, everyone should be happy at Christmastime, and we would keep the tree up and lighted and have Christmas till Daddy came, no matter how long it be!" And so with kisses and sympathetic pats they agreed that's what we should do. I am going to Midnight Mass in a few hours to give thanks for your keeping and pray for its continuance, so know, my dearest love, that I am with you in spirit. This Christmas, especially, I feel its true meaning more poignantly than ever in such a chaotic world. The Prince of Peace was born and lived to teach us that His kingdom was not of this world, but a kingdom of the spirit [John 18:36], and even though we live in this fighting, cruel world, we still can have His peace that passes all understanding in our hearts [Philippians 4:7]. And so tonight my prayer shall be that we may have:

Peace in our hearts, our evil thoughts assuaging,
Peace, while the world its busy war is waging.

Know my thoughts and prayers are ever with you, and that I am ever waiting with open arms and a heart full of love for you.

Your devoted Jacque

My Darling,

We have arrived at our usual first stop, and nothing eventful to report, except lots of ice all around.

The five weeks or so we have just completed together will always remain in my memory as a most happy one, and I am indeed grateful. I consider myself most fortunate to have been with you during that time, and I am so happy that you are willing to always be there when the ship comes in, although I know it is most inconvenient in many ways.

As the days and years go by, I become more grateful to realize that you are my wife and belong to me alone. I truly believe that true married love can only be after years of being together and when the realization comes that life would be very empty without your life partner. I have felt that feeling, now, since we left Washington, and I believe that it will grow stronger on down through the years.

We departed on Wednesday instead of Thursday, due to a change of orders. I was glad to go on the same day that I knew you were returning to Boston. I hope you made the trip without any untoward occurrence, and that you all are nicely settled in your warm nest once again. I am so glad you came to Portland, as it meant a few more happy hours with you and ours.

Now keep well and take good care of yourself. Don't worry about me, as I know your prayers will bring me back safely to your arms.

Yours forever,
Michael

Censored by U.S.N.

March 30, 1942 [postmark]

Sunday Night, 9:00 P.M.

My Darling,

We have just arrived here in Portland after our plans were cancelled for the night. I would give so much if you were over here waiting for me, and I could feel your arms around me. However, it is now 9:00 P.M., so I guess it's too late to call you and have you come up, especially since we are due to leave tomorrow. Otherwise, I would catch the first boat and get you started on your way.

I enjoyed our week together so very much. Each one becomes more dear to me, and someday I'll have you everyday, all day, and no more of this come and go.

Now take care of yourself and get fat and take it easy. I'll write you again from the usual first stop which should be in two or three days and then later on a cablegram.

I love you more each day and always will.

Yours forever,

Michael

Censored by U.S.N.

Thursday

2 April, 1942

My Darling,

Here we are again at the same old place ready to start another long trek. I am always glad to get started so that the time will pass the more quickly, and we are back home once again.

I was so sorry we did not get a day or two more together as we had planned, but I am thankful for the few days that we do have ever so often.

I hope you are feeling well and getting plenty of rest. Don't worry about me, as I'll be seeing you in a few weeks. Don't forget our arrangements concerning wires you may receive. There is no new news at this point.

I will always love you very, very much, and looking forward to seeing you ever so often is the bestest part of this war. I'll be thinking of you each day and night, and I'll know your thoughts are with me every mile of our way.

Forever yours,

Michael

I hope you have received word of mother's safe arrival by now. If you will, drop her a line and tell her you heard from me, and that I was inquiring about her and give her my love.

[On May 7, 1942 M.J. Klein was ordered to the Staff of Commander Destroyer Squadron Thirteen (Captain J.B. Heffernan). In the planning stages was the invasion of North Africa designated as Operation "TORCH."]

Monday

29 June [1942]

My Darling,

We arrived here last night all O.K. We were only in Portland a few hours, so did not get an opportunity to write. I have been rushed the past few days in connection with coming events.

I am enclosing a money order for $25 to repay that which you gave me on departure. I hope you will have enough to get you through.

I expect to depart early Wednesday morning. Keep our code in mind and will send you a message later on. I think you can expect my return on 30 July to <u>New York</u>. I hope you can be here to meet me, but, as that is the time you will be taking over your house, you may not be able to come. However, if you can arrange things, I would like to have you here on 30 July. I suggest, if you come, that you register at the St. George Hotel in Brooklyn, and I will inquire there for you. If you are not there, I will send you a wire. Hope you have a telephone in the new house by then so I can call you, in case you can't be here. Tell mother she can come next time, in case you can see your way clear to be here. We expect to be here only 3 or 4 days on our return, so it will be advisable for you to be here on 30 July, since the time will be so short.

I hope your new house is progressing nicely, and that it will please you on completion.

Our seven weeks together was divine, and I shall always remember them as most happy days. I shall hope and pray that there are many more such periods in store for you and me.

Now take care of your dear self and don't overwork or strain yourself. Don't let this new house get you all excited so that you will overwork. Nothing is more valuable than or important than taking care of yourself.

My dearest love to you and the children.

Michael

Passed by Naval Censor

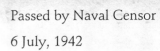

6 July, 1942

My Darling,

Just a note to let you know that I am well. The usual first leg has been completed, and everything is O.K.

I hope the house is progressing nicely, and that you are not overdoing in getting ready to occupy. Remember you must be careful and take care of yourself.

I can never forget our happy days together recently completed. I pray that many more will come to pass, as I love you very, very dearly.

I hope you will be able to get away on the date I mentioned in a previous letter. I hope to get word to you as I did in the past, using the system we have arranged. It perhaps will be wise for you to stay where you are, and I will get in touch with you as soon as I return. Just be ready on the date specified to catch an immediate train so that we won't miss a single day together.

Until then I shall be thinking of you every moment and for your well-being. Give our two darling girls a big hug and kiss. I think they are the best in this world.

Forever yours,
Michael

I suppose I'll have to wire you on or about the date I mentioned before. If you can arrange it, have a phone put in the house as soon as possible. When I return, I'll ask information for the number so I can get you by phone. Failing that, I'll call Ethel Johnston or the Washington Apts., if she has gone by then. If you aren't at the Washington [Apts.] and at the house, you should have the phone.

On August 22, 1942 the eastbound convoy was standing seaward from Halifax Harbor, Nova Scotia. Screen Commander was Captain J.B. Heffernan on the U.S.S. *Buck*. In thick fog the transport *Awatea* rammed the *Buck*, almost shearing off the destroyer's fantail. A dislodged depth charge exploded, causing more extensive damage. Seven of *Buck's* crew were killed in the collision. The *Buck* had to be towed back to port for repairs. See Roscoe 131.

To be opened on

22 September 1942

12 September, 1942

My Darling,

On September 22 we will have been married for 8 years. They have been a happy 8 years for me, and it actually doesn't seem that long--in fact, it seems only yesterday that I was courting you in Los Angeles in that bouncy little Ford. I want you to know that I have never seen a girl that I would have rather married than you, and I know that there is none that could have loved me more and given me such fine children. I can only love you the more as the years go by.

I know that there have been heartaches for you, but I hope they have been compensated for by the many happy moments we have had together. I only can pray that God wills for us to spend many, many years yet together.

I will thinking of you each moment after I leave, and I will pray that you will be all right when our child arrives. I will not be there in person, but you may know that my spirit will be just outside the door as on the two previous occasions. And I know God will take care of you. When you feel better, you might send a telegram to Naval Communications in Washington, D.C. and say something like this: "Please inform Lt. Comdr. M.J. Klein that he is the father of a baby boy or girl and that mother and baby are fine." I believe they may send it to me by radio.

Now, I want you to take this $10 and buy yourself something personal. You have spent and spent on the house, and I want you to buy yourself some pretty clothes and start with this $10.

Until I see you in October, know that I love you more than life itself.

Always Your
Michael

WESTERN UNION TELEGRAM

BROOKLYN NY. 10:43 A.M. SEPT. 22 1942
MRS. M.J. KLEIN
CARE CRAFTSLAND ROAD TELP BEACON 4349
CHESTNUT HILL MASS. I LOVE YOU EIGHT
TIMES AS MUCH AS I DID EIGHT YEARS AGO
TODAY.
MICHAEL

Passed by Naval Censor

Sunday

27 Sept. [1942]

My Darling,

I am thinking of you every minute of the day and wish that I could be at home with you at this time more than any other.

I haven't been over to see Mrs. Mason and do not expect that I will be able to, since I am so very busy here at this time. I will try to get over to call you by phone before we leave and find out how you are. This may be on Wednesday night, although you may be in the hospital by then. I pray that something will come up which will permit me to come to you, but it doesn't look like it at the moment. I'm afraid it will be some time before I see you.

I hope you have all your arrangements made by this time and are in all respects ready.

I love you more and more. I have your two sweet letters and will refer to them often. Just remember I'll be outside the door when our new baby is born, and I'll love you all the more.

Yours forever and ever,

Michael

WESTERN UNION TELEGRAM

1942 OCT. 2 P.M. 8:24 NORFOLK VIR.

MRS. M.J. KLEIN

70 CRAFTSLAND ROAD CHESTNUT HILL MASS.

THINKING OF YOU AND WISH I COULD BE

THERE. I LOVE YOU VERY MUCH

MICHAEL

My Own Sweet Darling,

I think you are wonderful! The good news reached me about noon today, and it was such a thrill. I just can't believe that I have a son. I would have loved a daughter just as much, but a son--it just escapes me. I hope the ordeal was not too hard, and I hope you are feeling fine when this reaches you. I am such a lucky man to have you and the fine children you have given me. God has indeed been good to me, and I am grateful.

I am going to call the hospital tonight to find out how you are and my <u>son</u> too, but it's <u>you</u> I want to know is really all right and will soon be up and around again. I wish I could speak to you, but I hope they will relay a message to you after telling me how you are.

As soon as you are able, write me a nice letter and tell me you love me, as I love you more and more and more as the years go by, and you give me more and more happiness.

Now, remember <u>don't get up too soon.</u> Even after you go home, you should lay around for quite awhile, so plan on doing it now. . . .

I'm afraid it will be some time before I see you again, but don't worry and always remember no one could ever love you as I truly do.

Michael

I am enclosing some forms I received in the mail in connection with renewal of your gasoline rationing book. I presume you will want to renew, so am sending them on to you to act on.

Also am enclosing an insurance receipt.

Also, please advise me if the new $5,000 government life insurance I requested has arrived. I want to be sure this policy is in effect.

Don't bother with all this until you are up and about. I just didn't want to forget it.

Your Michael

My Darling,

I called the hospital last night and hope you received my message. The nurse was very nice and gave me the information. Although I would have loved to talk to you, I am so glad that the ordeal was not a long drawn out affair. I was told you were getting along nicely which made me so happy. I am just too proud of our little Michael, but I could do without him, and I couldn't without you.

I am looking forward to hearing from you and getting all the news, but don't write until you feel able.

I would give so much to see you and our little one-- Michael, our son--I still can't believe, and I think you are wonderful.

All my love,
Michael

My Darling,

Your letter was so welcome. I had watched for several days with such eager anticipation, although I knew you would write as soon as you could.

I feel so lucky or fortunate or something when you say you love me. I'm not half good enough for you, but I am so proud that you do love me and consider myself the luckiest man in the world to have you for my very own.

Your description of our Michael just makes me want to see him all the more. I just think you are the most wonderful woman in all the world. I know that no other woman in the world could have a son--at least not our Michael. Now don't think I am going to be partial to Michael, for I wouldn't take all the world for our two sweet girls, Kay and Sissy. I just had it figured that we were destined to be sonless. But, I guess God just knew how much we both wanted a son, although we would have loved a daughter no less....

I'm afraid it will be about this [1 December] before I will see your own dear self and my wonderful Michael.

Now stay in the hospital as long as necessary and take it easy for a good long spell after you get home. I am planning on sending you a money order for $25 to help out just before departing.

I am just living for the day when I can put my arms around you and look down at our son. I am so lucky, and I love you so.

Michael (over)

I made arrangements for some flowers to be delivered to the hospital on Monday 5 October. Did you receive them?

When you get home, let me know if that govt. insurance policy I put in for has arrived or anything about it. If the policy has arrived, please give me the number of the policy.

My Darling,

I trust you are home by now, and how I would have liked to have been there to welcome you back. I expected to get a letter today, but hope to tomorrow,

I am planning on calling you by phone on Friday night. I hope I can get through, as this will be our last chance to talk to each other for some time. The lines are so swamped it is very difficult to get through even late at night, and I was only able to the night I called the hospital by saying it was illness.

I hope you found everything O.K. at home and that you are feeling better all the time. Now don't start working too soon, but take it easy for some time.

Mrs. Heffernan [wife of Captain J.B. Heffernan] arrived here on Saturday. Several other wives are here in Norfolk, and I am so jealous of the lucky ones, and I miss you so much. You would certainly have been here, too, if it had been possible at this time....

I am so impatient to see you and our wonderful son, but guess it cannot be at this time. You can never know how I love you. Until we meet again, take care of yourself and our family.

Your Michael

Passed by Naval Censor

22 October, 1942

My Darling,

Your two letters were waiting for me yesterday. It was so wonderful to hear from you and to know you are safely home with our children.

I am so proud of our son. He is such a beautiful baby, but all of your babies are beautiful, so he is just carrying on. I just can't tell you how much I love you--how much I miss you and long for you.

I am terribly rushed just now. This is just a note to let you know I am thinking of you and loving you always.

I'll call you Thursday or Friday.

Michael

My Dearest,

It was wonderful to talk to you last night, and I am so glad I was able to get through to you. The situation here in Norfolk is terrible, and it's very difficult to get a long distance call through. It was wonderful to hear your dear voice last night and to know you are safely back home--you and our son, Michael. I would have given so much to have been able to see you and him before I left, but conditions would not permit it this time.

I am so proud of yours and Michael's picture. I showed it to Mrs. Heffernan last night when she was aboard for dinner. She left today for Indiana. Many of the officers have had their wives here for this week, and I have been so homesick for you. Next time, however, you should be able to come down, if we are here again.

I wrote the Veterans Administration today about that Gov't Life Insurance Policy for $5,000. I sent the application with the premium for October about 1 September, and it should have been issued by now. I wrote them a letter and requested information. I am also sending the money order receipt for $3.75 which I forwarded in payment of the November premium. So, if the policy is issued or has been issued, it is now paid for until 1 December. When 25

November comes, you should send in $3.75 as payment of premium for December.

I am also sending you a money order for $20 which you can use as you see fit. I don't expect to need money for awhile.

I wrote the Goodyear people to forward the premiums to you.

I'll be thinking and dreaming of you and our sweet family every day and night for the next few weeks. I love you all so very much and am only living to see you all again soon. Now, don't get up too soon, but be sure you have your full strength back before starting work again.

I love you more than anything in the world.

Yours forever,
Michael

CONFIDENTIAL
United States Atlantic Fleet
Destroyer Squadron Thirteen
U.S.S. *Bristol* (453), Flagship
OF6-13/A4-3
Ser. (058)

At Sea, 19 November 1942

From: Commander Screen, Task Group 34.9
(Commander Destroyer Squadron Thirteen).
To: Commander Task Group 34.9 (Commander Transports,
Amphibious Force, U.S. Atlantic Fleet).

Subject: Recommendations for Special Recognition of
Officers and Enlisted Personnel in Connection with "TORCH"
Operations.

1.... The following recommendations are made:...

(m) Lieutenant Commander M.J. Klein, U.S.N., Gunnery and
Operations Officer, Staff of Destroyer Squadron Thirteen, was
indefatigable in the work of planning and carrying through the
screening and other operations of the destroyers. He was cool
and collected under enemy fire and carried out all his duties in an
efficient and commendable manner.

John B. Heffernan

SECRET
United States Atlantic Fleet
Destroyer Squadron Thirteen
U.S.S. *Buck*, Flagship
File OF6-13/P15
Serial (005)

Care Fleet Post Office
New York, N.Y.
April 17, 1943

FIRST ENDORSEMENT to CincLant [Commander in Chief, Atlantic Fleet] serial 00410 of March 30, 1943

From: Commander Destroyer Squadron Thirteen.
To: Lieutenant Commander Millard J. Klein, U. S. Navy.

Subject: Commendation.

1. Forwarded with the congratulations of Commander Destroyers, U.S. Atlantic Fleet and Commander Destroyer Thirteen.

E.R. Durgin.

[E.R. Durgin later recommended M.J. Klein to be placed in command of U.S.S. *Buck*.]

United States Atlantic Fleet
Flagship of the Commander in Chief
COMMENDATION
P15/(00410)
30 Mar. 1943

From: Commander in Chief, United States Atlantic Fleet.
To: Lieutenant Commander Millard J. Klein, U.S. Navy.

Subject: Commendation.

1. The Commander in Chief, United States Atlantic Fleet, notes with interest and gratification the report of your performance of duty as Gunnery and Operations Officer on the staff of Commander Destroyer Squadron Thirteen during the assault on and occupation of French Morocco ["TORCH" Operations] from November 8, 1942, to November 11, 1942.

2. You were indefatigable in the work of planning and carrying through the screening and other operations of the destroyers. You were cool and collected under hostile fire and carried out all of your duties in an efficient and meritorious manner.

3. The Commander in Chief, United States Atlantic Fleet, commends you for your highly creditable conduct and performance of duty.

R.E. Ingersoll

Passed by U.S. Naval Censor

15 December, 1942

My dearest,

It was wonderful. The best honeymoon we ever had, and I even love you twice as much as I did before it started-- which I don't see how is possible, but it is.

I am so lucky and fortunate that you married me and thus made me the happiest and luckiest man in all the world. I realize more and more that you are the best woman in the world as well as being the most beautiful.

I hope you arrived safely [from New York to Boston] and found our chicks in good shape. I'm so glad you had a bit of a vacation and hope you feel rested.

I love you more and more as the years pass on.

Hope to see you again soon, but will get in touch with you soon.

Your Michael

Passed by U.S. Naval Censor

19 December, 1942

Dearest,

It appears now that I may be able to come down on the evening of 24 Dec. and return during the evening of 25 Dec. Of course that is subject to change. Drop me a line if there is anything I can bring along. I probably won't be able to get a train until 6 or 7 P.M. 24 Dec. I will let you know what train I catch if I can come.

All my love and hope to see you soon.

Mike

From Jackie's Scrapbook:

A Daily Prayer in Wartime for Protection

He that dwelleth in the secret place of the most High shall abide under the shadow of the Almighty.

I will say of the Lord, He is my refuge and my fortress: my God; in him will I trust.

Surely he shall deliver thee from the snare of the fowler, and from the noisome pestilence.

He shall cover thee with his feathers, and under his wings shalt thou trust: his truth shall be thy shield and buckler.

Thou shalt not be afraid for the terror by night; nor for the arrow that flieth by day;

Nor for the pestilence that walketh in darkness; nor for the destruction that wasteth at noonday.

A thousand shall fall at thy side, and ten thousand at thy right hand; but it shall not come nigh thee.

Only with thine eyes shalt thou behold and see the reward of the wicked.

Because thou hast made the Lord, which is my refuge, even the most High, thy habitation.

There shall no evil befall thee, neither shall any plague come nigh thy dwelling.

For he shall give his angels charge over thee, to keep thee in all thy ways. Amen. Psalm 91.

IV

WARFARE IN THE MEDITERRANEAN THEATER 1943

Passed by Naval Censor

10 January, 1943

My Darling,

It was wonderful. I'm so glad you could come, as each moment was wonderful. I would not take a million dollars for each moment we have spent together, the time since I last arrived home. I can only look forward to more of them in the future.

I hope you arrived safely. I went down and got my zoot suit which I have aboard. It's one new suit I hope I won't have to wear.

I'll be thinking and loving you each moment of the days until I see you and our wonderful babies again.

All my love,
Michael

[Mike wrote to his mother on January 4, 1943 that he had been given the command of U.S.S. *Buck*.]

Passed by Naval Censor

12 January [1943]

My Darling,

How I miss you and wish you could be here. You didn't sound very cheerful last night on the telephone, and I have worried about you. I hope you are well and feeling all right. At sea I am resigned to be separated from you, but when I am ashore I feel that we should be together, and I resent anything that keeps us apart. I realize, of course, that we have spent quite freely of late, but money is so unimportant in wartime to me. The important thing is that I want you with me every available moment during the time I am ashore. I don't mean for you to neglect our children to do this, and I know you too well to think that they would be neglected, but it seems that we should be able to be together when the opportunity is there.

I love you so, ten thousand times more than when we were married, and it grows each day. It just isn't right for us to be apart. I'm so jealous of these other fortunate ones who have their loved ones close by.

This will be my last letter for some time. I will call you by phone tomorrow night (Wednesday) just to hear your dear voice once more and to tell you how much I love you, and I'll be thinking and dreaming of you each hour of the day until I return. I pray that those hours bring the day that much closer when I will be near you every day, and then life will be worthwhile.

Yours forever,
Michael

Passed by Naval Censor

23 February, 1943

My Darling,

I miss you so much already. Why do our meetings always have to end, and I have to go away with that lump in my throat?

It was wonderful being with you, and I enjoyed every minute so much. I only pray that the next time will come quickly.

I hope you arrived safely and everyone O.K.

I will call you from Portland if I get the opportunity, otherwise when I return to New York about 1 March.

I love you so very much.
Michael

My Darling Angel,

I am inclosing herewith our income tax blank all filled out. As you will note the amount of the tax, $55.60, is much less than I had at first supposed. This is due to the fact that I deducted taxes we had paid on the house and also interest on the mortgage, both items being properly deducted in accordance with the rules.

I guess I will have to pass this along for you to pay. Please forward the first quarterly installment $18.53 on or before 15 March to the Collector of Internal Revenue, Post Office Bldg., Boston, Mass. The remaining two installments of $18.75 will have to be forwarded on 15 June and 15 September respectively.

I miss you so. It was glorious to be with you for those 10 days, and it seemed to be only 10 minutes. Someday I'm going to have you all for myself all the time and not have to think about having to leave you and our family.

I'll be calling you either on 1 or 2 March.

I'll be loving you and you alone always.

Michael

Passed by Naval Censor

Sunday

18 April, 1943

[On February 28, 1943 M.J. Klein assumed command of U.S.S. *Buck*.]

My Darling,

I hope you arrived safely and found everything in good order. I treasure our being together, even though it was such a short time, and it only seemed like a day or two. I love you more and more as the months and years roll by. I am looking forward to the day we can be together all the time.

I arrived O.K. here yesterday afternoon. I am departing almost immediately. If you remember where I went in September and October, 1941 while I was with A.L. Pleasants,[1] you will know where I am for the next two or three weeks. I regret to say that I'm afraid I won't be back where Doris and Tony live, in accordance with the schedule I have been following the past few months. I expect to return to the place here which is near your old home when I was courting you. At that time I will call you and give any dope I can. This should be sometime during the first week of May.

I am enclosing a copy of the letter I have just received signed by Admiral Ingersoll which I thought you would be interested in. I'll put this with my letter of reprimand and consider myself even.

---

1. In the autumn of 1941 Mike was on destroyer *Benson* under the command of Lt. Comdr. A.L. Pleasants in the North Atlantic.

Take care of yourself and don't overdo in your garden. I'll be thinking of you and loving you each day. Give all our kids a big hug for me.

Yours forever,
Michael

[The letter Mike refers to is dated 30 March 1943 and is a commendation from R.E. Ingersoll, Commander in Chief, United States Atlantic Fleet, for Lieutenant Commander M.J. Klein's performance of duty as Gunnery and Operations Officer on the staff of Commander Destroyer Squadron Thirteen during the assault on and occupation of French Morocco from November 8 to November 11, 1942 (the invasion of North Africa named Operation "TORCH").]

U. S. S. BUCK (420) 19 April

My darling,

Your letter reached me just before I am to shove off. I was so happy to hear that you had safely arrived. Your letter was so sweet and the words of love so lovely to read. I am thankful and proud and happy that I possess such a love and I consider it my most prized possession.

Thank you for reminding me of Mothers day. I would appreciate your taking care of that

Passed by Naval Censor

U. S. S. BUCK (420) 19 April, 1943

My Darling,

Your letter reached me just before I am to shove off. I was so happy to hear that you had safely arrived. Your letter was so sweet and the words of love so lovely to read. I am thankful and proud and happy that I possess such a love, and I consider it my most prized possession.

Thank you for reminding me of Mother's Day. I would appreciate your taking care of that little item for me. Also I want you to get yourself and mother a small bouquet on Easter and consider it from me.

I'm rushed to get this off. I'll be thinking and dreaming of you each mile of the way there and back, and am just living until I again return to take you in my arms and tell you over and over how much I love you.

Michael

I am enclosing $3.00 for your Easter flowers.

Passed by Naval Censor

U. S. S. BUCK (420) [postmark May 4, 1943]

Thursday 2 P.M

IN REPLY
REFER TO

Dearest Darling,

Just a note before shoving off. Hope you arrived safely.

It was so grand to have you for these two days.

I love you more than anything else in this world.

Your

Michael

Passed by Naval Censor

IN REPLY
REFER TO

U. S. S. BUCK (420) 9 June, 1943

Wednesday 4 P.M.

My Dearest,

I have missed you so all day. I had the old lump in my throat when I saw you depart today worse than usual, and I felt as if I could not let you go. I hope someday to have you near me always and no more of these frequent separations.

I am so glad you came to New York with me, as it gave us three more precious days together. I would take no amount of money for them. I hope to always be able to take advantage of seeing you each possible moment, as that is the most important thing in my life--you and our darling children. That is why I don't care to spend all my life in the Navy, as I want a normal home life with you and watch our children grow up.

I hope you and Sissy arrived safely. I will be loving you each step of the way and will be praying for our speedy return to your loving arms. I love you more and more and more as the years roll by.

Yours forever,

Michael

IN REPLY
REFER TO

U. S. S. BUCK (420) [postmark June 10, 1943]

Wednesday Midnight

My Darling,

I can catch one more mail, so will drop you another line just to say how very much I am missing you. How I am longing for your arms around me as they were this time last night. I am looking forward to that day when I can be sure they will be around me every night.

I love you, I do, I do, I do, I do, I do.

Michael

Passed by Naval Censor

U.S.S. *Buck*

23 June, 1943

V-Mail

My Darling,

Just a note to let you know how much I think of you and looking forward to our reunion once more.

I am in good health and spirits and hope you and our little ones are the same.

I see the two angels you have put alongside our ship everyday and in them I see you, so I know you are always close by. I know you and they will bring us safely through.

I love you very, very much. It will be some little time yet.

Forever yours,
Michael

No.

To
Mrs. M. J. Klein,
70 Craftsland Road,
Chestnut Hills
MASS.

From
Lt. Comdr. M. J. Klein,
U.S.S. Buck
℅ P.M. Newyork N.Y.
7 July, 1943.

7 July, 1943.

My darling,

Just a note to let you know that I am well and in good spirits. I miss you so every hour of the day and night.

We will be depending on your angels and I know they will see us through.

I love you, darling, with all my heart and soul. Give our little ones a kiss for me.

yours forever,
Michael

V---MAIL

My Darling,

Just a note to let you know that I am well and in good spirits. I miss you so every hour of the day and night.

We will be depending on your angels, and I know they will see us through.

I love you, darling, with all my heart and soul. Give our little ones a kiss for me.

Yours forever,
Michael

Passed by Naval Censor

U.S.S. *Buck*

14 July, 1943

V-Mail

My Darling,

Just a line to let you know I am well.

I have had need of your angels, but they are seeing us through.

Kiss our darlings for me.

I love you.

Michael

CONFIDENTIAL

U.S.S. *Buck* (420)

DD420/A9/A4

Serial:172

July 20, 1943

From: Commanding Officer

To: The Commander-in-Chief, United States Fleet

Subject: U.S.S. *Buck*-Action Report Operation "HUSKY" [the invasion of Sicily].

1. U.S.S. *Buck,* with ComDesRon 13 [Commander Destroyer Squadron 13] embarked, approached the Southern Coast of Sicily to engage in operation "HUSKY," on D day (July 10, 1943). *Buck* was operating as part of Joss Attack Force whose objectives were the landing of troops and supplies on Red, Green, Yellow and Blue beaches in the vicinity of Licata.

2. Prior to H-hour (0245B July 10, 1943), *Buck* was steering course direct for Licata, in company with Tunisia Joss Slow Convoy. Commander Destroyer Squadron Thirteen in *Buck* was in command of this Convoy and Commanding Officer, U.S.S. *Buck,* was in command of Screening Units for this Convoy.

3. At 0300B July 10, 1943 (D day), *Buck* maneuvered in vicinity of Ten-mile reference vessel (U.S.S. *Bristol*) checking up on Units of Tunisia Joss Slow Convoy as they passed headed for their respective beaches. Shortly before 0300B July 10, 1943, it was learned that H-hour had been advanced one hour to 0345B.

4. At 0342B it was reported that *Swanson* and *Roe* had been involved in collision and would be unable to carry out their mission as Fire Support Vessels in Fire Support Area No. 1, supporting the landing of troops on Red beach. At 0343B *Buck* was designated by ComDesRon 13 to proceed to Fire Support Area No. 1 to replace *Swanson* and *Roe*.

5. At 0400B *Buck,* proceeding to Fire Support Area No. 1, heard roar of aircraft engines overhead. Aircraft flares were observed overhead and in the immediate vicinity shortly thereafter. At 0405B maneuvered radically at 25 knots and attempted to engage aircraft. Planes could not be seen but engines could be heard. At 0430B sighted enemy aircraft astern and opened fire on this plane. Plane disappeared. It is not known if any hits were obtained. At 0500B Coast of Sicily visible ahead and observed large amounts of anti-aircraft fire and flashes of gunfire from Coastal batteries and own forces. At 0505B enemy aircraft dives in on port quarter and straddles *Buck* with a stick of bombs. Closest bomb estimated at 200 yards. Opened fire on this plane with all guns which would bear but plane was visible only for a short time due to the visibility. First light was just beginning to show. At 0510B another plane dived in on starboard quarter and dropped a heavy bomb which missed by about 500 yards. Opened fire on this plane for the short period it was visible. It is not known if hits were obtained. At 0520B observed heavy anti-aircraft fire from other ships in immediate vicinity. At 0521B observed heavy explosion and huge column of smoke to seaward of *Buck*. It is believed that this was the blowing up of U.S.S.

Maddox. At 0526B opened fire on enemy plane going down port beam at a range of about 3,000 yards. Several 5" bursts appeared close and shortly thereafter plane disappeared. It is not known if any hits were obtained.

6. At 0555B approaching Red beach West of Licata, between Fire Support Area 1 and 2. At 0630B arrived on station off Red beach. Observed that troops landing on Red beach were under fire from Coastal batteries. Splashes were seen among the landing craft and on the beach. Attempts had been made since 0400B to contact the shore fire control parties on the frequencies assigned *Roe* and *Swanson,* but all efforts to establish communication had failed. These frequencies were 4670 Kcs and 4920 Kcs. At 0631B *Buck* was directed by ComTaskFor 86 in *Biscayne* to open fire on targets 27, 28 and 29 plotted on chart F1008 by means of overlays. These targets were known to consist of an AA light battery, a machine gun battery and a supply dump. From the size of the splashes landing among the landing craft it was estimated that the enemy battery consisted of 4" or 5" guns. At 0635B took station 3000-4000 yards directly off Red beach, speed 20 knots, and prepared to open fire. Fixed position by navigational fix and transmitted true bearing and range to Control parties. Since no communication was held with Shore Fire Control parties, the Control Officer was instructed to use a 500 yards continuous ladder in range and a 10 mil continuous spot in deflection. It was believed that this method would insure bracketing the target considering normal dispersion during rapid salvo fire at the 5 minute rate. At 0640B commenced firing with main battery, range 10,000 yards, bearing 050 deg.T. Sea was

calm, wind from SW, force 2, visibility and ceiling unlimited. No communication with shore fire control personnel had yet been established although attempts were continued. At 0645B checked fire and reversed course. Rechecked navigational position and gave control parties corrected true bearing and range to the target. At 0650B resumed rapid salvo fire. At 0655B checked fire and reversed course. Again checked navigational position and furnished corrected true bearing and range to control. At this time received word from ComTaskFor 86 on TBS [voice radio dubbed "Talk Between Ships"] that fire was effective and to apply a spot of up 1000 yards. Also at this time a visual message from ComTaskGroup 86.2 was received to apply a spot of up 1500. A spot of up 1000 was given the Control Officer and instructions given to continue use of the 500 yards continuous ladder. At 0659B resumed rapid salvo fire with main battery. Between check fire at 0655B and resuming fire at 0659B no enemy splashes were observed on the beach or among the landing craft. At 0705B ceased fire. No further enemy gunfire on Red beach observed. 340 rounds of 5" 38 Cal. H.E. ammunition was expended during this action with no material casualties. The rate of fire during the firing periods was at the five minute rate prescribed for shore bombardment. It is considered that the performance of the main battery during this bombardment was of the highest order, and apparently was highly effective as no further fire on our troops at Red beach was observed.

7. At 0730B patrolling off Red beach looking for targets. At 0731B began laying smoke screen off Red beach in accordance with orders from ComTaskFor 86. *Bristol* and *Edison* assisted in this work. At

0758B at last established communication with Shore Fire Control Party on 4670 Kcs. At 0759B asked Shore Fire Control Party if there were any targets to be fired on. Reply Negative: Wait. At 0758 ceased laying smoke screen off Red beach.

8. *Buck* patrolled off Red beach throughout the morning and afternoon of July 10, 1943. At 1320B observed enemy aircraft dropping bombs in vicinity of Licata. At 1639B shifted patrol to extend from Red beach eastward to Licata. At 1801B opened fire on enemy aircraft attacking shipping near Licata. No known hits. At 1848B opened fire on enemy aircraft near Licata. No known hits.

9. On July 11, 1943, *Buck* patrolling off Licata. At 0814B enemy fighter bomber scores direct bomb hit on LST [Landing Ship, Tank] 158 unloading on Blue beach. At 0921B Focke-Wulfe 190 dives in on port beam of *Buck* and drops bomb near LST in Licata harbor. At 0921.5B *Buck* opens fire on this aircraft. At 0922B enemy plane crashes off Licata harbor. As several other ships were firing at this plane it is not known who made the hits. At 0947B Focke-Wulfe 190 dives in on ships in Licata harbor but is driven away by AA fire by ships in and near the harbor. There were intermittent aircraft attacks by enemy planes throughout the morning and afternoon of July 11, 1943. At 2155B enemy planes dropped aircraft flares and several bombs in vicinity of Licata. Licata airport was apparently being bombed as many bomb flashes were observed in that area. At 2210B enemy plane apparently sighted wake of *Buck,* who was steaming at 15 knots, and straddled stern of *Buck* with

two medium bombs. No damage or casualties. Thereafter, patrolled at 10 knots to reduce wake.

10. From July 12, 1943 to July 20, 1943, *Buck* continued patrol off Licata harbor. No further actions with the enemy occurred during this period.

11. I consider that every officer and man did his duty. Their conduct during all phases of operation "HUSKY" which *Buck* participated in was in keeping with the highest traditions of the naval service. I consider that no special praise or censure is due any officer or man. In accordance with reference (a) no report of the Executive Officer is enclosed since he has nothing to add which is not included in this report.

M.J. Klein

Passed by Naval Censor

U.S.S. *Buck*

21 July, 1943

V-Mail

My Darling,

All is still well with me and the *Buck*. I miss you so very much. I wish I could say that we would be reunited again soon, but there is no prospect at the moment.

I think of you and our little ones each hour of the day and long to see you. What a glorious day it will be when I can tell you once more how much I love you.

Forever yours,

Michael

My Darling Angel,

All is still well. We have just about run out of everything, but are still holding forth.

I love you, I love you. I just can't wait to see you once again. No prospects as yet, however. Kiss our babies for me.

Yours forever,

Michael

Hitherto, Italian submarines had avoided waters where the United States Navy operated. *Argento,* a 630-tonner based on La Maddalena, was making a reconnaissance of the south coast of Sicily on the evening of 2 August when she encountered, within sight of Pantelleria, a convoy of six vessels en route Licata to Oran, escorted by United States destroyers *Buck* and *Nicholson.* Lieutenant Commander Millard J. Klein, *Buck's* skipper, challenged the boat. No reply. The target disappeared. *Buck* picked up sound contact, and dropped 16 depth charges at 2311. While the convoy passed on, Klein pursued his contact for over two hours, dropped another full pattern of depth charges at 0026 August 3, and had the satisfaction of seeing a submarine surface 1200 yards dead astern. *Buck* opened fire with all guns that would bear. *Argento* retaliated with a torpedo which missed. *Buck* turned to bring her forward 5-inch mounts to bear, and the C.O. with gratification observed a "hail of lead and steel hitting on, around and near the submarine," which fired a second torpedo and again missed. *Buck* closed to within 50 feet of the boat, already dead in the water. Shouts of Italian sailors who had abandoned ship were heard. After making certain that the submarine was abandoned and sinking, *Buck* lowered her motor whaleboat and spent an hour searching for survivors in the dark: she rescued 46 out of the crew of 49, including the Italian C.O., who informed Klein that *Buck's* "cannon fire" had blown a large hole in the base of the conning tower through which most of the crew had escaped. Morison, *History of U.S. Naval Operations* vol. 9: 42-43.[2]

---

2. For another exciting account, see Roscoe, "*Buck* Kills Submarine *Argento,*" *U.S. Destroyer Operations* 326. This report ends with the words: "This was the second Fascist sub downed by American depth charges in World War II. For his skillful direction of the attack Lieutenant Commander Klein was awarded the Navy Cross."

**M.J. KLEIN WITH BINOCULARS
ON BRIDGE OF U.S.S. *BUCK***

OFFICIAL NAVY PHOTOS OF *"BUCK SINKS ARGENTO,"* AUGUST, 1943
LEFT TO RIGHT: LT. COMDR. M.J. KLEIN, LT. GREMONINI,
LT. COMDR. G.S. LAMBERT, COMDR. LEO MASINA, ITALIAN NAVY

CONFIDENTIAL

U.S.S. *Buck*

DD420/A16-3/SS

Serial:184

4 August, 1943

From: Commanding Officer, U.S.S. *Buck* (DD420).

To: The Admiralty (Director of Submarine Warfare).

Via: Commandant Naval Operating Base, Oran, Algeria.

Subject: Destruction of Italian Submarine, R.SMG. *Argento*-Report of.

Enclosure: (A) Track Chart showing the action.

(B) List of survivors.

(C) Action report form "Anti-Submarine Action by Surface Ships" showing detailed data on the three depth charge attacks.

1. I take pleasure in reporting the destruction of the Italian submarine R.SMG. *Argento* by U.S.S. *Buck* at about 0030B August 3, 1943, in position Latitude 36' deg.-52.2' North, Longitude 12' deg.-08' East. This submarine was of 600 tons standard displacement and was about 200 feet in length. One survivor stated he thought other ships in *Argento's* Squadron are *Bronzo, Nichelio, Aciato,* and *Arco.* The armament consisted of six torpedo tubes, a 100MM cannon on main deck and also mounted two double barrelled twin mount guns (12MM). Eight torpedoes were carried, both electric and air, and were either of German or Italian manufacture or both. The submarine was commissioned in May, 1942, and departed on their last cruise from Sardinia on July 21, 1943. The submarine was on

a war patrol between Messina, Sicily and Benghazi. The information was obtained in informal conversation with the Commanding Officer, Captain Leo Masina (3 stripes). The rank of this officer is Tenente di Vascello, corresponding to the rank of Senior Lieutenant in U.S. Navy. The Captain stated that he had taken up a position off the island of Pantelleria in compliance with a radio message which informed him that a convoy would pass there during the night of 2-3 August, 1943. He stated further that hydrophone effect of the convoy had been heard by the submarine and he was preparing to attack when challenged by the U.S.S. *Buck*. He said he had not detected presence of *Buck* until blinker challenge was seen.

NARRATIVE

2. On the evening of August 2, 1943, U.S.S. *Buck* and U.S.S. *Nicholson* were escorting Convoy CNS-3, consisting of six liberty ships from Licata, Sicily, to Oran, Algeria. The six liberty ships were *Washington, Howell, Morris, Piez, Bell,* and *Webster.* The convoy was disposed in two columns of three ships each, 1000 yards between columns. *Nicholson* was patrolling on port bow of convoy and *Buck* was patrolling 4000 yards distant on starboard bow of convoy. At about 2230B August 2, 1943 *Buck* was patrolling station at 12.5 knots. Island of Pantelleria was looming up in the darkness on port bow, distant about six miles. Sea was smooth, visibility good with slight surface haze, dark night with no moon and no clouds, wind from the West, force 1. Commanding Officer was on the

bridge. Ship was darkened, in Condition of Readiness 2MS and Material Condition Able.

2245B- SG Radar contact, bearing 329 deg. T, distant 5500 yards. The Commanding Officer observed this contact on remote PPI scope on bridge, and immediately ordered General Quarters [Battle Condition I], assumed the Conn, and set course for the contact. DRT plot started. Sound operators and Control informed of contact. *Nicholson* came in on TBS and asked if *Buck* had contact. *Buck* replied in affirmative and reported that contact was being closed.

2246B- FD radar reported contact, bearing 328 deg. T, distant 5000 yards.

2250B- Bearing of contact drawing left. DRT plot reported course of contact as 293 deg. T, speed 12 knots. Ship's head brought to 318 deg. T. Range closing, now 4500 yards.

2254B- Control informed challenge was to be made. Be ready to open fire. Signalman instructed to make <u>three</u> minor war vessel challenges slightly on starboard bow. These challenges were made with no reply. Made no further challenges.

2255B- Range 3800 yards. Commanding Officer observing remote PPI scope on bridge, saw contact suddenly disappear. Reported to *Nicholson* on TBS, who verified. Increased speed to 15 knots and informed sound operators contact was submarine and to sound search very carefully ahead and to 45 deg. in each bow. Ordered depth charges to be set for base setting of 150'. This gives a staggered pattern, some charges set at 200', some at 150', and some at 250'.

2300B- Sound contact bearing 310 deg.T, distant 700 yards. Ordered ship's head to 285 deg.T and instructed officer at chemical recorder to drop a medium pattern of five charges to be fired by chemical recorder. Sound range was so short, the Commanding Officer did not receive but one more bearing and range before the pattern was fired. This bearing was 307 deg.T, range 400 yards. Sound contact lost at 300 yards.

2301B- Dropped medium pattern of five charges with base setting at 150'. Held course and speed and instructed sound operator to search down starboard side to the stern.

2305B- Began a turn to the right with standard rudder, and steadied on course 125 deg.T.

2308B- Regained sound contact, bearing 152 deg.T, distant 900 yards. Ordered ship's head to 152 deg.T. Bearing drew right. Steadied on course 200 deg.T, and ordered officer at chemical recorder to fire full pattern (11 charges) set for base setting of 200 feet. Lost contact at about 300 yards.

2311B- Dropped full pattern of 11 charges, base setting 200 feet.

2315B- Began turn to left with standard rudder and steadied on course 350 deg.T.

2321B- Regained sound contact bearing 185 deg.T, distant 600 yards. Informed sound operators I would open the range and we would then turn and deliver a deliberate attack.

2323B- Lost contact at 800 yards. Turned to right with standard rudder and steadied on course 165 deg.T. Intention was to circle area of last drop to regain contact.

2332B- Began slow turn to the right and steadied on course 050 deg.T. This course from DRT headed ship close to drop of second pattern.

2346B- Sound contact reported bearing 060 deg.T, but was classified as reverberations. No range obtainable.

2346B-0017B- Conducted box search around second depth charge attack point, using DRT plot to keep informed of ship's position with respect thereto. Planned to search area using box search, gradually extending the range from the reference point.

0017B- While on course 030 deg.T, obtained firm sound contact bearing 062 deg.T, range 600 yards. Announced intention to open range so deliberate attack could be made. Ship's head ordered to 082 deg.T.

0019B- Lost contact at 800 yards.

0020B- Began a turn to the right and asked DRT for course to steer to position of contact obtained at 0017B. This information was continuously supplied by the DRT as the ship turned to the right and at 0024B steadied on course 290 deg. T.

0024.5B- Obtained firm sound contact, bearing dead ahead, range 500 yards. Ordered sound officer to fire a full pattern of eleven charges, using a base setting of 300'.

0026B- Dropped full pattern of eleven charges, base setting of 300 feet.

0028B- At this time the Commanding Officer was observing the remote PPI scope on the bridge. The last depth charge explosion had subsided shortly before. Suddenly dead astern at a range of about 1200 yards there appeared a contact. I wish to state that at this time I experienced one of the greatest thrills of my life. Control was informed that submarine had surfaced. "Open fire with all guns which would bear." Full right rudder and 25 knots speed was ordered. I went to starboard wing of bridge and could observe submarine on surface.

0028.5B- 5" Gun No. 3 opened fire on submarine. Also starboard 40MM and after 20MM Gun opened fire. Fire from the machine guns provided excellent illumination for the 5" guns. The submarine stood out clearly and distinctly, fully surfaced and did not appear to be listed.

0029B- Torpedo reported approaching, bearing 150 deg.T by sound operator. The Commanding Officer could hear the noise of the approaching torpedo from the sound stack out on the bridge. The ship was already turning toward the bearing of the approaching torpedo with full rudder and flank speed so no other evasive action was taken. The torpedo track was observed to pass down the starboard side by several of the crew. The bearing of this torpedo was followed down the starboard side by the sound operator. At this time it appeared to the Commanding Officer that the submarine intended to fight it out and the decision was made to ram.

0030B- Forward five inch guns and two forward 20MM guns now bore and opened fire. It was very gratifying to the Commanding Officer to see this hail of lead and steel hitting on, around, and near the submarine. I knew the enemy would not be able to man their deck gun or machine guns in that withering fire.

0030.5B-Torpedo reported approaching by sound operator bearing South. The ship was still swinging toward the submarine. No further evasive action was taken. This torpedo by sound did not appear to come as close to the ship as the first torpedo. The sound operator states that he distinctly heard the sound of both torpedoes being fired and their subsequent run. The noise of the first torpedo was so loud it could be distinctly heard on the bridge. Word was passed on all circuits to standby for collision with submarine. After guns were now blanked but forward machine guns and 5" Gun No.

2 were firing rapidly and accurately at this time.

5" Gun No. 1 had rammer failure and only fired 2 rounds during the action. Hand ramming was used but gun had hangfire.

0031B- Submarine close aboard dead ahead. The rudder was not eased quite soon enough by the Commanding Officer and the intention to ram was defeated, the ship passing about 50' astern of the submarine. As the ship passed close aboard, no signs of life were visible on the submarine. The submarine was obviously stopped. The deck gun of the sub was still fore and aft and no machine gun fire was directed our way. Shouts of men in water were heard close by. It is believed that shortly after firing the second torpedo the submarine was abandoned. This decision was probably influenced by the effective gunfire and the close proximity of *Buck* approaching head on at high speed.

0032B- As the crew appeared to have abandoned the submarine, the decision to ram was abandoned, and control was informed that submarine would be circled at close range, every available gun would be brought to bear and the submarine sunk.

0032B-0037B- A hail of lead and steel was directed against the submarine. During lulls in the shooting, shouts could be heard in the water all about the submarine. The range to the submarine during this period was never more than 1,000 yards.

0037B- Cease firing was given. The submarine was still afloat but was obviously stricken, having a 45 degree list to starboard, and appeared to be settling lower and lower in the water.

0040B- Radar contact in submarine faded. Ship still circling with full rudder at 25 knots.

0041B- Slowed to 15 knots. It was decided to make a careful search of the area by sound and radar before accepting the risk of slowing or stopping to rescue survivors. Accordingly the area in the vicinity of the submarine's last known position was searched by radar and sound until 0100B. No contacts were obtained. Shouts from water were continuously heard during this search.

0100B- Position of survivors was closed and ship's speed reduced to five knots for lowering of motor whaleboat. While the boat was being lowered an object was reported in the water close aboard on starboard quarter. The Commanding Officer observed this object through binoculars. It appeared to be a long low-lying black shape and the waves could be seen breaking over it. Sea was flat calm. The officer in charge of whaleboat was instructed, before the boat cleared, to inspect this object. No sound or radar contacts could be obtained. A torpedo torch pot was thrown overboard to mark the spot. The boat officer later reported that the object was the submarine hulk. It was barely awash, and was either on its side or was bottom up.

0100B-0205B- Rescue of survivors continued. Ship circled area at 15 knots while boat was engaged in rescue operations. When boat was filled, boat signalled ship with blinker tube. Boat was then closed and survivors brought aboard over cargo nets, with ship making five knots. Forty-six survivors were rescued in three boat trips.

0205B- All survivors aboard. Area was now searched in vicinity of torch pot marker for submarine hulk until 0300B with the idea in mind of possible salvage of the submarine. Hulk could not be located. Search was abandoned at 0300B and course taken to rejoin convoy. A radio report to CINCMED [Commander in Chief Mediterranean] by *Nicholson* requested air search of area at daybreak for this floating hulk. Results of this search are not known.

3. The Commanding Officer of *Argento* has stated in conversations with the Commanding Officer that the first two depth charge attacks were ineffective. They were heard but did no damage and did not shake them up. He stated that the third attack was all around him. All lighting power was lost; engine room began to flood and submarine took a list to starboard. He gave the order to surface. He further stated that the "cannon fire" of *Buck* opened up a large hole in the submarine at the base of the conning tower through which many men escaped into the water after he gave the order to "Abandon Ship." He stated he did not know why he was fired on in such a concentrated manner as he was done for from the depth charge attack. He denied having fired any torpedoes at *Buck,* but in

the Commanding Officer's opinion the proof that torpedoes were fired is conclusive. Although the Commanding Officer of the submarine denied having fired two torpedoes at *Buck,* subsequent conversations with members of the crew of the submarine verify the fact that two torpedoes may have been fired. The sound of approaching torpedoes on the sound gear was unmistakable and the sound operator of *Buck* during this action was a man with over two years' experience on sound gear. The commanding officer also said he personally opened up sea valves before he abandoned ship, so it is believed that hulk must have sunk in a short time after being last observed by *Buck* at 0100B.

4. Three crew members of the total 49 on board the submarine are missing and were not rescued by *Buck.* Their names are indicated in Enclosure (B). Of the forty-six survivors who were rescued, one man died shortly after having been brought aboard from gunshot wounds in the chest. This man's name is Salvatore Orbi, radioman mate 2/c. He was buried at sea at 1400B August 3, 1943, in position Latitude 37 deg.22.5'N, Longitude 09 deg.22.5'E. A simple burial service was held on fantail. Prisoners were allowed to be present and colors were half-masted in all ships of the Convoy during the burial service. Seven other survivors are suffering from wounds but it is believed all will recover. The remainder of the survivors are all in good shape and spirits. They appear to be glad it's all over for them.

5. I believe it is obvious from this report the value obtained from the DRT [dead reckoning tracer] plot in this attack. It is my considered

opinion that this attack would not have been successful had not the DRT been employed. I say this mainly because of the extremely low effective sound range and have no intention to take away any share of the credit which rightfully belongs to the sound operators and the sound officer who manned the chemical recorder. The maximum effective sound range during this attack was never over 700 yards.

6. 110 rounds of 5"38 Caliber H.E. ammunition with MK 18 fuzes was expended against this submarine. Flashless powder was employed and cannot be praised too highly in reducing night blindness from gunfire. 338 rounds of 40MM ammunition was expended from the starboard 40MM gun. 707 rounds of 20MM ammunition was expended by the four 20MM which could bear during the action. 5" Gun No. 1 had a rammer failure after firing two rounds and later hangfire and did not figure in the action after that. 5" Gun No. 4 fired only 15 rounds due to a portion of the crew of this gun being employed in reloading depth charges. All 5" Guns were fired in local control and controlled by the gun captains. To quote one gun captain, "It was like Short Range Practice." It is believed that the machine gun batteries now installed in these ships are most effective weapons against surfaced submarines at close range.

7. The tremendous value of the SG ["Sugar George"] radar was again demonstrated. It is believed from experience that 5500 yards is a normal range to expect from a surfaced submarine with normal sweep. However, it must be borne in mind that ranges up to 800

yards may be obtained on surfaced submarines if "hand sweeps" are employed.

8. I consider that every officer and man did his duty in this action. Their conduct was in keeping with the highest traditions of the Naval service. I believe that the following officers and enlisted personnel are deserving of special praise for their part and I recommend them for special recognition.

OFFICERS

a) Lieut. Comdr. George S. Lambert, U.S.N.

Executive Officer

This officer supervised radar and sound personnel on the bridge during the radar approach, and subsequent depth charge attack. During the Gun action he was of great assistance to the Commanding Officer in checking to see that orders to the Wheel were carried out properly. He contributed further by helpful suggestions at various times during the action. He also was in charge of rescue operations of the survivors. The whaleboat was lowered and recovered with way on the ship in complete darkness. He was generally most helpful in internal administrative matters during the rescue and quartering and treatment of the survivors after they were on board.

(b) Lieut. R.K. Irvine, U.S.N.

Gunnery Officer

The 5" guns and machine guns delivered a highly effective fire against this submarine once it was on the surface reflecting a high state of training imparted by the Gunnery Officer. The promptness as well as the high rate of fire and effectiveness thereof undoubtedly discouraged any attempts by the submarine crew to man their deck weapons. 5" hits were obtained according to the commanding officer of the submarine and other survivors, and the machine gun fire can only be described as "withering."

(c) Lieut. G.H. Harrington, U.S.N.R.

This officer in addition to his duties as Navigator is charged with the state of training of the depth charge crews. The three patterns dropped during this action were all dropped in accordance with the prearranged plan. Loading after each drop was expeditiously handled, indicating a high state of training of the depth charge reloading crews in complete darkness. This officer also aided the Commanding Officer on the bridge during the rescue operations and provided several helpful suggestions. He kept the Commanding Officer continuously informed as to the ship's navigational positions. This was especially helpful as the Island of Pantelleria was nearby.

(d) Lieut. R. Scully, U.S.N.R.

This officer was in charge of the motor whaleboat during the rescue operations. He carried out his job efficiently and expeditiously, thereby keeping *Buck* in a suspicious area as short a time as possible.

(e) Lt. (jg) D.E. Crais, U.S.N.R.

This officer controlled the fire of the machine gun battery during the action and is jointly responsible with the Gunnery Officer for the high state of training of this battery. This officer's battle station is on the after deckhouse where he controls the fire of the machine gun battery. Shortly after the gun action started, the trainer of the starboard 40MM gun was blasted from his seat by the fire from 5" Gun No. 3. Lieut. Crais at once assumed the position of trainer himself and fire from the starboard 40MM gun continued until the regular trainer recovered himself sufficiently to man his station. This action of Lieut. Crais is highly commendable.

(f) Lieut. (jg) W.J. Conklin, U.S.N.

This officer is Communication Officer of *Buck* and his battle station is on the bridge. He was helpful to the Commanding Officer throughout the action in relaying the intentions of the Commanding Officer to the sound team and DRT plot team. In addition, when the Commanding Officer was on the wings of the bridge, this officer relayed information coming from the DRT and sound teams. I consider he performed all his duties in a commendable manner and materially assisted the Commanding Officer throughout the action.

(g) Lt. (jg) R.P. Lance, U.S.N.R.

This officer conducted the DRT plot and provided continuous and accurate information as to last known position of the submarine.

This officer without question contributed a great deal toward making the last depth charge attack successful.

(h) Ensign J.G. Andrae, U.S.N.R.

This officer manned the chemical recorder. He is Sound Officer and the efficient teamwork of the sound team during this action reflects a high state of training. This officer dropped the depth charge pattern when the correct time was indicated from the chemical recorder. Although the effective sound range was not over 700 yards the sound team furnished the Commanding Officer with the necessary data to effect a successful approach.

(i) Ensign D.W. Crawford, U.S.N.R.

This officer was designated as interpreter for the survivors. He was most helpful in looking after the general welfare of the survivors and in obtaining much of the information from the survivors included in this report. This officer also made the first trip in the whaleboat to rescue survivors and assisted Lieut. Scully in this task.

(j) Lieut. T. Boyt, U.S.N.R.

This Medical Officer did an excellent job in caring for the wounded and in looking out for the general welfare of the survivors.

ENLISTED MEN

(a) M.J. Vradenburg, U.S.N.

This Chief Petty Officer assisted Lt. (jg) Lance on the DRT and materially assisted by his experience on this instrument in supplying the Commanding Officer with the information which made possible a successful attack. He accomplished the actual plotting of own ship and submarine track and thereby materially assisted in making the attack successful. He furnished immediately any bearing and distance requested by the Commanding Officer during the box search to regain sound contact.

(b) Smith, W.M. Jr., U.S.N.

This enlisted man manned the QC sound gear throughout the depth charge attacks. He demonstrated that he was familiar with proper sound procedure and executed "lost contact" procedure on the several occasions that sound contact was lost. The short effective sound range existing in the action area was a handicap, but Smith furnished the Commanding Officer with bearing, ranges and width of target, quickly and accurately. It is considered by his performance of duty that he contributed materially to the success of the action.

M.J. Klein

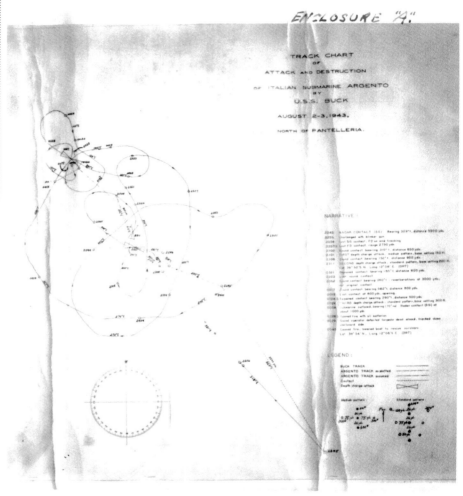

**TRACK CHART OF ATTACK AND DESTRUCTION
OF ITALIAN SUBMARINE *ARGENTO* BY
U.S.S. *BUCK* AUGUST 2-3, 1943
NORTH OF PANTELLERIA**

My Darling,

Just received two V-Mail letters from you, and it was so good to hear after so long. They were dated July 15 and July 18.

I miss you so as the days go by and only pray for the day to come when we shall be together once more.

Do you remember our code we made up last year? I hope you still have it. Look up and see what "All my love" means. I hope that is a good approximation. You may have to add another 10 days. You can expect a call from Ralph Johnson about 24 August. I have asked him to call you and tell you I love you. I always have and always will.

Yours forever,

Michael

Bright Harbor

by Daniel Whitehead Hicky

I have known harbors at the earth's far rim
Scented with oleanders pale as dawn,
Ports hushed with starlight when the dusk grew dim
And mandolins struck a tune to dream upon.

I have plowed into the sunset, sails aglow,
Burning with color under the south wind's spell,
Shouted with joy to see the first far row
Of harbor lights, to hear the first faint bell.

I have come home. I bring you lotus flowers,
A shell the sea's wild music burst apart.
I have dropped anchor until my dying hours
Deep, deep within the harbor of your heart.

**LAST PICTURE OF MIKE WITH FAMILY IN BOSTON,
SEPTEMBER, 1943:
MIKE AND JACKIE, KAY, CISSY, AND MICHAEL**

Passed by Naval Censor

U. S. S. BUCK (420) 16 Sept., 1943

Thursday Night

My dearest Darling,

We arrived today on the first leg of our journey. We had a rough time in the storm.

I've missed you so since leaving you. It was so wonderful being with you. The time was so short. How I dread the parting, but look forward so eagerly to our next meeting.

I'll be thinking of you each hour and minute of the day. I love you more than life itself.

Michael

It will be about 10 days before I can send you another letter.

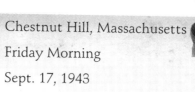

Chestnut Hill, Massachusetts

Friday Morning

Sept. 17, 1943

V-Mail

Michael, dearest,

I wrote you at length last night via air mail and am mailing this and it together this morning to see which reaches you the quickest. Just told you how much I love you, how wonderful it was having you home that lovely two weeks, and how much I miss you now that you are gone. Also told you how fortunate I am to have you for a husband and how proud to have you for the father of my children. It seems our family will remain the same size a little longer, but even though I am relieved, I am also sorry we are not in a position to have just as many as we could, for they are the dearest and finest anyone could wish for, and I don't know what I'd do without them when you are away. They keep me from slipping into the slough of despondency and give life back some of its meaning until you come and bring all the meaning and happiness life can hold. God bless and still keep you, my dearest, and speed the day of peace and your return to

Jacque

IN REPLY
REFER TO

U. S. S. BUCK (420) 21 Sept., 1943

Passed by Naval Censor

Darling,

Please sign this and mail to "Office of Collector of Internal Revenue," Boston, Mass.

Instructions issued by the Navy state that premiums paid on life insurance can be applied against current tax liability, which means we owe them nothing. Just sign and forward.

I am half way. I love you so and miss you so.

Michael

P.S. The Sept. 15 deadline does not apply to those on active service.

22 September, 1943.

My darling,

Today we have been married 9 glorious years. It seems only yesterday. How I wish I could be with you on this day, even more than any other, to tell you that I love you even more than I did 9 years ago. I have learned what real love is and the greatest thrill of my life was the day we were married. I wish we could go back and relive each happy moment over again but when I think of our lovely children I am content to go on and watch them grow up to manhood and womanhood.

Every year that passes I feel more fortunate in having had you for my wife. I know that no other woman could

MIKE'S LAST LETTER DATED SEPTEMBER 22, 1943

Wednesday Oct. 6th

Michael, darling,

How wonderful to get your sweet letter today and to know our hearts and minds were full of the same dear thoughts on Sept. 22nd! And how wonderful to hear that you love me the way I love you. There aren't enough roses grown in all the world that mean as much to me as this dear, lovely letter telling me your thoughts and love for me. That's the most wonderful anniversary present you could have sent. And I shall treasure it through the years and show it to my grandchildren to tell them how much their grandfather loves me all through the happy years. I know God is going to see you through this frightful war, Michael, for your safety and nearness means so much to me

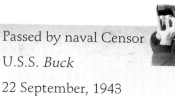

Passed by naval Censor

U.S.S. *Buck*

22 September, 1943

My Darling,

Today we have been married nine glorious years. It seems only yesterday. How I wish I could be with you on this day, even more than any other, to tell you that I love you even more than I did nine years ago. I have learned what real love is, and the greatest thrill of my life was the day we were married. I wish we could go back and relive each happy moment over again, but when I think of our lovely children, I am content to go on and watch them grow up to manhood and womanhood.

Every year that passes I feel more fortunate in having had you for my wife. I know that no other woman could have made me as happy as you, or made as good a mother to our children. I can only thank God that He has been so good to me, and ask Him to preserve me so that I may return to you and our children for many more years of happiness.

I wish I were there today. I would send you the biggest bunch of roses I could find. To be frank, I would have made the necessary arrangements before I left, had I thought of it in time. The hours and days just passed so quickly, I did not realize they had come and gone. However, you can rest assured that on our anniversary that I am home I will make it up in good measure. I do wish you would make yourself a purchase with the money I gave you and consider it my

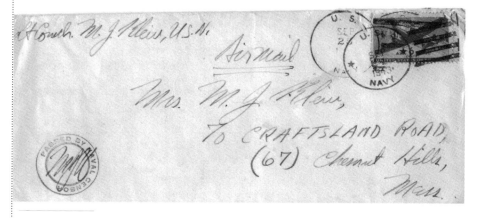

present on this happy day for me. I love you so, my darling. Life for me will be perfect if we can only be together uninterrupted once more.

I will mail this on arrival which will be two days hence. I will shove right off shortly to go up further and do my share in the struggle. It may be some little time before I can write you again, but I will be thinking of you each hour of the day and night, and your spirit will be here with me at all times. I know your angels will carry us through, aided by your prayers.

Write me often and just tell me often that you love me--that's what I really want to know, along with knowledge that you and the children are in good health and want for nothing.

Be patient with mother, and you will be rewarded.

My undying love to you, my dearest and sweetest.

Yours forever,
Michael[3]

3. This was Mike's last letter to Jackie.

Chestnut Hill, Massachusetts

Sept. 21, 1943

V-Mail

Michael, darling,

Tonight marks the close of nine years of my being married to the dearest, finest man in all the world. If I could go back and choose again my partner for life, I'd make the same choice even quicker than I did before. I thought I loved you then, but after nine years of happiness with you, I realize I didn't know what love was and am just beginning to realize how wonderful a thing love can be. How I wish you were here tonight to relive in memory that mad, wonderful Sept. 22nd of nine years ago in Mexico. I am so very, very glad I did it. I'm closing my eyes and kissing you across the thousands of miles between us, for I know you will be thinking of the same things I am on this day. God grant that we may spend our tenth, twenty-fifth, and Golden wedding together in a happy and peaceful world. God also bless you, my dearest one, and keep you.

Jacque

Chestnut Hill, Massachusetts

Sept. 21, 1943

Air Mail

Michael, Dearest,

I'm writing you both ways again tonight, as I am celebrating a wonderful day in the year for me. Nine years ago tomorrow I made the best decision of my life, and I am so very glad I did. Do you remember that mad but wonderful night in Mexico, my darling? I wonder sometime how I was so sure it was the right thing to do, for I really didn't know you but so well, and I knew the difficulties involved in making such a step, but some inner voice told me to go on, and some unseen force seemed to urge me on. How glad I am that I heeded them, for living with you has been the happiest, most wonderful experience of my life. Being your wife and the mother of your children is what I'd rather be than Queen of the universe! How I wish you were here that I may tell you how fortunate I feel I am. I close my eyes and kiss you across the miles between us in spirit and whisper how much I love you and how glad and grateful I am that we belong to each other. God grant that we may celebrate our tenth, twenty-fifth, and Golden wedding together in a world of peace.

Everything here is going along O.K. We are having some lovely Indian summer weather, and it is hard to stay indoors. I mowed the lawn yesterday and fiddled around my planters today awhile. But I must get to painting my windows. They're all here and waiting to be done. Sunday night the Forbes had me to supper with the Farleys, Fasslers, Thomas' and Ginly's. I enjoy getting out and laughing at their jokes and antics, but miss you so much all the time and never do anything that I don't wish you were here so that I could enjoy it completely. That's being made "one" by marriage, I suppose. I only half enjoy the pleasures of life, for my "better half" is away with you. God bless you and keep you, my darling, and bring you safely and quickly home.

Jacque

Envelope stamped "Return to Sender" "Navy Department Unable to Deliver"

Chestnut Hill, Massachusetts

Sept. 26, 1943

V-Mail

Michael, darling,

Your sweet letter arrived on the 22nd and was the nicest anniversary present I could have gotten. Nothing is so valuable to me as your love, and to hear you profess such love for me after nine years of married life is a priceless treasure to me. I missed you even more frightfully than usual on that day, but feel we celebrated it a bit earlier in New York. I'm going to take my $20 present and dress myself up for you by the next time you come home. It just happened that Lee Cutler invited me over to supper that night. That helped so much to alleviate my lonesomeness for you. Mother wrote that she appreciated and enjoyed your letter, but hoped you hadn't exhausted yourself writing such a long one. I'm in the midst of painting my storm windows. The days are getting chilly now, so want to get them finished. Am writing this before I go to church this morning to thank God for keeping you and our little ones safe and well, and to ask Him to always do so. With my heart full of love for you.

Jacque

Envelope stamped "Return to Sender"   "Navy Department Unable to Deliver"

[Chestnut Hill, Massachusetts]

Monday, Sept. 27th, [1943]

Michael, dearest,

You've been gone ten days now, and it seems like a year! Each day I wonder where you are on that particular day and today am supposing you are across by now, if you are going where I imagine you to be. The news on the radio is encouraging, but hard fighting is in progress, and I dread what that means--but I have implicit faith that God has given His angels charge over you to keep you in all your ways, and pray it may be over soon and you may come back to live the rest of your life in peace and joy. It's this thought that keeps me going when I feel like sitting down and howling for lonesomeness for you. But then I think how fortunate I am that I have you to wait for. Mrs. Farnsworth brought me up a lovely bouquet of fall flowers that filled the house and make it so sweet. Lee Cutler had me over for tea yesterday, and last night the Farleys had the "play reading" group in to hear "The Man Who Came to Dinner." Your mother went to that also--and, by the way, she went to the Red Cross last Wednesday. Saturday night the Thomas' had a party--and so the neighbors are helping to pass the weary hours until you come home, and I begin to live again. I got a letter from Kay Franz saying how nice it was to see us and a card from Rue in Santa Cruz, Calif., where she had a vacation with Howard who had a few days in 'Frisco awaiting transportation. Frank Hoye called and said I owed him $6 more for the scotch. He said it had gone up. Cissy seems interested in going to real school now and by the papers she brings home seems to be doing well. Kay is saving her perfect papers with gold stars for you. Michael is standing alone now when he wants to use both hands, and doesn't realize he's doing it and has taken a couple of faltering steps alone. Sally Hadden, Lee's sister whose husband is on Joe Foley's ship, had her baby yesterday. It was a little girl. That seems to be my "thirty" in neighborhood news. We are all well and miss you so very much. Hurry home again, my darling, to one who loves you and your little "chips" more than all the whole wide world.

Jacque

Envelope stamped "Return to Sender" "Navy Department Unable to Deliver"

Chestnut Hill, Massachusetts

October 2, 1943

V-Mail

Michael, dearest,

I can't realize it's been only a little over two weeks since you left—it seems so long! It was just a month ago today you came in, and yet it seems so long ago. Time races so when you are here and drags so when you are gone. I miss you more every day and am praying you'll get back before Xmas. They say, "Faith moves mountains," so I'll just believe you are coming, and so you will.

All of us are getting along O.K. It has rained most of this week, and the children miss getting outdoors so. Evie Leeson called me and said she had recently taken a house on Laurel Road. It's just over the parkway from here. She said she and Bob saw Virginia and Blackie in New York, and Virginia was expecting her third baby. She's going to bicycle over soon to exchange all the news. Said she heard of your fine exploits. I'm so very proud of you and feel so fortunate to be loved by you. God bless you and keep you. I love you, I do.

Jacque

Chestnut Hill, Massachusetts

October 6, 1943

V-Mail

Michael, my dearest,

How wonderful to get your sweet letter today and to know our hearts and minds were full of the same dear thoughts on Sept. 22nd! And how wonderful to hear that you love me the way I love you. There aren't enough roses grown in all the world that mean as much to me as this dear, lovely letter telling me your thoughts and love for me. That's the most wonderful anniversary present you could have sent, and I shall treasure it through the years and show it to my grandchildren to tell them how much their grandfather loves me all through the happy years. I know God is going to see you through this frightful war, Michael, for your safety and nearness mean so much to me and our little ones--and it is something right to pray for--that I know He will see that you are restored to us in a world of peace for which you have so valiantly fought. He said, "Ask and it shall be given you" [Matt. 7:7], and if your faith is so big as a mustard seed, "thou canst move mountains" [Matt.17:20]. And I have asked Him to preserve your <u>body</u> and <u>soul</u>--with every breath I pray it--and I do believe He will. I shall keep the home fires, which you are so bravely protecting, still burning and looking with longing eyes for that day of peace that shall be the fruit of your labours, and will mean you are home to stay with those who love you so much. For I do love you, my one and only love,

I do, I do, I do! I kiss you Good night, dearest, across the many miles between us and ask God's angels to hover near that bridge always.

Jacque

Am sending this V-Mail too. Let me know which reaches you first.

V-Mail: Envelope stamped "Returned to Writer" "Reason Checked: Deceased"

Air Mail: Envelope stamped "Officers Mail Room, Bureau of Naval Personnel-Returned to Sender" "Unclaimed"

NAVY CROSS AND PURPLE HEART

[On October 9, 1943 Lieutenant Commander M.J. Klein was killed when the *Buck* was torpedoed and sunk off Salerno, Italy. Three survivors later reported the details of the sinking in personal letters to the family.

Lt.(jg) J.A. Hoye recalled that the *Buck* "was running down a submarine contact when a torpedo struck just forward of the bridge on the starboard side, blowing up the ship's magazines. The vessel sank within four minutes of the time of the torpedo explosion, the stern disappearing under water last. Only two survivors who had been on the bridge came through the explosion. One of those, Lt. D.T. Hedges, was standing on the port side of the bridge at the time of the explosion and was blown over the side unconscious and came to when being carried up through the water by his life jacket. He knew nothing of the explosion and thought he had fallen overboard."

Lt. D.T. Hedges was the last survivor to see Captain Klein, who was standing and giving orders on the starboard wing of the bridge. Lt. Hedges wrote: "I got to the bridge about five minutes after G.Q. [General Quarters] sounded. I went to the starboard wing of the bridge, and Captain Klein was already there. I heard one his talkers give him a range on the target (surface) which had caused him to order G.Q. Then the Captain ordered the depth charges set and the searchlight manned. The target was still some distance away, and finding myself somewhat engulfed in the confusion normally attending a night G.Q., I then left the starboard wing and walked around to the port wing. I had not been there more than three minutes when we were hit. The whole forward section of the ship simply disintegrated. The torpedo must have detonated our forward magazine. The blast was terrific." Captain Klein and the officers on the starboard wing of the bridge were killed instantly.

Ens. E.M. Buchanan gave the following report in his letter: "After we were hit, we waited for instructions from the bridge, but found that communications had been cut off. The order to stand by to abandon ship was given by word of mouth. When I reached the main deck, the first thing I noticed was that the bridge was missing and the ship had already started to heel forward. All available life rafts were cut loose. All hands that were able went over the side and started swimming for the nearest raft. About a minute after I left the ship, there was an underwater explosion presumably from our own depth charge. As a result of this explosion, the number of casualties was increased."][4]

4. See in Appendices: Bill Brinkley, "Three Men on a Raft," *The Stars and Stripes Weekly* 6 Nov. 1943; full text of letters from survivors; letter from German U-boat captain. For the account of the hunt for and destruction of the German submarine *U-616* that sank the *Buck,* see Roscoe, "U.S. DD's and British Aircraft Kill *U-616* (`Operation Monstruous')," *U.S. Destroyer Operations* 371-73 and Blair, *Hitler's U-Boat War* 524-25.

Chestnut Hill, Massachusetts
Monday, October 11, 1943

My dearest,

How I wish you were home, now that Fall is really here. I think I love this season best of all, for it reminds me of when I first fell in love with you. And too, we started our married life in that season, and all our babies were born in the Fall and early winter. Do you remember that first November? Little things come back to me so vividly of that wonderful November at Annapolis—when I couldn't listen to your explaining the mechanism of an airplane for wondering about you as you talked, and the strange, new feeling that came over me in the cosey [cozy] bridge of the subchaser. And then the glorious words I heard you say in Mrs. Leich's living room the next afternoon, and we two sitting before the kitchen stove watching the glowing ashes conjure up wonderful pictures of our future. Could it be that was thirteen years ago! And then the Fall of 1934 saw us starting life together in Vallejo. Do you remember how we'd romp and fall laughing and exhausted into each other's arms? And then the next year in December, Kay came to make our love complete—and then October two years later, Cissy, and last October, Michael. No wonder Fall is the most beautiful time of the year! And it always reminds me of you in hunting togs with Shadrack [family dog], me, and two little ones trudging at your heels, looking for a coney [cony] or quail. I've seen several pheasant but no quail about here. The trees are lovely though. Last night we had our first frost, and it was a big one. My morning glories and tomato vines looked so forlorn that I couldn't stand it, so went out this afternoon and pulled them all up and cleared the trellis. I had picked all the tomatoes, even the green ones, and have one-half bushel basket of ones to ripen and made three quarts of mincemeat and three quarts of piccalilli with the very green ones. I'm saving some for your next visit home. I've just about finished my painting, and the men on the street say they don't see why I pay anyone to install the windows, since they'd be glad to do it for me, particularly if I give them a chicken dinner. The Fasslers had me in to Sunday nite supper last night, and the Farleys had a sherry party yesterday afternoon. They include me in everything and are so nice to me. It is the friendliest street I ever saw. Mrs. Morison called me this week and said they had just gotten home again from Maine and wanted to know if I could come out to spend the day again when daughter Elizabeth arrives. The Commander [Samuel Eliot Morison] and she heard about your achievement, and she sent congratulations. I asked her how they heard, and she said, "Scuttlebutt." I haven't seen the Heffernans since we were over there.

Mother sent me a snappy herringbone suit today--said it was a present for my anniversary. That was just an excuse to give me something. I'm taking your $20 present and getting hat and shoes and gloves to match. So I'll be dressed up for you when you come back. Please God make it soon! For I do so much

love you and miss you so very, very much. And God bless and
keep you, my dearest one, and bring you safely and swiftly
home to me, who loves you and your babies more than anything
in all the wide world.

Devotedly,
 Jacque

Envelope stamped "Return to Sender" "Navy Department Unable
to Deliver"

The filing time shown in the date line on telegrams and day letters is STANDARD TIME at point of origin. Time of receipt is STANDARD TIME at point of destination

BAH91 73 GOVT=WUX NR ARLINGTON VIR OCT 13 555P

MRS JACQUELINE COLEMAN KLEIN=   OCT 13 PM 6 50

70 CRAFTSLAND RD CHESTNUTHILLS MASS=

THE NAVY DEPARTMENT DEEPLY REGRETS TO INFORM YOU THAT
YOUR HUSBAND LIEUTENANT COMMANDER MILLARD JEFFERSON KLEIN
US NAVY IS MISSING FOLLOWING ACTION IN THE PERFORMANCE
OF HIS DUTY AND IN THE SERVICE OF HIS COUNTRY THE
DEPARTMENT APPRECIATES YOUR GREAT ANXIETY BUT DETAILS NOT
NOW AVAILABLE AND DELAY IN RECEIPT THEREOF MUST
NECESSARILY BE EXPECTED TO PREVENT POSSIBLE AID TO OUR
ENEMIES PLEASE DO NOT DIVULGE THE NAME OF HIS SHIP OR
STATION=

    REAR ADMIRAL RANDALL JACOBS THE CHIEF OF NAVAL
    PERSONNEL.

THE COMPANY WILL APPRECIATE SUGGESTIONS FROM ITS PATRONS CONCERNING ITS SERVICE

"MISSING IN ACTION" TELEGRAM

Western Union Telegram [two red stars stamped] (34)

BAH91 73 GOVT=WUX NR ARLINGTON VIR OCT 13 555P

MRS JACQUELINE COLEMAN KLEIN=1943 OCT 13 PM 650

70 CRAFTSLAND RD CHESTNUT HILLS MASS=

THE NAVY DEPARTMENT DEEPLY REGRETS TO INFORM YOU THAT
YOUR HUSBAND LIEUTENANT COMMANDER MILLARD JEFFERSON
KLEIN US NAVY IS MISSING FOLLOWING ACTION IN THE
PERFORMANCE OF HIS DUTY AND IN THE SERVICE OF HIS COUNTRY
THE DEPARTMENT APPRECIATES YOUR GREAT ANXIETY BUT DETAILS
NOT NOW AVAILABLE AND DELAY IN RECEIPT THEREOF MUST
NECESSARILY BE EXPECTED TO PREVENT POSSIBLE AID TO OUR
ENEMIES PLEASE DO NOT DIVULGE THE NAME OF HIS SHIP OR
STATION=

   REAR ADMIRAL RANDALL JACOBS THE CHIEF OF NAVAL
PERSONNEL.

MISSING IN ACTION following the reported sinking of the destroyer Buck last week was the word received by the family of Lt.-Comdr. Millard J. Klein of Craftsland road, Chestnut Hill. With Mrs. Jacqueline Coleman Klein, formerly of Tennessee, are their children, Virginia, 6, left; Michael, one year, and Kathleen, 7.

ARTICLE *Boston Herald* 20 Oct. 1943

To One Missing In Action

I put you in God's loving care,
In His great Universe somewhere
You are still there.
You are o'ershadowed by His wing
In heav'nly climes; or in this ring
Of earth's circling.

He can restore you to my sight,
The battle's angry roar despite,
He has the might.
Though Laz'rus, death's dark valley trod,
It was within the power of God
To raise from sod.

Yet it may be this earthly span
Is but a test for mortal man;
A race you ran.
Who, in the fight, all sacrificed,
Have stood the test and gained the prize
Of Paradise.

-If He returns you to my breast,

I shall rejoice in thankfulness,

And be e'er blessed.

But if He wills you wait me there,

Serene, the test of life I bear,

Expectant here.

Jacqueline C. Klein (1943)

POSTSCRIPT

After the sinking of the *Buck*, Jackie left Boston as a young widow of 33 years of age and went to live with her three children in the Blue Ridge Mountains of Loudoun County, Virginia. She never remarried. In 1948 she moved to Richmond in order to educate her children in good schools. Her last home was in Coral Gables, Florida. Her eight grandchildren knew and loved her, and she told them all about their grandfather who was a brave naval officer. She died in November, 1971 at the age of 61.

My Balm of Gilead

I came to Loudoun when my soul had need of balm,
And in her strength'ning hills I found my calm.
From war's hurt and cruelty I fled
Facing life, bereft of love, with dread and longing to be free.
And there 'neath Scotland's homey hill
My eyes with breathless beauty filled
And overflowed the pent-up tears.
I felt, from all my grief and fear, my soul at liberty.

God's still small voice I hearkened to and heard
Within the throats of thrush and mocking-bird,
And in the gnarled and laden apple tree
The smiling, cheerful face of God did see, and saw His
footsteps pass
Along the country road in neighbor's errands trod,
Along the ploughman's track of upturned sod.

And saw His flowing garment trail across

The fieldstone land embossed, as wind-swept orchard grass.

There in a house beside the road I made my home,

And from the neighbor gardens' black and richly loam

Came off'rings of Nature's plenteous store

Almost daily brought through open door by work-worn, giving hands.

Across the rose entwined fences flowed

Miracles from kitchens; cellar-stored

Treasures in earthen crock and canning jar.

How remote the famine and the war, how distant ravaged lands.

And lifting up my eyes to mountain-side

I found my Gilead at even-tide,

Looking out to where Catoctin stood,

Bidding me to be still and brood. Soul, whatever harms

And trials come, have not faithless fear,

For aught save loss of God be alway near;

Beneath it all His spirit keeping station

Before the mountain was, a firm foundation, the everlasting arms.

Jacqueline C. Klein (1946)

His Everlasting Arms [Deut.33:27]

My selfish, narrow, little world
Was so upset today.
Life seemed so very futile,
And God seemed far away,
When Someone asked me questions,
"Does God His own forsake?
Have you ever really hungered?
Has your thirst ne'er found its slake?
Have you ever been a stranger
That no one would let in?
Have you ever been in prison
For any human sin?
Are you sick and maimed in body
And have no one to care?
Have you ever had any cross that
Jesus didn't help you bear?"
"Yes," I could not answer,
So I fell upon my knees,
And asked forgiveness for distrust
And found my heart at ease.
In thankfulness I lay me down
To sleep in perfect rest,
And feel His everlasting arms
And know His plan is best.

Jacqueline C. Klein (1954)

APPENDICES

At Sea

U. S. S. BUCK (420)   24 March, 1943

From: Commanding Officer.

To: All Officers.

Subject: Instructions for Officers.

1. The following instructions will clarify the general policy of the Commanding Officer with regard to the general performance of duty and deportment of all officers. Some of these instructions have already been brought out at recent conferences.

(a) Uniform at sea. On deck any uniform consistent with the weather is acceptable for both officers and men. Officers will wear a complete uniform at mess table. Khaki shirts are acceptable provided insignia of rank are displayed. Blue shirts and blue trousers are authorized also provided insignia of rank are displayed. No mixed uniforms at the mess table and no sleeves rolled up.

(b) Uniform in port. In port I expect all officers to be either in complete blue uniform or a khaki uniform. If khaki uniform is worn, then the coat must be worn. I have noticed officers appear on deck in khaki shirt with no hat, no insignia of rank and shirttail hanging out. Officers must be careful of their personal appearance on deck, in the wardroom and elsewhere. The men follow your example. The only exception to the above is in the case of officers assigned engineering duties who are authorized to wear clean dungarees or khaki, as they prefer. If khaki is worn, insignia of rank should be displayed. Other officers when actually doing work around guns or inspecting may also wear dungarees or khaki.

(c) Uniform for crew. I expect O.O.D.s to enforce requirements for the crew to be in uniform. Every day I see men going about the decks without hats and in very dirty dungarees. See that this is corrected. Do not permit dirty dungarees or torn dungarees to be worn. If the word is passed to shift into uniform of the day, enforce the order and do not permit men on deck out of uniform. I do not expect to have to come on deck and observe deficiencies. If I do, it is a direct reflection on the O.O.D. These deficiencies include beside uniform such items as men lounging on the rail, decks not swept down, colors foul,[1] irish pennants,[2] absentee pennants not flying if Commodore or Captain are absent. O.O.D.s be smart in your appearance and deportment and the men will quickly follow your example. Be alert. Take charge and follow through.

(d) Quarters for muster. I expect officers to consult the Plan of the Day for the next day and plan their movements accordingly. If Quarters are scheduled for 0800, I expect officers to be at their quarters station a minute or two before 0800 and then require the crew to be at their quarters in a reasonable time. The other day I observed Quarters at 0800 from the bridge. The crew straggled up to quarters, some not wearing hats, others smoking cigarettes as they fell in. In most cases they didn't fall in but gathered in a knot. It was 0810 before I observed the first officer on deck before his division. Be there on time yourself and require your division to muster quickly and smartly in uniform prescribed. Require them to fall in and be military. It will be good for them as Quarters is about the only military operation which they are required to perform.

---

1. The national ensign or flag not clear.
2. An untidy loose end of a rope.

(e) I expect all officers to be in uniform in the mess room. If you want to undress do it in your room.

(f) I expect all officers to cooperate in keeping the mess room in a neat and orderly condition. Do this by not leaving your caps and other articles of clothing lying about the wardroom. If any officer sees the mess room untidy he should call the mess boy and have the mess room straightened up. Clear the wardroom table one half hour before the scheduled hour of the next meal to permit the mess boys to set up. Do not lounge in wardroom during the morning after breakfast so that the mess boys cannot clean up. The officers at that hour should be inspecting their divisions.

(g) Be at meals on time. If the Commanding Officer is not present at five minutes past the scheduled hour of the meal, the senior officer present go ahead with the meal.

(h) Read over Ship's Orders. Publish them to your divisions. Require that they be carried out. An order which is not enforced is worse than no order at all.

(i) Effective immediately all officers will be called at 0700 daily both at sea and in port. Breakfast will be served from 0700 until 0815. At 0815 breakfast will be cleared and mess boys proceed with daily field day in wardroom.

(j) I expect the O.O.D. or J.O.O.D. in port to inspect to see that reveille is executed promptly by all hands. All compartments on the ship will be swept down before breakfast is piped down. This fact will be determined by the J.O.O.D. If any compartment is not swept down on the inspection the entire division effected will be called to the compartment concerned. Upon completion of the sweep down, the division will then proceed to breakfast.

(k) I expect all division officers to require that the junior division officers inspect all spaces in their respective departments both morning and afternoon as a minimum requirement. Point out defects during these inspections and follow through to see that the defects are corrected. Know your men and see that they turn to at the specified time. The junior officers should be in their parts of the ship frequently during working hours to see that work is progressing. If the contents of this paragraph are carried out, it will be unnecessary for the ship to make frenzied efforts to prepare for an inspection. The ship will be ready for an inspection at any time, which is the condition I want. I believe that much work on deck is unsupervised, which accounts for lack of visible results. I expect the officers to provide this supervision.

(l) Every space on the ship should have some man or men assigned to that space as a cleaning station. All division officers see that this is carried out and hold responsible the ones concerned for the cleanliness and upkeep of the space involved.

(m) I desire that every Thursday the Executive Officer require that heads of departments inspect a department other than their own and turn in a list of defects noted to the Captain and the Executive Officer.

(n) All junior officers will begin immediately to take the General Information Course under the direction of the Executive Officer. Upon completion of the General Information Course the officers will take the course which corresponds to the job they are under training for. Failure to comply with this paragraph will result in officers being restricted to the ship upon arrival in the United States.

(o) All reports will be completed and in the hands of the Captain not later than the 10th of each month. I expect all heads of departments to keep all records such as Alteration and Improvement program, repairs required, machinery records, etc., up to date at all times.

(p) If any man is observed by the O.O.D. or other officer on deck in dirty, filthy, or ragged clothing, the division officer will be informed. The division officer will proceed immediately and inspect the bag of the man concerned. The man will then and there be required to wash all dirty clothing in his possession. The division officer will make a list of deficiencies in the man's bag and require the man to draw the missing articles as soon as possible.

(q) All officers must be prompt in handling official mail. Take care of your mail the same day it reaches you. Do not leave official mail lying around wardroom. Keep a tickler file on all mail requiring an answer.

(r) The Executive Officer will be in charge of training of officers. Lectures will be scheduled daily whenever operations permit on such subjects as damage control, Tactical school including mooring board problems, local control of 5" guns and torpedo battery, Coding Board instruction and Communication Procedure, naval etiquette and customs, ship control, steering casualties, proper procedure on battle telephones. I expect all officers to discuss over gunnery and fire control problems so that the O.O.D.s may act promptly and effectively in cases of contacts at night. In many cases this action will have to be taken before the Captain can reach the bridge.

(s) Be military in your bearing and deportment when standing watch. Be on deck at least ten minutes prior to the hour when you relieve. The officer you relieve will feel better as well as yourself.

(t) Planning. I expect Commissary Officer, Mess Treasurer and all other officers to plan ahead in connection with supplies for long voyages. There is no excuse for running out of any commodity three or four days out of port. It indicates poor planning and in most cases no planning on the part of the officers concerned.

(u) Do not permit the crew to lounge on the lifelines. No officer should ever be observed lounging on the lifelines.

(v) In the future, when in port other than that of a United States port, The O.O.D. watch will be continuous, as at sea. I expect the Chief Petty Officers and petty officers standing watch at the gangway from 2200 to 0800 (the period when no officer will be there in a U.S. port) to fully understand their responsibility and carry out their duties or otherwise the O.O.D. watch will be continuous all night in U.S. ports. I intend to make inspections to determine that the watch from 2200 to 0800 in U.S. ports is effective.

(w) General Rules.

1. Familiarize yourself with ship, fleet, and Navy regulations.

2. Do not criticize your seniors.

3. Learn the names and faces of leading petty officers as soon as possible and extend this to include others as soon as possible.

4. Division officers inspect lockers frequently.

5. When ship's work is in progress, the junior division officer should be in his part of the ship.

6. Never call an enlisted man anything but by his name or rate. His name is much better.

7. Before making a decision, weigh it well, but once having made it, stick to it. Be quick, however, to admit if you are clearly wrong.

8. When a delinquent is before you, always make him stand at attention.

9. There are many cases of minor discipline which can be handled without taking men to mast, but the "popularity jack" who never reports a man is a menace to discipline and a nuisance to his brother officers. Report whom you must.

10. Know when and how to say "NO."

11. A nod of praise is usually a better spur than a growl of censure.

12. You should be self-confident, firm, courteous, and at all times, military.

13. If an order is to be given that you think will be unpopular, do not try to stand from under with "The Captain or Commodore says."

14. Don't let the men on this ship see an officer who is-

   (a) Lolling or indifferent.

   (b) Careless or non-regulation.

   (c) Diffident or afraid to speak up.

   (d) Blustering or browbeating.

   (e) Giving orders in a "won't you please" manner.

15. There are no limited working hours for us in the Navy.

16. Your men will size you up before you learn to know them. Strive to learn and train yourself in the qualities of a leader. Study your men, and try to learn each man's individuality. Keep your men interested and stimulate them to strive for new records of performance.

17. You are always subject to critical examination by your fellow officers. Conduct yourself accordingly.

18. Devote a portion of your time to study.

19. One of the best things I can say about you is "When you are given a job I can always count on getting action NOW."

20. The messroom is the home of your messmates. Do not invite people there you would not take to their homes ashore.

21. Do not go into the messroom out of uniform. Always remember that your mess will be as clean and orderly as the officers make it and no more.

22. Do not fuss because you have to be at meals in uniform. You will look better and feel better.

23. Do not play musical instruments during working hours.

24. Until you have had experience as Mess Treasurer, do not be too ready with complaints.

25. Do not have enlisted men to your room.

26. When you enter the Captain or Commodore cabin, remove your hat and do not lounge unless you are invited to sit down. Do not say "Yeah" in answer to a query or as an affirmation to a statement.

M.J. Klein,
Lieutenant Commander, U.S. Navy,
Commanding

THE STARS AND STRIPES WEEKLY
Saturday, November 6, 1943, page 5
"Three Men On A Raft: They Met In Sea By Accident And Talked Of Life At Home" by Bill Brinkley

Navy Lt. David T. Hedges was standing on the bridge of the U.S.S. *Buck,* patrolling off the American-held Italian mainland. The next thing he knew he was under churning water flailing his arms furiously to get to the surface.

He came up half dazed and wiping fuel oil from his eyes with his good left hand.

That was the beginning of a battle for life which Hedges, Coxswain Anthony Pepponi and Officer's Steward Leroy Highe were to make in the open sea for 19 hours, after they were knocked overboard after the U.S.S. *Buck* had been torpedoed.

The raspy general quarters call shook Hedges out of his bunk at 0100. He glanced at his watch and yawned: "They're a little early tonight." GQ's had been coming pretty regularly at 0300.

Pulling his life jacket over his clothes, he hustled to the charthouse. It was crowded so he didn't go in. Not going in was to save his life. When the ship was torpedoed five minutes later, the charthouse was destroyed.

Instead he went on out to the port wing of the bridge ten feet away peering into the night for enemy craft. Then he was in the water with no memory of how he got there. His right wrist was limp. From base of ribs to hip bone there was no feeling in his left side.

His first thought was that he had fallen off the bridge. Presently he noticed he was in a thick overlay of oil. It occurred to him the ship might have been hit.

Piece of Wreckage

A curve-topped piece of wreckage floated by six inches out of the water and he grabbed it. It turned out to be half a small raft split lengthwise. Though badly shaken, he managed to hang on to the raft by throwing his arms over the side, remaining chin-deep in the sea.

He clung thus for about an hour before seeing a few yards away what appeared to be the other half of the raft. Tightening his grip on the one section he swam one-armed for the other. He got an arm over each piece. Soon he heard a faint voice.

"Ahoy! Ahoy!"

"This way! This way!" he shouted back.

"Ahoy ! Ahoy!" the voice repeated.

Hedges kept yelling, "This way! This way!" as a guide. In about a quarter hour a man swam up to him. The man twisted his life belt and in the black, blowing night this conversation took place:

"Who are you?"

"Anthony Pepponi, coxswain."

"I'm Lt. Hedges."

"Gee, I'm glad to find you, sir."

"You can forget that 'sir' stuff. We're just two guys with a life raft, or I hope a life raft. We've got a hell of a job to do. We've got to try to lash these pieces together. Do you have a knife?"

"Yes, sir. A jackknife, sir."

With the jackknife Hedges and Pepponi cut small strips of line hanging from one section of the raft and tied them together. Holding on for life to the two sections, they situated themselves one at each end for the lashing.

Just then they saw dimly a ship's silhouette and were about to call for help when they squinted their eyes and shut off their speech in their mouths. The silhouette was a sub. Grabbing tight to the raft parts, they ducked behind them for a few tense wordless moments until it had slithered by. Then they went back to their lashing job.

Here began a ticklish business, one that might easily prove calamitous. A strong northerly wind was beginning to blow up an even choppier sea. The two sections of heavy wood were banging together. A hand caught between one of these contacts would be seriously smashed. And they were always in danger of losing the potential raft. Huge waves were crashing over them.

Strong as Ox

Fortunately, the 22-year old Pepponi is "strong as an ox," as Hedges put it. After several tries the two managed to pull the sections together. They looked and their hearts almost collapsed within them.

Two large chunks of board in what they thought was a complete raft were missing. The sections would not fit.

They conferred a moment, hit upon the idea of turning the semicircular pieces over and up. This gave the raft a high prow and very much the appearance of an old Viking ship. More important, it brought the sections together at both ends and thus made them lashable. The raft would not close in the center. But being together at the ends, perhaps it would stay fast anyhow.

"We didn't do a hell of a good job of lashing," Pepponi said. "But the raft looked like it might hold. And to us right then it looked as beautiful as the U.S.S. *Iowa.*"

They struggled aboard and sat on the curved sides gingerly. A high wave caught the raft for her first test. They held their breaths. The cone of the wave shattered against the little Viking. The craft came up high upon it, rode the wave and descended. Triumphantly the lashing held. The two men exhaled the biggest sigh of relief of their lives.

All that miserable night on a choppy sea they clung to the raft, now straddling it, now sticking both feet between the two sections in the center.

Hedges' hand was beginning to ache badly. Whenever he turned, his bruised side made him wince. Pepponi's eyes were almost swollen shut from oil and water and just about driving him mad. To bear the pain he would cup his hands tight behind the back of his head and grit his teeth. The back of his neck was swollen like a puffed-up sack from a blow received when he had slipped on deck at his powder loader battle station. The torpedoing had picked him up out of the water and shaken him "like a big hand squeezing me and then hurling me down." Hedges now noticed his steel-band wrist watch was gone--blown off by the explosion. Both men were shivering from shock.

Hedges kept telling Pepponi and himself, "We mustn't give up, we mustn't give up."

On into the night they kept hearing far off a kind of "out-of-the-world warbling, pitiable sound" which they first thought might be the wind but which they soon decided was a human being.

Some of the boards that had been the bottom of the raft were still hanging loosely to one section of it. Two of these they pried off with Pepponi's knife. Using them for paddles, they tried going in the direction of the warbling.

Somehow, though, the direction of the warbling kept seeming to change. At dawn a heavy rain poured down, chilling the men and reducing visibility. When it cleared, they saw a speck on the water.

Coming into sharper view after an hour's paddling they could see a Negro lying with all but his head in water in a Navy cork and net type life raft, constructed in such a way that the net bottom stays slightly under water, receiving its support from small cork floats.

His head resting against one of these floats, the man was lying there as if in all comfort, chanting a rich-voiced, "Oh, Lord, I'm in Your Care."

Flashing Smile

The man sat up in the net and gave a flashing-toothed "Hello, man, am I glad to see you!" Pepponi recognized Leroy Highe, officer's steward second class on the *Buck.*

His net was lashed onto the raft in case more survivors should be sighted and Highe came aboard the Viking. Stories were exchanged again. Highe related how he had almost been trapped by a sprung door in the after dressing-station, how he had escaped by wrenching the door open and then grabbing onto a mattress which had floated off the torpedoed destroyer.

Presently he yawned, crawled over between his two new comrades to sitting position on one side of the raft, leaned the upper part of his body across the little gap of water, laid his head on the other side and promptly fell asleep.

Up in the morning planes began coming over. Hedges, Pepponi and the awakened Highe started shouting.

"I don't know what we yelled," Hedges said. "We just opened our eyes and made the loudest noises possible. Pepponi stood on the edge of the raft and began waving his arms. His eyes would stay open only when he held the lids with his hands. This he would do to spot the plane, then would drop his hands from his eyes and start yelling again.

"I was afraid he would make the raft split standing up there but it held. He fell into the water several times but each time would climb back on.

"None of the planes saw us, apparently. We could hear a motor first before we saw anything--the sky was cloudy. Then high up through the clouds we would see a plane. We kept waving and screaming and the plane kept right on going. Everything got more and more hopeless.

"It got to where it made us sick just to see a plane go over," Pepponi said.

Mid-morning they spotted a pack of cigarettes floating on the water. They had no dry matches so they chewed the cigarettes, their only food of the 19 hours.

At about 1000 a plane came out of the clouds directly toward them. If the men had shouted before, they almost yelled their lungs out now. Hedges began giving the fighter's handshake, raising his arms high over his head and pressing his hands together until his sprained wrist quivered with pain.

"Suddenly the plane swept to about 50 feet over us and the back door opened," Hedges related. "We could see a man standing in the door. He waved to us and we waved back. We almost cried for happiness."

Chuckled Highe, "That door opening like that was like the pearly gates swinging wide."

The plane turned up again and tailed away. Assuming help would be out soon, Hedges directed that all paddling cease, so that present position might be retained. Highe began to sing, "We're Drifting Back to Dreamland."

"We talked about everything," Hedges said. "About home and about Burlington, N.J., where Pepponi lives, and Jackson, Tenn., where Highe lives, and about Cedar Rapids, Iowa, where I live."

We talked about the steaks they would give us when we were rescued," Pepponi added. "Survivors always get steak first thing, we had heard. We were the happiest people anywhere. We talked a streak for two hours."

"As a couple of hours began to peter away," said Hedges, "the happiness and conversation dribbled off. No one said what we were all thinking--that someone should have come to pick us up if anything was coming. When the hours kept on going by and nothing came, we stopped talking and were deep in ourselves again and if our eyes happened to catch each other's we would look away quickly."

When they had waited six hours and nothing had come, they decided to cast off the net they were towing and start paddling east toward Italy.

With what doubtless would have seemed futile slowness to anyone else but with each stroke taking them forward a few inches or so, the three oil-soaked men headed the jagged prow of the fantastic little ship in the direction of land.

At about 1930 they could hear a faint thrum of motors. The sound was from the surface, not the sky. They sat dead silent, tense and anxious. Suddenly they could see the silhouette of a destroyer off their port bow.

"Isn't that a ship?" yelled Pepponi, jumping up and holding open his eyes.

"It ain't no minnow," chirped Highe.

Moon Glow

"The moon!" Hedges screamed. "Paddle for the moon!"

Frantically all three men began paddling to get the raft into the path of the moon to spotlight her for the destroyer.

"That tincan must have been doing 25 knots," Pepponi said. "She whizzed on past us a half mile away before we could reach the shaft of moonlight. That was our worst moment. We were in for another night of it, we knew. And with my eyes hurting more and more from the effects of that fuel oil and salt water I wasn't at all sure I could take another night out there."

A few minutes later the men saw three bright red flares burst into the sky. They didn't know it then, but those flares were from a Very gun in a life raft carrying other *Buck* survivors.

Presently the destroyer was back and at reduced speed. This time they got their Viking raft square onto the bright funneled stage cast by the moon and began desperately beating the water with their crude oars, hoping the ship would see the white splash.

Pepponi stood up on the raft's edge and waved wildly. He fell into the water and climbed back on. The destroyer heaved over toward them.

A rope ladder was down. Highe, Pepponi and then Hedges started up. Hedges, exhausted, started tumbling back toward the sea and just in time was able to throw his arms through two loops of the rope and cling there. A member of the ship's company scurried down, secured a line to his body. He was hauled aboard.

Hedges volunteered immediately to go to the bridge and direct her to an area where he thought might be other survivors of the sunken *Buck*. He received quick medical treatment and then guided the ship. More survivors were picked up.

Lt. Comdr. F.W. Hoye, USN
Navy Department
Office of Supervisor of Shipbuilding
United States Navy
Bethlehem Steel Company
Quincy 69, Massachusetts
20 December 1943

Mrs. Martha Klein [Mike's mother]
Knoxville, Tennessee

Dear Mother Klein:

My brother John [Lt. (jg) J.A. Hoye] has returned home; in fact, he has been here for a couple of weeks, but I have been ill at home and my whole family has been ill and I have been unable to write until now. I am going to give you the facts just as John gave them to me, but there may be information in it which the Navy Department would not want released, and I wish you would treat it confidentially for that reason.

At the time the *Buck* sank she was about 40 or 50 miles offshore, roughly northwest of the Island of Capri. She was running down a submarine contact when a torpedo fired by another submarine struck just forward of the bridge on the starboard side, blowing up the ship's magazines. My brother feels that there is very little chance of any survivors who were stationed forward of the after fire room. Only two survivors who had been on the bridge came through the explosion as far as is known. One was a signalman who had been standing near the signal bags on one of the after corners of the bridge and was blown all the way back to the main deck at the stern of the ship, suffering several broken ribs and a fractured collarbone, but who was placed aboard a life raft and was saved and has recovered. The other known survivor was a passenger, Lieutenant Hedges, who was standing on the port side of the bridge at the time of the explosion and was blown over the side unconscious and came to when being carried up through the water by his life jacket. He knew nothing of the explosion and thought that he had fallen overboard.

While my brother feels that the chances of Millard's survival are not good, there is a chance, because the submarine which torpedoed the *Buck* did surface for a few minutes and was

definitely seen by my brother and other survivors and may have picked up Millard as they certainly would have done had they suspected him of being the Commanding Officer. There is also a strong possibility that there were German E-boats in the vicinity, and he may have been picked up by one of these. My brother John feels, however, that the chances are not good, but he is certain that all those who were on the bridge were either blown clear of the ship or died instantly, not knowing what had happened and suffering no pain.

At the time of the explosion John was aft at the after conning station; he was thrown into a gun mount by the force of the explosion, ripping open one leg. He tried to get forward to ascertain the amount of damage to the forward part of the ship, but was unable to proceed further forward than the amidships deck structure, due to wreckage. The vessel was obviously sinking, and John being the senior surviving Officer ordered all survivors to take to the two remaining life rafts and all shore timbers thrown over the side and for all survivors to abandon ship. He and two torpedo men set all depth charges to safety before leaving the ship. John was the last one to leave the ship and swam off the fan tail with the water standing up to his waist when he left. The vessel sank within four minutes of the time of the torpedo explosion. A few seconds after the stern of the vessel disappeared under water, one of the depth charges which apparently had a faulty safety set exploded, injuring thirty or forty men in the water. My brother was blown up into the air and then drawn under the water and was carried to the surface by his life jacket in a semiconscious condition. He made his way to one of the life rafts which had been blown up by the depth charge, but whose balsa wood ring was still intact, and he carried with him an injured sailor whom he had picked up in the water, pushed the sailor up on the balsa wood float, and climbed up on it himself before losing consciousness. He recovered consciousness about one-half hour later and took command of the life raft and another life raft, attempting to gather together all the survivors, lashing timbers together to form rafts. Several of the men who were survivors at that time (the vessel sank about one o'clock in the morning) died later as a result of injuries incurred following the explosion of the depth charge. When daylight broke, none of the survivors could see or hear well, due to fuel oil being in their eyes, ears, noses and mouths. A seaplane flew over about ten

o'clock in the morning and dropped life rafts containing needed medical supplies and drinking water, and about ten o'clock the following night two destroyers combed the area, picking up all living survivors that they could find. The following morning, the entire area was searched thoroughly by aircraft and patrol boats, but no living survivors were found. My brother was the last one to leave the water to go aboard the destroyer, passed out as soon as he climbed aboard the destroyer *Gleaves,* was given two blood transfusions, and delivered to the Army Hospital at Palermo the following morning. His left side had been paralyzed. He had coughed up a sizable quantity of blood, and his chest had been blown in three inches. He recovered rapidly and left the hospital in about three weeks and has overcome all his injuries, except he has very little feeling in his left arm, although he has muscular control, and occasionally has lapses of memory which, however, he has been assured by the Medical Officers he will recover from within six months to a year. He is now on thirty-days leave and will report to the First Naval District for duty after a thorough checkup at the hospital.

I am sorry to have to give you so little hope, but felt that you would prefer to know exactly what happened, as far as is known....

You may be sure that I will write you just as soon as I have any further news, and please do not give up hope because there is always a chance, no matter how remote, that things may not be as bad as they seem.

Sincerely yours,
Frank

Lt. Comdr. F.W. Hoye, USN
Navy Department
Office of Supervisor of Shipbuilding
United States Navy
Bethlehem Steel Company
Quincy , Massachusetts
3 January 1944

Dear Mother Klein,

I received your letter and will answer your questions first and in the order that you asked them. First, John last saw Millard about a half hour before the ship was hit. He had been on watch when the submarine contact was made and the ship's company went to battle stations. At the time of the explosion Millard was standing on the starboard wing of the bridge just above and a little aft of where the explosion occurred. John himself was back in secondary conn by number 3 gun mount at the time of the explosion. That is back on the afterdeck house. The submarine was not sighted before the ship was hit. It is not known whether or not it was the same submarine that sank both the *Buck* and *Bristol*. The *Bristol* was sunk two days after the *Buck*.

Hedges did know where Millard was. He knew he was on the starboard wing of the bridge. Anderson, as far as I know has not come back to Boston, but no one knows as much as John about what happened, as he was the only surviving officer who saw everything and he became the commanding officer.

John has gone back to duty. He is the intelligence officer at Martha's Vineyard and Nantucket and will remain there until he has had a chance to recover from his injuries. He had his right leg gashed open, and his chest was blown in three inches, but has expanded back to normal. He cannot feel anything in his left arm now. Sometimes his mental reactions are not as quick as normal for him, but he is improving. It will take him a few months to recover. I don't think we will know if Millard is a prisoner for at least six months….

As John has given me the full story about the *Buck,* I think I can tell you anything that is known. Don't hesitate to let me know anything that I can do.

Best regards,
Frank

Lt. David T. Hedges, USNR
530 East 90th St.
New York, N.Y.
April 13, 1944

Mrs. M.J. Klein
Richmond, Virginia

Dear Mrs. Klein:

Your letter to Mrs. Hedges arrived recently, and I am glad to give you what information I can regarding the loss of the *Buck*. I remember with pleasure meeting you aboard the ship in New York just seven months ago today.

First of all allow me to dispose of my own experiences in short order. While it was not nearly as harrowing as some of the other men, John Hoye for one, the *Stars and Stripes* chose to report on it in one issue. Perhaps you have already seen it, and if you haven't, it may be bad taste to send it to you. On the other hand it is a report of the experiences of three more *Buck* men, and I shall take a chance that it may add to your "piecing together" of the entire picture.

I am now an instructor in communications at a naval training school in New York. Aside from a somewhat weak left leg, I have fully recovered from the disaster.

It is with the deepest regret that I report that I did not see the Captain in the water after the ship went down. I personally questioned most of the survivors and not one had seen him. It is my frank opinion that he did not survive--I am taking you at your word that you want the truth, painful as it may be.

I got to the bridge about five minutes after G.Q. sounded. I went to the starboard wing of the bridge, and Capt. Klein was already there. I heard one of his talkers give him a range on the target (surface) which had caused him to order G.Q. The Captain ordered the depth charges set and the searchlight manned. I believe Mr. Lambert and George Harrington were also there, but in the darkness I could not be sure. The Captain was the only one I heard speak. The target was still some distance away, and finding myself somewhat engulfed in the confusion normally attending a night G.Q., I then left the starboard wing and walked around to the port wing. One signalman and myself had it all to ourselves. I had not been there more than 3 minutes when we

were hit. I would estimate that there were 8 or 10 men on the starboard wing with the Captain, and just the signalman and I on the port wing. Of that group only two were seen again. The signalman 3/c (a Polish boy named Gryzch) who had manned the searchlight (lit, but shutters closed, of course, until further orders) was blown clear back to the fantail where he <u>and</u> the light landed. He survived, as John Hoye has probably already told you. The signalman over on my wing was not seen.

The whole forward section of the ship simply disintegrated. The torpedo must have detonated our forward magazine. The blast was terrific.

The submarine which the *Stars and Stripes* mentions did not come close enough for me to be sure whether it picked up any survivors or not. The light I saw, which I assumed was the submarine but could not swear to, stayed visible about 15 minutes. In that time it could have picked up survivors, but, due to the number of Allied craft in the vicinity, it could not afford to stay up long.

As you know, I was a new and very green officer aboard. The Captain was at all times helpful, patient and considerate. He took a personal interest in me and kindly acceded to my request that I be considered part of the ship's company until such time as the staff returned to the ship--technically, I was only a passenger, as my orders were for duty on the squadron commodore's staff. It was a gracious thing to do, helped me feel I was doing my part and aided me in absorbing a great amount of knowledge in a short time.

Such things were typical of Captain Klein, and I shall always have the greatest respect for him. He had the full respect and affection of his men too, and on every side I heard them express their sincere grief at his loss. I don't want to make you feel worse by saying these things, Mrs. Klein, but I want you to know that he was a real credit to the Navy and to his country. No more able naval officer ever lived and the service could ill afford to lose him. I know that I shall always consider it a real privilege to have known him. No one hopes more than I do that my guess as to his loss is proven completely false.

I shall be glad to answer any specific questions you may have. It looks as though I would be ashore for another couple of months anyway, so please feel free to write again.

Kindest personal regards,
David T. Hedges
Lt., USNR

Passed by Naval Censor
Lt. (jg) E.M. Buchanan, Jr.
U.S.S. *Ingraham* (DD-694)
c/o Fleet Post Office, N.Y.C.
May 31, 1944

Mrs. Millard Jefferson Klein
Round Hill, Virginia

My dear Mrs. Klein,

Your letter finally caught up with me, and I shall be only too glad to give you any information I can concerning the disaster of the *Buck*. My knowledge as to what happened to the men topside is very limited, since I was in the after engine room at the time of the accident.

After we were hit, we waited for instructions from the bridge, but found that communications had been cut off. The order to stand by to abandon ship was given by word of mouth. When I reached the main deck, the first thing I noticed was that the bridge was missing, and the ship had already started to heel forward. All the available life rafts were cut loose, and the order to abandon ship was passed. All hands that were able went over the side and started swimming for the nearest raft. About a minute after I left the ship, there was an underwater explosion presumably from our own depth charge. As a result of this explosion, the number of casualties was increased.

During the twenty hours I was in the water I didn't come in contact with any of the personnel who were on the bridge. After being interned in the hospital, I met Lt. Hedges who was on the bridge at the time the ship was hit. He told me then that two members of the crew and himself were the only known survivors of those on the bridge.

Only recently I met Lt. Hedges in New York, and he told me then that he had written to you giving you information which would be more accurate than mine, since he was actually on the bridge.

The possibility that any of the survivors were picked up by the enemy, in my opinion, is far remote. I wish I could give you some assurance of Capt. Klein's safety, but under the circumstances I am afraid he was lost when the ship was hit. I am sorry I must be so blunt, but you asked for an honest opinion, and I think it is only fair to give one. The loss of the Captain was deeply felt by all who served under him, and I sincerely hope that somehow you may receive some news of him. If I can ever be of any assistance in the future, please feel free to call on me.

Sincerely yours,
E.M. Buchanan, Jr.

Kay Klein Brigham
Miami, Florida
September 1, 1999

Dear Dr. Koitschka:

I am the daughter of Lt. Cmdr. M.J. "Mike" Klein who was the commanding officer of the destroyer U.S.S. *Buck*. In 1998 a new book, *Hitler's U-Boat War,* by Clay Blair revealed that you were the commanding officer of the German submarine *U-616* which torpedoed and sunk U.S.S. *Buck* on 9 October 1943 in the Tyrrhenian Sea off Salerno, Italy. *U-616* was sunk east of Cartagena, Spain on 17 May 1944, and you and your crew were saved and taken aboard two American destroyers, U.S.S. *Rodman* and U.S.S. *Ellyson*.

My family has learned that you are coming to the United States in September to attend the reunions of the *Rodman* and the *Ellyson*. We thought that the article I wrote about the *Buck* would be of interest to you. We want you to know that our hope and trust in God has sustained us in the loss of our father, believing that in all things God works for the good of those who love him (Romans 8:28).

Sincerely,
Kay Brigham

Siegfried Koitschka
Lohra, Germany
September 7, 1999

Dear madam,

Thank you very much for your letter. I am very sorry that just I caused so much harm about your family. You must know that we did not fight against sailors; we fought against ships. We had war and the commanding officer of the *Buck* tried to kill a submarine which he found by radar. We only anticipated him for some minutes.

Now I want to tell you how I experienced the sinking of the *Buck*. I remember this October 9, 1943 very well. It was a smooth Mediterranean night. The sea seemed like a duck's pool, and there was some mist over the water. We prowled around on the surface off Salerno. In the Mediterranean submarines only were able to surface during the night. During the day submarines submerged, because there were aircrafts everywhere. At night also the batteries were charged. At that night Oct. 9 0036 we got contact with the radar of a destroyer. A few minutes later we could see a one funnel destroyer moving with high speed to our position. I think she came with malicious intent, and we suspected that the destroyer crew was already arming their depth charges. We found ourselves in a miserable situation for firing torpedoes, because the destroyer approached in a very acute angle nearly position zero. With our normal torpedoes we could not do anything in that situation. But we had got an [T-5] acoustic torpedo. It was the first one, and nobody knew something about it and nobody trusted this torpedo.

The torpedo should react on the sounds of the ship's propellers. And when it had found the ship by its sound receiver, it detonated below the ship on account of the mass of the ship. But in this situation we had no alternative. We fired the torpedo out of the stern tube and waited for the result. The distance was 2000m. After a few minutes we saw and heard a detonation, and the destroyer became very small and at last she disappeared. Our torpedo had electric traction, and the wake could not be seen. Because a destroyer is never on her own, but in company with others, we disappeared as fast as we could. We did not find persons or debris. I am sorry that so many sailors of the *Buck* had to cross the bars, but what should I do else? In the other way the *Buck* would have killed me by her depth charges.

From Sept.16-21 we take part in the reunion of *Ellyson* in Charleston and from Sept. 22-26 in the reunion of *Rodman* in Washington. May be it possible we shall meet there.

The enclosed picture of *U-616* was painted by the British navy painter, Geoffrey Hunt. I myself own the original. My British friends presented it to me years ago.

Smoothly sailing
Your

Siegfried Koitschka

GERMAN SUBMARINE *U-616* **THAT SANK DESTROYER** *BUCK*